THE GIFT!

A Tool to Explore One's Divine Connection

Sebeline

INDIA · SINGAPORE · MALAYSIA

Notion Press

Old No. 38, New No. 6
McNichols Road, Chetpet
Chennai - 600 031

First Published by Notion Press 2018
Copyright © Sebeline 2018
All Rights Reserved.

ISBN 978-1-64429-866-4

DEDICATION AND ACKNOWLEDGMENTS

In times where feminism has lost its true meaning and the efforts of good men go unappreciated, I acknowledge the contribution of the two most important men in my life, without whom, I wouldn't be the woman I am today!

Battling the norms of a conservative society while disregarding the mysteries and controversies revolving around my existence, a childless man took under his wing a fatherless child 40 years ago. Unlike those who secretly wished I perished, sacrificing the pleasures of life he could have had, *Michael Ignatius D'souza*, my mother's uncle, became my saviour and guardian angel giving me the *'gift of life'* in the true sense! For his unconditional love and support, I am eternally grateful! I feel blessed to have the privilege to serve him at his ripe age of 83!

I dedicate not only this book to him, but also my life to ensure that he always has a smile on his face and the spark in his eyes, because he was the only one, who couldn't bear to see my tears, until *Bjørn Erik Sorhus Arnesen*, came along.

Escaping the demons of my past, this once shy and timid girl found herself across seven seas working on a cruise ship where she met a Norwegian sailor who helped her get out of the box.

One windy afternoon, stuck to the phone booth in Skagway, Alaska, talking to Bjørn who was home on vacation, our conversation lead in the direction of kids. I said, *"I am open minded and all, but out of respect for my grandfather, I need to be married to have children."*

Seeing the sacred union of marriage losing its charm, I had long decided I was better off without that label, and when the time came I would happily adopt! Bjørn never saw himself getting married either. His beautiful daughter *Gina* was two when we met.
As a wise person once said, *"Never say never."*

Destiny had brought us together for a reason! This special man from another corner of the world, understood the significance of my saviour in my life. So, in *2006*, we ended up tying a knot without him officially proposing!

He made sacrifices of his own, making India his new home. But, the irony of life came a full circle when we found that there were complications for me in the 'conceiving' department.

In my country in this modern age, a girl child is widely accepted. But, if procreating becomes a challenge, wives and daughter in laws are subjected to various medical procedures with the intention of producing an heir, since adoption is not an option to orthodox minds. As for women like me who come to terms with our calling of not forcing something that is meant to naturally flow, we are stigmatized by the 'society' for the choices we make.

"Your blood, carries on your legacy!" I grew up hearing this often, not realising then, it was meant to be a taunt.

Therefore, to prove a point of my own, I decided to carry on my saviour's legacy by capturing the essence of his life in my stories, and immortalize him by imprinting his name '**MICHAEL IGNATIUS D'SOUZA**' in the pages of my books!

For he, will always be my Dada, and I will forever remain his Baby!

***

The journey leading to the conception of my first book, '*THE GIFT!*', which you hold in your hands, has been nothing short of a magical one!

Having found solace in my poems while growing up alone, there came a point in my life when I wanted to write about women empowerment. In *May 2015*, a chance encounter with a French man, *Pierre Paul Sylvain Hirbec-Goumot,* gave my unsatisfactory life a direction. After a few heartfelt exchanges, he said to me, *"Why only women? We men also need a nudge and push in the right direction. Why don't you tell your story?"*

His words steered something within me, and by *July 2015,* my blog, *Rolesoundcameraaction.com,* came to be. Wanting to make a difference in someone's life somewhere, I embarked upon a journey which not only made the impact I hoped for, but also proved cathartic for me by helping me shed my baggage.

In *Feb 2016,* I attended a workshop called ***Wild Roots Vocal Journey*** conducted by an Israeli musician ***Amit Carmeli.*** I needed to work on my breathing, because when I concentrated on something, I felt like I forgot to breathe. However, we got off on the wrong foot when he said, *"no one forgets to breathe."* My feathers were ruffled, since I felt he didn't understand where I was coming from. Still, I attended his workshop knowing what I needed, *'or so I thought'*. Although, I was clearly the biggest sceptic in the group, I did receive a lot from his subtle teachings. So much so, that I am eternally grateful to him for showing me the mirror at that stage of my life without him lifting a finger.

In *Jan 2017,* watching the finale episode of ***BIGG BOSS*** season 10, (*The Indian version of the reality show* **BIG BROTHER***. I never ever dreamt to be a part of it. Yet, I religiously followed it, because I like conducting social experiments in my personal life!*) when the promo for season 11 popped up, a voice within said, **'Go for it!'**

Apparently, I was born in ward number **11** on bed number **11** on the **11**th **of November!**
And, for reasons unknown, my connection with this number has been very strong. Therefore, there was no questioning the higher purpose!

Growing up alone, the idea of being in that chaotic space with strangers was *madness.* From concealing my identity on social media and remaining in hiding for almost two decades because of an obsessed ex-boyfriend, to now putting myself out there in the public eye was *absolute insanity.* Nonetheless, I embraced this *madness* and *insanity,* because I trusted the *Divine* within me to lead me to where I needed to be. Knowing this would be a great exposure to make the difference, I intended to make it by leading by example. *So, all excited, I embraced that thought.*

Seeking blessings from my beloved husband for this unforeseen twist in my life, it was a challenge I had to overcome. Since we are a team, without his consent I couldn't take that crucial step. Although very sceptical, the one who has always supported me in my craziness gave me a green signal keeping in mind that without any contacts or influence, it was a slim chance to be shortlisted in a crowd of millions.

Miraculously, all doors opened for me, and I set off to pursue that platform, thinking it was my destination to reach. I made it through all rounds of auditions. I strongly believed it was my time to shine, simply because this journey made me see myself in a different light, giving me innate confidence.

Therefore, imagine my plight when I didn't see myself in that house when the show began.

Still, I didn't give up hope. I comforted myself with the thought that, '*No wild card has ever won the show. Maybe, my limited mind doesn't see the bigger picture…*'

I didn't give up and I persevered even though, by that time, my dreams had become a joke to many people around me. But, at the same time, many good things came of that first step that I took. *The one who never left loved in her life, found so much love that she started counting her blessings thanking all the angels in the past and present for making her who she was!*

Taking a challenge upon myself, I decided to have a children's book published by the time of the next auditions to prove to them that**, '***Hey, the last time we met, I was just a blog writer. Now, I'm a published author. So, how do you want to play this?*' Confident in my ability to deliver, I applied again!

Even though it was season 12 this year, I told myself, '*It is still a special year because **2018** adds up to **11**. On **11:11:11** I will be **40,** and maybe, re-launching myself at this age on that platform is the higher plan!*'

You might be questioning my madness right now. But let me tell you, I didn't even get shortlisted for an audition this time. Surprisingly, unlike last year, I wasn't desperate to chase that platform anymore. Because let's face it, *in real lives where everyone is walking around with masks, how did I expect originality to be appreciated in a reality show?*

Thanks to the voice which prompted me to walk on that path, and my full faith in the Universe which made me take that big leap; you are here reading my words today!

Had it not been for all the circumstances leading to this stage, I guess the notion of writing a book would linger in my head for years, and it would probably take a lifetime to deliver a book.

Therefore, although I didn't make it in **BIGG BOSS** house in season 11, I'm grateful to them for indulging me for as long as they did. And as for season 12, I'm grateful that they didn't shortlist me for an audition. *Why?* Because, had that happened, I'd be rushing my first book and not doing it justice in return!

So, thank you, **BIGG BOSS.** Moreover, thank you, **BIGGEST BOSS!**

$$***$$

A special thanks to those who senselessly ruin the beauty of my **Mother, Nature.** Because, if it wasn't for your disregard, the fire within me wouldn't have ignited the way it did transforming a children's book into one for older children and adults.

Besides all the angels from the different walks of life who bestowed me with their blessings and showered me with their love...

I, especially, thank *Shobha Nayak Krishnan,* my friend since the *11ᵗʰ* standard, for helping me lift the weight of not bearing a child.
"Sabby, don't ever feel sad for not having a baby. Maybe, you are not meant to invest your energy in one soul. You are born to touch many more! Consider yourself to be privileged to be able to live your dreams, and go do it for the rest of us!"
Thank you, Shobha, for being my voice of reason!

Thank you, Deepa Patel Gosalia, for being the Goddess that you are and for sharing my excitement and madness with me. It's been an absolute pleasure sharing this magical journey with you!

Thank you Ashish Phaldesai, an aspiring artist full of zest to explore the unknown! Thank you for coming to my rescue and to help me bring my vision to life in the form of illustrations for this book when another person abandoned me. And, I thank this other person for rejecting my plea, because if you hadn't done that, I wouldn't have connected with Ashish!

Everyone at Notion Press, thank you for your patience!
Thank you for indulging me to see my vision come to life!

A special mention to **Sandra Sherin**, an ex-employee of notion press, for the warmth you showed besides doing your job. It impressed me into tying up with **Notion Press**.

A special mention to **Ahiraj Pratap** from **Notion Press**, who, just like Sandra, went that extra mile to make me feel at home!

Last but not the least, *I THANK YOU BJØRN ERIK SORHUS ARNESEN* for your faith in me. Thank you for reminding me that, *'When I put my mind to something, consider it done!'*
You are the best life partner I could ever ask for!
THANK YOU FOR BEING AN IMPORTANT PIECE OF MY PUZZLE!

And, you there! I Thank you too!
THANK YOU FOR JOINING MY TRIBE!

In a country blessed with abundance…
Where the first rays of the eagerly rising sun,
Kiss the snow-capped mountain range of the Kanchenjunga,
Making it glitter, like gold;
Then, nourishing and sustaining life with its energy, throughout the day…
This majestic ball of fire spell binds its spectators; pulling a Houdini at the horizon!

A horizon where the glorious skies,
Blend in with the mystic waters of the Arabian Sea,
Making it dawn upon us at dusk how blessed we are!

Blessed to be able to witness the magic of this Universe!
Blessed to be one with the amazing beauty bestowed upon us by Mother Nature!

In this diverse country which flaunts different cultures…
Traditions, religions, languages and a variety of spices,
People from around the globe are drawn in with different desires and varied
intentions.

Some come to explore the ancient civilizations,
Some seek adventure; some tantalize their taste buds!
While others travel for work,
Many more come here to find their spiritual connection!

A connection which a very few manage to make;
Since, money mongers are ever eager,
To exploit lost souls in the name of 'Spirituality.'

Don't drift away reading a word such as 'Spirituality!'
This profound word has lost its simple meaning in a world full of greed.

This isn't a history, geography or a religious lesson either!

This is a lesson of life which I wish I had received at a younger age!
Against all odds, fortunate to receive unconditional love.
I wish to share a story of special bonds and amazing connections!
This special connection, I pray, everyone experiences at least once in their lifetime!
For there is where you might be yearning to be!
This is what you might be waiting to see!

Buckle up;
Let the adventures begin!

CHAPTER 1

N̶ot so far away, in an exotic land…
Grey clouds took over the bright blue sky, and just on cue,
A bunch of alluring peacocks flew low over the paddy fields;
Turning the open clearings of their sparse jungle into a landing strip!

Nearby, a large family of langurs swung from branches to branches, trees to trees,
filling their tummies with wild berries and ripe mangoes. In the bushes beneath,

smaller critters, eagerly awaiting fruity blessings to be bestowed upon them from above, were easily distracted by the sudden action around them. Intentionally drawing attention, the perky peacocks got ready for their magnificent performance, inviting audience with joyous calls!

Noticing the mesmerizing birds spread out their hypnotic feathers, from high up in the air, Dadu, the elder of the langur clan, rejoiced too!
With each scar on his ageing body telling a story never told before,
Humility and kindness still reflected in his soulful eyes.
Eyes which had seen life prevail in what was once,
Their ultimate paradise of luscious vegetation untouched by man;
Oblivious to the ways of those who reside in the concrete jungle...
As a boy, Dadu found himself in sudden despair when he had spotted primates clad in funny attire trespassing onto their territory and tearing down ancient trees.
Trees which had taken centuries to blossom.

Witnessing the rainforest deplete within the blink of an eye,
Young Dadu had dreaded the day they would all be forced out of their natural habitat.

Once concrete found its way into the jungle,
Building up walls unlike anything they had seen before,
He knew the moment of distress wasn't far away.
With the direction of water changing all dynamics of life,
Villages started flourishing around the water bodies forcing its natives to, eventually, drift away in search of new homes and resources to survive.
To make matters worse, monsoon would shy for the next many years to come, literally sucking out rain of what used to be a 'rainforest' leaving them for dead.
Seeking aid from the villages around had proved fatal on many occasions, because the villagers felt threatened by the inhabitants that refused to migrate.
Since then, only the reckless ventured into the forbidden land to play with fire.

Life had been tough for many species,
But, the ones who trusted their elders' instincts had thrived.
The dry spell had lasted for so long that like most creatures, Dadu too,
Had forgotten the taste of pure flowing water.

But, all that was about to change!

Bedazzled by the hypnotic dance of the enchanted creatures,
A few more vivacious voices joined in setting the tone for their orchestra to begin!
With synchronised music echoing through the jungle...
A huge gust of wind passed on the symphony like wildfire to those who were wound up in their own existence, oblivious to the world outside of their own.
Slowly, yet steadily, almost every life that prevailed in the wild gathered around the clearing with hopeful eyes staring at the sky which got darker by the minute.

It was indeed a time to celebrate!
Monsoon had arrived!

While the curious langurs quickly descended to lower grounds,
Dadu heard the youngest of the lot whimper,
"Wait, wait. Don't leave me behind. I just got up here."

"Akeli, try to keep up with the rest.
If darkness falls, you will lose your way;
You are too young to be left alone..."
Dadu expressed his concern.

"Dadu, I try, but Chikoo and Kaju are so fast that I can never keep up..."
Akeli grunted, swaying in mid-air.

"They say that I am the slowest langur in the history of langurs.
Is that true Dadu?"
Making herself cozy next to her beloved grandpa, Akeli anticipated his reply.

"Well,"
Dadu chose his words wisely knowing the motherless child was a sensitive soul,
"It is your fears that hold you back.
But, once you overcome them,
I am certain, you will lead this tribe someday!"

Giving his wise words a thought, she questioned,
"But, how will I overcome my fears when I am afraid of almost everything?"

Reliving her struggles to fit in, she moaned,
"Besides Kaju and Chikoo, the others also antagonize me in your absence.
Sometimes, I think they are right, and I don't belong up here on trees.
I am better off with the critters down there."
Akeli sulked pointing at the bushes, too nervous to look down.

"Oh, cheer up sweetheart!
I know what this fuss is all about…"
Dadu smiled, affectionately stroking her unusually coloured head.

"You tread carefully while climbing up and for the most of it, you enjoy it too!
Your problem is that, you are unsure of the ways to get down trees.
That is what scares you!
You fear falling."
Surprised to hear Dadu's accurate observations, the timid one shied away.
"I feel your heartbeat my precious!
I am always watching;
Even when you think you are out of my sight,
I feel your heartbeat!"
The prudent langur held her close to his own.

Dadu's every word meant a lot to Akeli who knew him to be her mother and father, besides the protective guardian that he was.

"Come on now, let's not be late for the party!
It's time to celebrate!"
In a long time, Dadu was cheerful!

"But, what are they celebrating Grandpa!?!" her young mind was curious.

"The gift that Mother Nature is going to bestow upon us very soon!"
Dadu's worries seemed to fade.

"What gift? I want a gift too! I never get a gift.
Whenever I am close to getting something, everybody beats me to it…"
Grumbled the naive one.

Feeling responsible for Akeli, in every way possible, Dadu was glad to continue their little chat, **"Eleven months ago, you got the biggest gift one could ever receive...**
This is just a consolation prize.
A present which will ensure us all a bright future!"

Still fixated on the notion of a gift, Akeli frowned,
"What do you mean?
I received a big gift that I don't know of?
If it was that big of a gift, I would have remembered for sure."

"So what according to you is a perfect gift!?!" inquired the astute.

"A big bunch of bananas!" squealed a familiar voice from above.

Following the sound of Kela's voice, Dadu chuckled,
"Bananas! I should have known!
Your instant love for this simple, easy fruit is how you got your name boy!"

Signalling the naughty langur to join them, Dadu continued sharing his wisdom,
"Now, bananas are the consolation prize.
The perfect gift you both received is much before that."

"Why do you always speak in riddles Dadu?" grunted the impatient soul.

"I am not the brightest flower in the garden, I'm repeatedly told..."
Scratching his head, he innocently revealed.
"So please just tell us what you mean.
See Kaju, Chikoo, Narangi and Mosambi are already enjoying themselves;
I want to go dance with them too!"
Urged Kela, who regretted the situation he got himself into.

Coming straight to the point, Dadu emphasised,
"You can go pretend to have fun down there, or...
Rise up higher with us to seek the knowledge you secretly desire."

With Akeli attached to his hip, Dadu effortlessly leaped towards a skinny conifer which seemed to kiss the sky. This enticed Kela to leave the comfort of the big Peepal tree.

Although Kela always put up a brave front,
Dadu knew that he dreaded the company of Narangi and Mosambi.
Who, in spite being his older siblings, took wicked pleasure in bullying him,
Just like they did to the rest.
Spotting Kaju and Chikoo being terrorised on lower grounds,
Kela fought back his anxiety for riddles,
While he followed Akeli and Dadu to conquer new heights.

Reaching almost the tip of the tallest tapering tree he'd seen,
Kela held on to a tiny branch for dear life, as he struggled to find his footing.
Dropping his uncommonly long tail, which was indeed the talk of the town,
Dadu facilitated a strong rope for his grand-nephew instead of making him sweat.

Though Kela displayed great courage by venturing on a journey that others only dreamt of, his trembles had made the tree shiver scaring him to death.
"Make it stop Dadu. Make it stop. I don't want to die without receiving my gift."

Hearingthe brave one panic, Akeli started crying too,
"Dadu, I don't want any gift. Please, can we go down now?
Please, I'm getting dizzy."

Dadu, being as wise as he was, couldn't be fooled. He knew it was the expectation of a gift more than the thirst of knowledge that made Kela linger around.

"*Calm down, Akeli.* You are both safe in my arms!
I promise, I will never let you fall!
Come on now, close your eyes and breathe like I always ask you to.
Inhale deeply... Exhale slowly..."

Dreading his demise, if he were to fall from that height, Kela's nervousness reflected in his behaviour when he ignored Dadu's teachings.

"Kela, don't look down...
When you have done as I say, I will present to you your precious gift."
Owlishly, Dadu gained his confidence.

As obedient as she was, Akeli followed her idol's instructions letting out a deep sigh. But, Kela's frivolous mind stood in the way of his growth.
Even though he didn't take a conscious breath as asked, Dadu kept his promise.

"Good! Now open your eyes slowly…
And tell me what you see.
Explain to me how that makes you feel?"

Masking his anxiety with the expectation of receiving a gift,
Kela, thoughtlessly, proclaimed,
"I feel like the KING OF THE JUNGLE!!!!
Because, from where I sit, everyone beneath me look like ants!"

Closely observing a sight new to her soulful eyes, Akeli failed to express herself,
"I see, I see, Hmmm... I see...
Actually, I don't know what I see.
Mainly, because, I have never seen this sight before!"

Struggling to see what his cousin's soulful eyes were seeing,
Kela, who was eager to impress at all times, frowned.

Unaware of the baggage, he chose to carry along with him wherever he went...
His vision was blurred with excitement, but Akeli guided his eyes to what he needed to see, even though she didn't understand what she was looking at herself.
Gratitude wasn't a part of his practice;
Therefore, inflating his ego furthermore…
Kela dismissed her efforts, and lost himself to the wonders of a world unknown to him.

Dadu's tumultuous lifetime had trained him to be vigilant, making him a great observer of restricted minds. At that moment, high up in the sky, Dadu observed the silence and the chaos, all at once, addressing them both.

"That fine line you see;
The line which separates the soon darkening sky from the glistening salty waters…
It is called the horizon!
And, beneath the dark clouds…
Is yet another world waiting to be explored!"
Dadu enlightened the young minds.

"The sandy shore you see;
That used to be our playing ground long ago;
Before humans found their way in there, and the exploitation began.
Once again, forcing us farther and farther away into the diminishing woods;
Depriving us of the serenity we once knew…"
Dadu lost the twinkle in his eye.

"What is it, that you saw there Dadu?"
Inquired Kela insensitively, looking forward to new adventures.

Tapping into his desperation, Dadu indulged Kela's challenged spirit,
"Just like we thrive in the forest,
Captivating creatures, reign the underwater world!
Just like we set off on expeditions early in the morning,
Dreamy dolphins make their presence known at the break of dawn, enthralling the spectators on land who eagerly await the arrival of the majestic ball of fire.
A ball of fire, which we call the Sun!"

Interrupting again, the restless langur started to make plans,
"I want to see the show as well someday. When can we go there?!?"

"Yes, Dadu!
I would like to see the mermaids too!!!
Aunty says that they live in the water! That water!!!"
Akeli expressed her enthusiasm, clapping.

"Someday, we might be fortunate enough to see mermaids riding the dolphins!
But, not just yet," Dadu's eyes moistened recollecting a painful memory. "When

you children are ready to face the harsh reality of this lost world, I will take you there myself." he said.

The sensitive soul, who was always thoughtful of others despite their inhibitions, hugged her dearest Dadu tightly sensing his pain.
"If going there makes you sad, I never want to ever go there... Ever!"
She muttered.

Upon which, nudging her, Kela frowned since he was adamant for a new thrill.

"Today is a special day! Such a very special day!!!
Soon our rivers and ponds might be full of water!
And this dying jungle...
This dying jungle, might just flourish once again!"
Dadu's lost spark was back!

"Come! Come! Let's go shake some booty down there!
Hurry, before the rain gods endlessly shower us with their divine love!"
Gathering his emotions, Dadu escorted the little ones to safe grounds.

Guiding them to the centre of the circle, and lifting the shy one on his shoulders, Dadu, gracefully mimicked the dazzling peacocks, using Akeli's delicate arms to depict their wings.
Dancing and singing in harmony, all the creatures of that jungle dropped their animosity that evening. Blissfully welcoming the pitter patter of the first rain in a long, long time!

CHAPTER 2

Sheltering themselves from the glorious downpour...
All inhabitants of the jungle scrambled to find their safe haven.
And, Dadu, he led his clan to the ruins of an ancient cave situated in the heart of the mountains only he knew the way to, to retire for the night!
Curling up next to each other for warmth, the protective mothers comforted their younglings from roaring thunders and the blinding flashes of light.
Seeking solace in Dadu's arms, unlike every night, Akeli didn't wonder,

'*Why she was the way she was?*'
Instead, she was concerned about what was bothering Dadu...
Who aimlessly stared into the dark night as his tribe slowly drifted away to sleep.

While Kela tossed and turned,
Dreaming dreams of riding mythical creatures underwater just like the mermaids,
Akeli stayed up all night contemplating on how to approach a clearly sensitive subject whilst trying hard, to catch a glimpse, of her early memories.
Respecting the wishes of the elders, Akeli had stopped questioning her existence.
But, knowing that Dadu was carrying a huge weight on his chest, she was tempted to break the silence.

The bullies in the clan came of all ages, shapes and sizes;
For reasons unknown to her, they had mocked her on a daily basis...,
Forcing her to feel unwanted.

Narangi insinuated several times that Akeli was jinxed because of the way she looked.
That was his lame reason for not making her feel accepted.
Mosambi always had a hearty laugh pushing her around claiming she was so ugly that her parents were petrified of her and ran away.

Calling her 'Dadu's pet,' Chickoo had once aggressively shoved her aside.
According to him, Dadu was only protective of her since he had found her in a village, as an ailing baby, without a father and mother in sight.

As timid as she was, Akeli always swallowed everything with a pinch of salt.
But, her wicked uncle's words had pierced her soul.
He always claimed that she was the reason for her mother's demise.
Her dilemma was as to who to believe;
The ones who wished ill upon her, or Dadu, who stood by her side against all odds.

Her existence, to her, remained a mystery.
A mystery, which only Dadu could solve.
But, she had come to realise that this topic was not up for discussion just yet.

She'd have to wait until she was older, she had been told.
Hence, she wasn't ready to face the harsh reality of life, she'd gathered.

Wondering, what could be worse than what she had already heard...
Akeli was now afraid to close her eyes, dreading the recurring nightmares she couldn't make sense of.

At the break of dawn, with every leaf in the jungle now rejuvenated!
The curious elders, wondered if it had rained enough to make little streams flow into the rivers which had remained dry for the last couple of years.

Sliding off the slippery slopes of what was once a cascading waterfall, while the rest of the langurs rejoiced in the mist, Akeli found herself following Dadu who leaped fearlessly while navigating his way to the waterhole. Her tiny limbs struggled to keep up the fast pace, and soon, she found herself lost in unchartered territory.
Fearing the presence of ferocious predators she had heard stories of, she screamed for dear life when a blue creature she had never seen before startled her from behind.

It was none other than her mischievous cousin Kela wrapped in blue plastic.
Plastic he had found by the dying waterfall, laying lifeless, next to empty bottles of alcohol, of which, he had sucked out the last remaining drops.
Recognizing the screams to be of the one he treasured the most, Dadu rushed to her rescue following the sound of breaking bottles.

"Kela stop that!
You will end up hurting yourself and other animals in the jungle.
Stop that right now!"
Dadu commanded furiously while snatching the bottle off Kela's hands.

"But, Dadu there is no one here, and this Akeli, she is scared of everything.
I'm just playing with my new toys!!!" exclaimed the naive one.

"This is no toy, this is garbage. Garbage that doesn't belong here."
Dadu shrieked in anger.

"Those humans... They think they are so much better than us.
Still, they fail to clean up after themselves...

Shamelessly putting our lives at risk at every turn.
First, they drove us away from our safe haven...
Now, they have the audacity to make our new home into a garbage dump.
How dare they?" the adulated langur, trembled in fury.

"Oh Dadu! Don't be so dramatic. Calm down!"
Intoxicated, Kela crossed all his boundaries.

"Kela, you never talk to Dadu like that. What is wrong with you?!?
Why are you acting so strange?"
Akeli stepped in, unable to tolerate her grandpa being disrespected.

"This is what happens when you get sucked in to the dark side..."
Dadu let out his frustration while picking up the shards of broken glass hastily.

"This is what happens when they invade our space..."
He sighed in distress at the smell of liquor.

"They mess with our minds and turn us against each other...,
Just like they do to their own kind.
We must be smart... We must be smart.
We can't let temptation create a rift between us."
Dadu looked extremely troubled.

"Claiming to be civilized while acting like ferocious animals...
They've forgotten the simple pleasures of life.
Appreciation, kindness, thoughtfulness, compassion, harmony...
Have been erased from their memories altogether, because greed, has consumed their being.
Procreating senselessly they boost their population...
Then, selfishly they exploit all our natural resources.
They've hunted our brethren down to the verge of extinction...,
And, they have the gall to call themselves the mankind???"
Dadu's thunderous pitch echoed through the jungle bouncing back from the treacherous mountains alarming every soul in the vicinity of his wrath.

"We in the animal kingdom shed blood to survive and protect.
But they…,
They not only torture innocent souls in our kingdom for guilty pleasures,
They also consider the less fortunate in their own world a nuisance.
Anxious to erase our existence they forget that we also have emotions.
We too feel pain. Excruciating pain.
Why don't they just leave us alone? Why???"
Dadu expressed his dismay.

"They pretend to be brave.
But, the reality is that they are threatened by things they do not care to
understand.
They worship idols, not because they are spiritual,
But, simply because they fear the wrath of God.
They take pride in labelling themselves the superior being.
Yet, all they do is exploit the meek instead of becoming their voice.
Such a shame. Such a shame…"
Dadu cried out loud letting out a deep sigh while fighting hard to hold back his
tears,
"SUCH A SHAME!"

Witnessing her guardian and mentor having a meltdown, Akeli, who never shed
a tear in Dadu's presence before, rushed to his side, sobbing. Her tears were the
one thing he couldn't bear. Therefore, Dadu tried to regain his composure as she
wiped his bleeding fingers with a medicinal leaf.

Kela sobered up standing there like a statue, in shock, racking his young mind.
Wondering, what he had done to infuriate Dadu?
According to him, all he had done was, keep himself entertained with the objects
he had found. Never in his wildest of dreams did he expect this kind of terrifying
reaction to his mindless mischief.

The one who was accustomed to always hide her tears…
Understood there was more to the elder's pain than he revealed.
She sensed he was definitely hiding something…
That secret, he wouldn't share, was weighing him down.

Her heart ached to see him that way. So, she instantly asked Kela to apologize to Dadu for his madness rolling her buttoned eyes.

Wrapping themselves around the revered soul, they tried to comfort Dadu.

"I am sorry Dadu...
I never meant to hurt you.
I will never ever play with garbage again.
I promise!" Kela's sincerity touched Dadu's kind heart, and he anxiously hugged his grandchildren pleading with them to be careful.

Ceasing the opportunity to dig deeper into his soul, the usually shy and timid Akeli blurted,

"Dadu, this isn't all about the blue plastic and glass bottles is it?
There is something else you don't want me to know.
I can feel it in your deafening silence...
I can see it in your saddened eyes...
And today, for the first time, I sensed the pain in your voice...

You are angry at the humans. You always tell us to be away from them.
Today, I want to know why???

The tribe mocks me and bullies me...
Everyone tells me that it's my fault that my parents are gone...
Because of me, you lost your daughter...
Tell me, grandpa... Did you find me by the river?!?"

Already vulnerable, and now caught off guard by the directness of Akeli's questioning, Dadu didn't know where to begin as he aimlessly stared into her hopeful eyes.

"Dadu, I'm not as small as I look. I am not weak either.
I know this, because every day, you tell me what a big, tough girl I am!"
The introvert had found her voice.

"Please, Dadu... Please unfold the mystery that my life is..."
She looked into his eyes, but he looked away.

"I know something terrible has happened, and bottling it all up, is killing you from inside."
Akeli's observations took him by surprise.

"Just like you do...
I hear your every heartbeat too, my precious grandpa!
I hear it every night as you gaze away in the dark unable to sleep.
I keep myself awake not only because I'm afraid of the nightmares I have...
I'm awake, because you are not sleeping.

I've told you about all my nightmares, Dadu.
Now, it's time you tell me yours.
You know I can handle anything that comes my way.
So, please, Dadu! Allow me to comfort you...
Comfort you, while you share with me your NIGHTMARE..."

CHAPTER 3

Tending to a motherless child had been hard on Dadu.
Especially, after the horror he had witnessed not so long ago.
Now, forced to answer questions laid out by a pure soul who put him on a pedestal,
Missing his missus by his side for what felt like multiple lifetimes…
Memories of his beloved Gayatri engulfed Dadu's entire being, making him tremble in angst.

Transporting himself back to the Valley of Hope where his story had first begun, Dadu lost himself into the impressions of his past.

Named *'Dhairya'* by his mother,
A mother, who was mostly absent from his life…
His patience was tested every step of the way, as a toddler yearning for her love.

His father was around, yet, he felt neglected by him...
Because, his older brother Bhram, sought their father's undivided attention.

Practically raised by his grandmother who he affectionately called Dadima, the matriarch of the clan, fostered him to be a valiant langur, encouraging Dhairya to erase his mother's memories in order to maintain his sanity as a child.

As an adolescent, he went to seek adventures of his own helping those in need along the way. Even in darkness, he managed to find light living up to his name wherever he went.

When the atrocities of the corrupt and the betrayal of the loved became hard to handle…

He drifted further and farther away from his tribe, eventually, meeting his match under unusual circumstances. And to her quirks, he had instantly lost his heart!

A free spirit that he was,
Adamant to have Gayatri accepted by his tribe, he had defied his grandmother.
Unable to reason with the elders who were set in their ways...
Disappointed in them, he drifted away from his family while embracing Gayatri's tribe as his own.

Chief Kanu, who was once a force to be reckoned with,
Welcomed Dhairya with open arms this time instantly inviting him to fill in his lost son's shoes.
Since the mysterious disappearance of her older brother, Gaya…
The pressure to produce an heir weighed heavily on Gayatri shoulders.
Now, Dhairya was under the same pressure, because, he was the son-in-law of a frail Chief.

But, as luck would have it, it wasn't easy for them to procreate;
Giving Gayatri's cunning uncle Vyakul, a perfect opportunity to weasel his way to the throne.

Scheming since he was a little boy...,
In his middle age, Vyakul, finally set his plan in motion in order to attain the crown which his power hungry mother had always claimed as rightfully his. In her obsession with the throne, she had begun planting seeds of deceit in her underachieving son, even before he had learnt to walk.

Whispering more gossip in the ears of a gossip monger, Vyakul had successfully ignited a full-fledged fire in the usually peaceful tribe. Insinuating that the Chief's daughter was infertile.

While majority of the tribe had accepted Dhairya's role in their lives...,
Vyakul's children, who were as wicked as their father, if not more, always tried pushing his buttons making him feel like an outsider.
Still, Dhairya, didn't pay any heed to their antics.
His only concern was, Gayatri's happiness!

One morning, navigating his way through the dense forest, chasing the first rays of the soothing sun while enjoying the mist kissing his cheek, Dhairya was excited to fetch Gayatri's favourite water lilies from an emerald pond!
Because, it was his beloved's birthday!

But, all the excitement fizzled away in a heartbeat,
When, he overheard gossip not meant for his ears...
Fired up by the wrong assumptions and false perceptions, relating to Gayatri's ability to bear children, Dhairya lost his cool and confronted the instigator, Vikaar.
Vyakul's oldest son, who was secretly smitten by Gayatri ever since they were kids.

When forced to face the jury for the little blood that he had shed of a bully, who was clearly disrespecting the Chief's daughter and the love of his life, Dhairya was caught off guard witnessing the inconsideration of the tribe he adored.
With everyone pointing fingers at Gayatri, calling her a bad seed;
Defending his darling from being labelled barren...
He did the unthinkable when he announced himself to be sterile.

Shocked at this absurd revelation, and upset by his outburst…
Giving in to the pressure created by his cunning cousin Vyakul, Chief Kanu, announced the exile of his own son-in-law without thinking things through.

Taken aback by her father's declaration, breaking all barriers, Gayatri heavy heartedly bid farewell to her friends and family…
Following the one she worshipped aimlessly into the woods.

With gossips and rumours spreading like Chinese whispers…,
They often battled the stigma of not bearing fruits.
They were greeted with taunts and mockery almost everywhere they went.
Against all odds, their love had only grown stronger;
Because, each time they hit a wall, they found solace in each other's arms instead of playing the blame game.

Wandering further and further away into the wilderness, happy to be in hiding,
The langurs were in bliss creating a paradise of their own;
Unaware, of the dangers lurking around every corner.

Instead of sustaining the valuable resources and preserving what was left of the rainforest, the humans were exploiting every inch of the land rich in minerals.
Hunting was no longer a means to feed families…
It had become a senseless sport for the wealthy.
Majestic mammals such as elephants and rhinoceros, were being brutally hunted down for their tusks while magnificent cats were being stripped down for their skins...
In a world where hoarding currency and coins had become a lifestyle, anyone who came in the way of their black marketing business was undoubtedly toast.
An overall peaceful life had been disrupted…
And, hooligans from both worlds were out causing destruction.
Escaping the scorching heat which had gotten unbearable over the years, the primates of the jungle had to scour for patches of shade to cool down their overheating bodies.
As for Dhairya and Gayatri,
Her favourite Gulmohar tree had become their love nest, where they affectionately performed their daily ritual of grooming each other silly!

One early afternoon, after filling their tummies with berries as they retired on a huge branch of the Mayflower tree, a family of deers grazing under its shade was suddenly spooked by a monstrous roar.

Dhairya, who was the master of mimicry, was forced to wonder,

'Which unknown creature, had set foot in their territory now?'

Just then, another unfamiliar roar, followed by a familiar explosion, shook them to the core, forcing Dhairya to the highest peak in order to get an eagles view of the eroding landscape.

Noticing birds frantically circling over one particular area of the forest, chirping in distress, Dhairya's sharp eyes caught a glimpse of a goon with a gun camouflaged in green. Recognizing the attire which helped them blend in with the surroundings like a chameleon, he instantly recollected the horrible moment he witnessed as a child, when darts had first pierced the chest of Bholu's gentle mother followed by her cubs. Chained and shackled, the last of the bear family were being kidnapped from their homes.

When the little langur had attempted to stop the poachers, he was rendered unconscious by a metal object which he later identified as a deadly weapon called the 'gun.'

Sensing the gravity of the situation,

And, the wind steering faint cries of helpless inhabitants in his direction…

Feeling the scar on his forehead with his sweaty palm, he knew he had to act right away.

Pleading Gayatri to stay put while he checked on a matter not so far away from them,

Dhairya, catapulted himself over the canopy of trees in utmost urgency.

But, not before gently planting a kiss on Gayatri's perspiring forehead.

Seeing animals run helter-skelter in all directions, he fearlessly dashed towards the disaster. Closing in on the site of terror, his vision was blurred by the smoke which rose above the flames. To his dismay, it was a cruel nightmare occurring in broad daylight.

Unable to bear the thought of separating from her soulmate…

Fearing the worst, Gayatri recklessly followed her lifeline into the heart of the fire while dodging the eyes of dreaded humans. There, she saw him risk his life to rescue souls in agony. Quickly grabbing a little macaque, who had latched onto Dhairya's tail terrified, Gayatri's maternal instinct kicked in. Rounding up younglings of various species trapped in the blaze, while Dadu focused on reaching their parents, she bravely assisted in the rescue operation.

A spark started by heartless humans;

With the intention of clearing that patch of the jungle by scaring away the resident animals, had now, spread like wildfire resulting in the loss of countless lives, orphaning innocent children, who screamed in vain for their loved ones.

Stealthily escorting the wounded and traumatised away from the dark clouds hovering over their heads, the daring duo nursed their new tribe back to health for weeks and months to come, in the safety of a mysterious cave.

A cave situated at the mouth of an enchanting waterfall.

A waterfall which they had stumbled upon on one of their many adventures!

Besides Gayatri and Dhairya, to whom parenting and nurturing came naturally…,

Their instant family now consisted of Berri, the sneaky squirrel!

Perry, the inquisitive parrot!

Ravi, the sharp raven!

Monty, the mighty monitor lizard!

Mannu, the lazy mongoose!

Soni, the sassy snake!

Beety, the beautiful wild boarlet!

Capu, the naughty leopard cub!

Along with a few of their surviving relatives!

Forgetting their petty differences of regular life, the new tribe learnt to live in harmony, graciously adapting to each other's quirks!

Mantra, the only surviving macaque...
Who was barely a few days old when Gayatri found her attached to Dhairya...
Were now, inseparable!

A motherless child...
Was in the safe arms...
Of a childless mother!

CHAPTER 4

She had secretly yearned for a little one of their own…
Ever since Dhairya had stolen her heart!
After being bound together as one in wedlock, Dhairya often made her blush;
Playfully teasing her how awesome their offspring would be!
They could dream all they wanted…
But, the reality was crude, and the pressure was on.

Eventually, coming to terms with the daily challenges they faced due to the ignorance of misled minds, they gave up on this once exciting topic all together considering the plight of their partner. Yet, every now and then when loose tongues thoughtlessly lashed out at them testing their patience, the soulful couple would turn a deaf ear. At times, when the ruthless crossed all limits of decency by mocking his beloved senseless, Dhairya would lose his cool.

Which is when, comforting her darling husband who displayed unconditional love by bearing the burden of being childless, Gayatri would hold him close and whisper in his ears…

"Don't let these menial minds crawl under your skin my love!
I am very blessed to have you by my side!
Therefore, I strongly believe,
Mother Nature will give us the pleasure of parenting someday!"

Although he had simply smiled at her optimism every time,
The realist in him always wondered,
'Where a baby would fall in their laps from?'
Now, seeing his Goddess at work, spreading laughter and joy;
To those who had lost their twinkle,
Dhairya was, indeed, proud to be her langur!

In the arms of pristine beauty,

Together, they had spent countless days;
Tending to the open wounds of their unconventional family.
At night, the guardians of the new tribe had taken turns succouring the damaged souls from their recurring nightmares of that godforsaken afternoon.
There was no time to be selfish under those circumstances.
No time to dedicate to oneself.
Therefore, Dhairya ended up suppressing his own visions of terror…
Staying courageously strong.

Seasons changed, enhancing their mystical landscape!
While those like him and Gayatri became one's saviour,
Planting seeds of compassion and empathy within their tribe…
Insecure bullies, not so far away,
Took up the role of savages threatening the survival of their own.
It wasn't only the human race which was turning against each other…
The animal kingdom was facing a siege too.

Oblivious to the carnage going on in her original clan,
While the moon shone brightly above them, Gayatri realised that Perry and his entourage hadn't returned home for the night yet. Worried sick, she investigated as to when was the last time anyone had seen the explorers.

"I have told them, several times, not to just wander away. But, only if they listen."
With Mantra attached to her hip like an extra appendage, Gayatri rushed to seek answers from Dhairya who lay under the stars in awe of the Universe.

"Did you see which direction Perry, Poppy, Pascoe and Boscoe took this afternoon? They've never been out so late before. I'm afraid that something unfortunate must have happened. Please, can you go check on them? Hurry, hurry, hurry!"
Insisted Gayatri forcing Dhairya to his feet.

"Calm down my love! You are scaring Mantra…"
He who fit perfectly in a father's shoe, tickled the little Macaque distracting her from her mother's anxiety.

"Look at this magnificent moon;
Full to its potential! Spreading light in abundance!
How can anyone lose their way under her radiance!?!"
Comforting Gayatri, who seemed on edge, he pointed towards the sky.

"The kids are kids no more;
They are blossoming into adolescence!
They must have lost track of time engaging in youthful adventures.
Don't worry so much, they will be back soon! I promise!"

Before Gayatri could scold her laid back langur, Capu, the once tiny leopard cub who had now grown to become intimidatingly huge, came bearing good news.

"I saw them at a distance, they will be here within no time!"
The gentle giant chuckled, getting Mantra to hop onto his back.

Upset still, Gayatri continued pacing up and down anxiously awaiting their arrival.

Perry was the first one to touch ground followed by Poppy and Pascoe.
But, little, chubby Boscoe, was nowhere in sight.

"What's going on?"
"Where did you birds wander away?"
"Where is Boscoe?"
Bombarded by a million questions at once, the rest were rendered speechless.

"He is right here. He is fine!
He seems to have clipped a wing...
I saw them struggling to carry his weight. So, I gave him a ride!"
Ravi, the astute raven, successfully calmed everyone's nerves.

Sternly warning them to be back by dusk next time, Gayatri, holding back her tears, stepped out of the cave for some fresh air followed by Dhairya and Ravi.

Standing at the edge of a treacherous cliff…
As Dhairya and Ravi maintained the peace and tranquillity of the brightly lit night…
Spooked, by a shadow cast far away…
Gayatri, who hadn't left that vicinity for almost 9 months, curiously asked,

"Ravi? Have you noticed anything unusual lately???
When you've been cruising above the trees, I mean.
My gut says, 'Something horrible is happening somewhere.'
Have your sharp eyes caught a glimpse?"

Caught off guard by her concern, Dhairya softly spilt a secret of his own not wanting to wake up Mantra who had dozed off in the breezy night without a worry.

"I've been getting recurring dreams of my grandma.
She seems worried…"
He tried in vain to control his jittery voice.

"She repeatedly calls my name from a distance.
I can never clearly tell if she is signalling me to come close,
Or, get as far away as possible.
By the time I stagger to our favourite big Banyan,
Where she groomed me, nurtured me and taught me aerial tricks as a child,
She is gone.

I never seem to reach her on time;
Her voice gets distant, and I am deafened by countless groans and moans.
When the ringing in my ear stops,
Dadima appears before me calling out my name again.

Excited to reunite with her, as I try to take a leap,
I am unable to lift the weight of my body, and I find myself utterly helpless.
Helpless, to see my dearest Dadima wither away…
Wither away along with the sacred tree of eternal life."

Surprised by his revelation, the intuitive Gayatri wondered how long he had been having these nightmares while Ravi tried to make sense of his dream.

"It's been too long.
They started right after the catastrophe we faced which brought us a new family.
Since we had our hands full at that time, I didn't pay attention to them.
I thought they would eventually stop.
Stop, just like the nightmares did for Ravi and the rest of the tribe.
But, they haven't…"
Dhairya lost himself in his thoughts.

"My love! Why have you kept your nightmares from me for as long as you have?
Recurring visions aren't supposed to be taken lightly. We both know that.

We chose to come to these caves with the wounded and the traumatised because we wanted them to heal. Heal, while they slept in peace without having to scramble for their lives.
Initially, we didn't sleep a wink since we had to nurse our babies and brethren to health.

But, as you wisely put,
They are blossoming into adolescence!
Some fortunate souls have also reunited with their loved ones!
Their loved ones, who are here, to support us and share our responsibilities as a tribe."
Gayatri, reassuringly, stroked his tense back.

"If your family's well-being has been on your mind,
Let's go pay them a visit! It has obviously been too long."

"Yes Chief. Mrs. Chief is right!"
Ravi, the wise raven, seconded Gayatri's suggestion.

"You don't have to worry about us.
We will all be fine!
Up here, we are invincible!
No human will risk his life climbing up these treacherous mountains.
Which is why you brought us here, didn't you!?!
You must go check on your family now.
They will indeed be happy to see you!"
Said Ravi with conviction!

"Happy?!?"
Dhairya recollected that unfortunate moment when his tribe turned their back on him,
"You don't know how pleased my brother was to see me leave.
And my father…
He didn't utter a word.
What had I done wrong?
I simply wanted to follow my heart…
Be together with the one I loved!
But, no!
Her need to have her way…
Her thoughtless commitment…
Meant more to them than my happiness!
Our happiness!
How could she decide my fate before I was born?
How was that fair to me?
Can you explain???" Dhairya was conflicted, keeping in mind the suffering he dealt with, along with the anxiety of separation.

"We all make mistakes, don't we?
I am sure, she missed you dearly after she let you go.
You were her favourite grandson after all!"
Gayatri hoped to give him solace in her arms, but Dhairya wasn't at peace.

"Favourite???
Come on, Gayatri…

Weren't you there, when we were shunned?"
Stepping away from his beloved in haste, Dhairya displayed his distress.

"My love,
Look where we are now?
We have all the love in the world we need right here!!!
With our new family!
Everybody makes mistakes! Even your perfect Dadima!"
Gayatri attempted to cheer him up.

"Wouldn't you expect her to forgive you for your mistakes?!?
So, you are the younger one and she is the older one;
Can't we be the wiser ones and let go of all this unwanted anger and
animosity?

She might have had her reasons to make a promise all those years ago.
Maybe, she considered you to be their saviour even then.
Maybe, she succumbed under pressure just like my father did when he
banished us.

Although you've misplaced the love you had for her after you felt betrayed,
I know that your heart still beats in her name.
Just as you love us... I know, you still love her too!

Don't allow your false pride to get in the way of your kindness.
The way you describe your visions,
It seems like your Dadima needs you.
Don't dismiss her voice, for I very well know...
You will later regret."
Gayatri, owlishly, gave him something to think about while understanding her
husband better than he did himself.
"What do you say, Sir Ravi?
Am I reading the signs correctly?!?"
Gayatri sought the raven's valuable opinion, because his wisdom had kept her
strong in times of darkness and despair; reintroducing her to her inner voice.

"You read fairly well my lady!"
Ravi smiled turning his attention to Dhairya.

"Be willing to let go of all the old baggage,
In order to make space for new memories to blossom;
Open your heart and invite warmth into your soul!
Yet,
Never disregard the shrills which might send chills through your spine.
Do not become a barrier and cage your own free spirit.
Until you get to where you need to be...
Every other thought is a distraction!
Distraction, eluding you from your priority.
And, what is your priority?
That, only you can tell when you are in control of your emotions."
The prudent raven, looked splendent in the dark...
As if he had absorbed the moon's radiance, before she bid them adieu.

"What about your tribe, Gayatri?
Don't you miss them?!?"
Ravi hoped his disciple was ready to share.

"You are my tribe now, and I shall miss you all when we are gone..."
She masked her pain behind her beaming smile.

"But, what about Mantra?"
Like a concerned father, Dhairya questioned immediately.

"I know all the reasons you will lay down to leave her behind.
Yet, you very well know...
No matter what anyone says, I will never leave her side."
Gayatri was honest about her feelings.
"She is our responsibility now! **We are the only parents she knows!**

Unlike our family, who chose to abandon us…
We shall never abandon our child!"

Gruesome pain reflected in Gayatri's words as she rocked her darling daughter back to sleep, allowing tears to flow freely this time.

CHAPTER 5

At the break of dawn, praying to the spirits of their ancestors to guide their
way…
Taking a moment to admire their world in the light of the rising sun,
Dhairya and Gayatri, soon, discussed their departure,
With the responsible grown-ups of their tribe.

Following Ravi's instructions, Capu, Beety and Perry, along with their companions,
Took off to arrange a farewell feast for their beloved guardians!
The sleepy heads and lazy bones, who took their time to open their eyes…
Were surprised to wake up to a lavish spread of fancy food!

Curious to know what was being celebrated…
They gathered around the enormous flat rock outside the cave,
Eager to pounce on the elegant table full of treats.
But, no sooner did Ravi raise a coconut shell toasting to the trio's safe return,
The younglings were bummed.

Besides Dhairya Pa and Gayatri Ma,
Who they had grown to love and adore unconditionally…
Their mate, Mantra, was leaving too.

"Why does Mantra have to go on your adventures?
Can't she stay here and play with us???
We promise to take good care of her, Gayatri Ma!
Please let her stay! Please, please, please!"
Shani, the baby squirrel who enjoyed Mantra's company, pleaded.

Kaku and Maku, the koyal twins, expressed their disappointment in the only way
they could think of…
"Mantra can't leave; We are a band!"

"Yes, that's right! We are a band!"
Sprung to their side, sassy Soni, attempting to build a case.
"The twins sing! We dance! Don't we?!?"

"Yes! Yes! Mantra is the one who teaches us the moves;
She is the most important member of our band!
Without her, we wouldn't be able to groove." Monty's youngest, Shanti, who
could barely carry the weight of her tail, concocted a story.

"Yes, yes. That is correct! Mantra is irreplaceable!
You can't break up a band.
Can you? Can they???"
The twins screeched seemingly puzzled.

Feeling responsible for the way things were unfolding overnight,
Boscoe couldn't help himself but cry.
"It's all my fault…
Had I been attentive while flying, I wouldn't have clipped my wing.
And, you wouldn't be leaving us all behind like this…
I'm sorry. I promise, I will never leave this cave. I will never fly again.
I'm sorry. Please don't go, please…"
Begged the heartbroken parrot, soaked in tears by now.

Mantra, who rarely uttered a word yet, paid close attention to the elders' teachings,
Took the assembly by surprise when easing his grief, she thoughtfully said,
"You are a bird Bossy, you are meant to fly!
Don't ever say you won't spread your wings.
Don't you know how lucky you are?!?

I wish I could glide like you do…
But, I am not even ready to take a big leap yet.
You are the brave one, I am not.
Besides, I cannot fly, because, as you keep reminding me…
I do not have wings now, do I?!?"
She tried hard to get her dear friend to smile,
Rendering her parents speechless with what she announced next.

"It's not because of you we leave;
We have to go, because Pa's grandmama needs us."

Encouraged by her honesty, hopping onto her tiny shoulder, Boscoe tried again,
"Alright! I will never forget who I am...
A lucky bird!" he blushed.
"But, please stay until my wing heals...
I'll need a buddy to hang with when the rest are out taking flight.
Please say yes! Please, please, please. Pretty please!"
His moist eyes stared down Dhairya anticipating an approval.

"It's never easy to say goodbye. Especially, to the ones we love, little one!
But, every now and then, we must find the courage to follow our heart,
In order to fulfil our purpose of this lifetime!"
Dhairya carefully stroked Boscoe's chipped wing with his healing touch.

Addressing the future of their diminishing world, their guardian continued,
"It is so easy to get settled in our comfort zone...
Forgetting how unpredictable life can be.
Hence, keeping our senses wide open...
We must dive within ourselves!
We must be prepared!
Prepared for our calling!
Which, we never know when one might receive."
His warm smile spread contagiously amongst the children...
While his words left an imprint on their young minds.

Slowly, turning his attention to the older lot in the tribe, Dhairya continued,
"As awkward as our bond might seem,
To those who don't understand the circumstances that brought us together,
It is only us, who know what we mean to each other!

Therefore, as we are about to venture on a journey into my past...
I want you all to know, we love you dearly!
We accept each and every one of you, the way you are.
Because, thanks to you, we are now a family!

None of us are perfect beings.
We all have our flaws.
Yet, we complete each other in ways unthinkable.
Although we might not be together in flesh…
Our souls will always be connected!
Like it's been, since forever into infinity and beyond eternity!"
Raising his coconut shell up in the air, Dhairya toasted to his family.

Ravi followed in with his pledge too!
"SINCE FOREVER! INTO INFINITY! BEYOND ETERNITY!"

Causing a ripple effect;
Enticing the entire tribe to follow his lead,
Sending out strong vibrations of togetherness echoing through the cosmos;
"SINCE FOREVER! INTO INFINITY! BEYOND ETERNITY!
BEYOND ETERNITY!
BEYOND ETERNITY!
BEYOND ETERNITY!"

"You are all my children, and I am grateful that you regard me as your mother.
With you, I leave a very special piece of me behind.
My heart, which I will soon return to collect!"
Gayatri winked at the younger lot;
Who giggled at the idea of holding on to a priceless possession.

"We wish we could take you all with us.
But, our destination is far away.
So far away, that we are unsure of the ways to get there…
Simply because our forest, isn't the forest we knew, anymore…
We might encounter unfathomable obstacles,
Which you little children might not be ready to face just yet…"

"If that is so, then why is Mantra going with you?"
Interrupted Berri, the most inquisitive member of the tribe,
Unhappy with the idea of staying behind.

"Because, Mantra is always attached to Gayatri Ma's hip, you silly!"
Exclaimed Mannu the mongoose anxious to tame his growling tummy.

"I have to go...
My presence might melt great grandmama's heart!"
Mantra was hopeful.
"And, if it doesn't,
Then, at least, Ma will not feel lost with me by her side!"

Surprising everyone with her awareness and understanding,
The little macaque made believers of the sceptics!
Gathering love from her tribe along with their blessings...
The congregation huddled together in a group hug,
Wishing their dearly loved safe travels!

While a father was proud of all his children,
A mother's heart melted, sensing the impact her adorable angel had had on those who not only cherished her company, but also regarded her highly despite her age!

She was no longer a little girl who needed protection.
She was to make a difference in their world simply by being who she was;
A pure soul considerate of her tribe's feelings!

CHAPTER 6

Feeling blessed, to have established lifelong connections with beautiful souls…
The three musketeers embarked upon an unforgettable journey of their lifetime;
In hopes of reuniting with their estranged relatives.

Gayatri had inwardly blamed herself for driving Dhairya away from his family.
But, in reality, it was the ego of both Dhairya and his elders,
That had created a rift in their relationship, resulting in uncalled for anxiety.

Their inability to acknowledge the other's sentiments,
Had ignited a full-fledged fire, scaring their hearts forever.
It was their stubbornness, which had driven them away from each other;
Not the lack of love.

Although Dhairya had instantly regretted his outburst then,
His pride, had pushed him away from what he treasured the most…
'His tribe.'
Now, reading into his nightmares as a sign to reconnect with old souls…
His soul mate had convinced him to make amends with the ones she knew,
He secretly missed, every day of his life.

The idea of meeting her Pa's extended family excited Mantra!
The little macaque couldn't help herself but hop, skip and jump with glee!
Trying different stunts to impress her idols while admiring God's creation…
All the little soul could think along the way was,
'How she could be 'the glue' holding her estranged relatives together?!?'
Because, to her, family meant everything!

Despite her adoptive parents being discreet of their problems…
The smart one very often took them by surprise,

When she accurately deciphered their pain.
She was indeed a special soul, whose goal was to see everyone happy!

With uncertainty swinging over his head like a double edged sword…
Dhairya battled his dubious doubts and arising fears with grace,
Seeking solitude in his daughter's heart-warming laughter.
Successfully taming his mind to maintain its calm,
Gayatri's divine smile melted his heart furthermore…
Reminding him to hold no grudges!

Willing to overcome any obstacle which might arise on this unpredictable journey,
Dhairya was determined to make their first expedition as a family, a memorable one!

A free spirit that he was, he had realized at a young age that,
'One's destination might be the goal;
Although, one might not get there as planned…
The experiences one gains along the way, are priceless!!!'

Eager to impart this wisdom,
To the soul who was meant to carry on their legacy against all odds…
Dhairya believed in leading by example, rather than simply making strong statements - statements which had made no sense to him as a child…
Since he had seen those preaching the gospel, lead a dubious life.

"We need to be the change we intend to see."

Had emphasized the brawny Bhram!
Dhairya's role model growing up.

"It's a waste of our precious time…
Trying to convince those, who are accustomed to blindly follow the herd…
Therefore, breaking all barriers of inequality…
We must rise above our differences, to protect the weak!"

Rallying his entourage who were scattered along the Big Banyan one afternoon,
Bhram's voice reflected rebellion...
He was adamant to bring peace into all clans.
Especially, after the unfortunate loss of a meek langur's life...
Who, Bhram claimed, was tortured by ruffians of an unruly tribe.

"Making it our motto to eradicate pain altogether,
We must become each other's voice!
We must follow in the footsteps of the brave!
Allowing ourselves to display compassion to its fullest,
We must do right by another being, no matter where they might come from;
After all, we are here to support each other and become the meek's crutches..."

Bhram's powerful words had impacted everyone present!
Especially, Dheer who always bragged of his older son to be a born leader!
While, thoughtlessly labelling his younger boy, to be a vagabond!

Aiming to follow in the footsteps of his brother ever since he was little...
Bhram's words had inspired Dhairya towards the path of righteousness,
As he went along his daily adventures;
Spreading smiles and touching lives regardless of their origin!

Hearing subtle groans, coming from shrubs near the river banks one morning,
Dhairya, instantly dropped the deliciously ripe papaya from his hands and charged
towards the prickly bushes, with full intention of conducting a rescue operation
if needed.
Noticing an eaglet struggling to survive, missing the warmth of its mother's wings,
Dhairya was adamant to reunite the blinded baby with its certainly worried sick
mother.
Picking up on the scent of a wicked wolf in the vicinity...
The young soul's instincts forced him to hurry, not caring for the cuts and bruises
he gained as a result of his haste. Disregarding the sharpness of the thorns cutting
through his tender flesh, Dhairya's existence lit up when the baby eagle was safely
tucked in his tiny palm.

Scanning the area, wondering, where the helpless soul must have fallen from,
A huge mahogany tree caught his attention.

Spotting a restless serpent eagle high up in the sky desperately calling for what sounded like her baby, Dhairya lost track of time treading carefully to the top of the canopy.
His priority was to reunite the sobbing baby with its weeping mother;
And, he was ever willing to risk himself for the divine cause!

Appreciating the little langur's courage, Sakshi the eagle, was grateful for his valiant effort bestowing blessings upon him in abundance. Accepting her gratitude graciously, then planting a gentle kiss on the baby's forehead, Dhairya left their cosy nest blushing!

He was never the one to brag about his selfless endeavours;
Yet, his eagerness to share his enthusiasm was often misunderstood.
His journey through life was an open book for anyone and everyone to read...
But, he soon realized that he remained a mystery to those who were disillusioned by their false perceptions - perceptions which remained far away from his reality.

Never allowing immature minds to dampen his exuberant spirit,
Dhairya looked forward to sharing his story with Dadima who, he felt, understood his every heartbeat! Taking a minute to enjoy delicious raspberries along the way, he thoughtfully collected a few berries for his idol as a token of gratitude for his teachings.

Losing track of time along with his way, in the soon darkening dense patch of forest,
Dhairya stopped to feel the direction of the evening breeze on his bruised skin.

Unable to make up his mind as to which way to go…
He closed his eyes and opened his hearing;
With the intention of grasping onto a sign.
A sign which would point him in the direction he needed to take!

Focusing on his breath along with the outside chitter chatter of the forest, as he tried to make sense of where he was, a familiar voice close by caught his attention.

It was Lobhika;
Bhram's lady love enjoying a hearty laugh at the expense of Pheni,
A young langur from another clan who was literally crying for dear life.

Apparently luring Pheni away from her troupe by tossing exotic fruits her way, Lobhika had successfully cornered the shy and timid soul with the intention of scaring her.

Mimicking a leopard, known to create carnage wherever he went...

The temptress had chased Pheni farther into the woods, away from her family.

The thought of being ravaged by a hungry beast triggered panic in her fragile stature, forcing her to step onto a dying branch which snapped without warning.

Sending the terrified soul free falling for a distance...

Luckily, thorny creepers down below broke her fall, saving Pheni from certain death.

But, Lobhika's wickedness knew no bounds...

Because her devious plans, were always laid to perfection.

She disliked Pheni's mother Hasina whose mesmerising beauty was the talk of the animal kingdom. Always desiring to be the subject of fascination herself, the cruel langur intended to cause unfathomable pain to the beautiful soul, by making her only child vanish without a trace in a deadly pit of unforgiving muck.

Hearing her distress calls in time,

Dhairya descended closer to the forbidden territory.

But, he was soon struck by absolute grief of his own,

Witnessing his role model/idol/brother, who he put on a pedestal...

Hand in glove with the perpetrator.

In order to please his mate the one who talked the talk...

Clearly, failed to walk the walk;

When instead of showing compassion,

He senselessly threw pebbles at the quickly sinking soul; while enjoying it too.

"Brother stop that. You are hurting her..."

Screamed Dhairya in dismay.

Immediately grabbing a sturdy vine hanging in plain sight, the brave one rocked back and forth, desperately attempting to make contact with the withering Pheni.

"Hang in there, Pheni. I am going to get you out of this mess.

Hang in there!

Hold your arm high and try to stay still; I'm coming. I'm coming.
Don't give up on yourself;
I'm coming…"
He urged, holding back his tears.

"Dhairu! Are you crazy? What are you doing?!?"
Bhram was caught off guard by his brother's presence.

"Do you want to get yourself killed???
She's already sunk too deep. There is no hope for her.
You stop that stupidity right now.
Go home! I command you to go home, and not utter a word."
Besides fearing for his sibling's safety, Bhram was afraid of being exposed.

"No I won't; Not until I get her to safety.
She wouldn't be fighting for her life had you been true to your preaching.
She wouldn't be sinking so quick, had you attempted to save her.

It was your job to protect her…
You are supposed to be our saviour, not her tormentor.
What is wrong with you???"
Dhairya snapped in disgust.

Sensing the stubbornness in his tone, Bhram, although consumed with shame, felt obligated to help his younger brother. Yet, the one who had lost his vision to the tricks of a temptress, acted only after he sought a half-hearted approval from his misleading maiden.

"Have you forgotten your own words, or must I remind you now?"
Dhairya yelled in fury gasping for breath.

"'Breaking all barriers of inequality,
We must rise above our differences to protect the weak!
Making it our motto to eradicate pain altogether, we must be each other's voice…'

Remember these words?
They came out of your mouth brother. They came out of your mouth..."
Dhairya's disappointment reflected in his voice.

Taking it upon his inflated ego, Bhram grabbed onto a vine himself.
Coaxing Pheni to somehow pull her other arm out of the mess that he got her into the first place, he ordered Dhairya to follow his lead. Forgetting his anger against his dubious brother, giving Pheni priority, Dhairya obediently complied displaying great teamwork.

It wasn't an easy rescue operation...
More bruises, more scrapes spoke of one brother's courage and bravado;
And, the cowardice of the commanding sibling, reflected in his jittery actions.
Instead of showing remorse for his actions,
Lobhika still acquired all of Bhram's attention as she sulked in the corner,
Upset with him for acting against her wishes.

Carrying the mission on his shoulders alone...
Not once did Dhairya think of giving up.
Risking his life over and over, almost falling into the sinking sand himself,
He continued to try and try, until he finally succeeded to pull Pheni's limp body onto dry land. Then, he collapsed by her side feeling the exertion in his aching bones.

Instead of taking accountability for his actions by sincerely apologizing to Pheni, Bhram totally disregarded the traumatised soul, and rushed to Lobhika's side to woo her. Baffled by his idol's behavior, Dhairya was rendered speechless furthermore as he escorted Pheni to a stream nearby, holding her frail body close to his broken heart.

Gently pouring fresh water on her badly bruised eye,
The one who always felt faint at the sight of blood, played nurse for the very first time!
Carefully tending to the grave wounds on her scrawny body,
Dhairya flaunted a thick skin as he cracked jokes to hide his anxiety.

With night falling upon them quickly,
The cool breeze made the fragile being tremble like a leaf...
Dhairya, who always liked to keep dry,
Wrapped himself around the survivor like a blanket,
Promising not to leave her side, until she was in the arms of her loved ones.

Embarking upon yet another important mission, he paid no heed to time.
His inner voice was telling him to take as long as it took;
'Put in all the effort required without cutting corners' was the message...
And, diligently, so he did!

Gathering more blessings from grateful parents, whose souls were beautiful inside and out;
Although he plastered a smile on his face wishing Pheni a quick recovery, his heart hurt...
Because he knew, the idol he put on a pedestal, was responsible for all their suffering.

He staunchly believed,
Whenever he got back home, his selfless deeds would be appreciated.
He was looking forward to seek solace in Dadima's bosom, as the unfortunate incident which transpired before his eyes, had shattered his faith.

Replaying different scenarios as to how he would subtly question his icon,
The sincere soul was shocked to see a council led by his grandma, serenade a bully for his bravery allowing a tormentor to fabricate fiction, taking all the credit.

"Had my hero not risked his life,
The poor soul would have vanished right in front of our eyes.
I'm so proud of my beloved Bhram! And, so must you all be!
He is the bravest! He is the best!
Everyone is blessed to be in his presence!
My Bhram is unlike any ordinary soul...
In his compassionate heart, forever, I wish to rest!"
The power hungry beast feasted upon deception...
Encouraging everybody to sing praises of their future Chief.

In a male dominated world,

Dadima had taken charge of her tribe after the unfortunate demise of her esteemed husband. A husband whose tales of valour were still told by those who were fortunate to witness his grandeur.

Dadima was one strong primate who took pride in her uncanny ability to look through the facade of goodness. Unlike the wisdom she imparted upon the children of her clan on a daily basis, always ending her sermon with the words, *'Never say never!'*

She who claimed that she couldn't be fooled,

Was now blinded by the charisma of her successor.

Seeing his Dadima being brainwashed by the best in the business, Dhairya silently wept behind a ripening jackfruit, heartbroken at the dishonesty of his role model.

"Dhairya, get down here right now!

Where have you been gallivanting the whole day?!?

Look at the state of you; all bruised up and muddy.

Who have you been wrestling with?

When are you going to stop your antics and follow in your brother's footsteps?!?

Always getting yourself into trouble; what is wrong with you?"

His usually loving Dadima expressed her disappointment while Lobhika, shamelessly, added fuel to the fire knowing Dhairya would never rat away his idol.

"Yes, Dhairu, where have you been???

Where have you been, when your elder brother was saving those in distress?

Why are you all bruised up and muddy?!?

I hope you weren't responsible for getting Pheni into trouble.

She would have most certainly died today if it wasn't for Bhram!

You must learn something from your lionhearted brother instead of wasting your precious life hiding on trees."

The mean monkey mocked a saviour while she glorified a sissy.

Honest to the core, Dhairya bit his lips...

Not wanting to cause further embarrassment to his role model who couldn't lock eyes with his younger brother anymore; since he had been exposed for who he really was.
An oppressive coward, who was a puppet to the crude.

Witnessing the duplicity of Bhram's words and actions,
Dhairya swore never to allow himself to be brainwashed ever again;
No matter who preached…
He had learnt a valuable lesson of life that day,
'*Actions, indeed, spoke louder than words.*'

As days passed by, Dheer wondered,
'*Why my once inseparable sons are now drifting apart?!?*'

Yet, he didn't make an effort to get to the root of the problem.
Because, he was too wound up in the worldly ways.
He simply believed the lies being fed to him by the beautiful Lobhika,
Distancing Dhairya, who eventually embarked upon his own expeditions.

After being away from home for a long period one time,
He had hopelessly fallen in love with the compassionate yet sassy Gayatri!
And, since then, Dhairya dreamt dreams of a big celebration upon his return.

But, when the day arrived, he received nothing more than cold shoulders.
Lobhika, who bore a dark soul under her flawless fair skin,
Had remarkably managed to hide her bitter heart behind a sweet tongue,
Successfully fooling everyone, for as long as she did.

But, Gayatri's innate confidence and astounding beauty had instantly ruffled Lobhika's insecure feathers, seeing her bond with the matriarch with great ease. Whispering sweet poison into his ears…
The wicked primate, easily convinced Bhram who she had wrapped around her tainted fingers, to get Dhairya banished for good.

With the puppeteer setting stage for a game of flashbacks in honour of the prodigal son's return, the puppet, promptly, played his cards!

Entrapping Dadima, with the promises she made in the past...
Bhram, cleverly got Dheer to admit to a commitment.
A commitment made by them, to their faithful friends of the south.
A commitment which deprived Dhairya, of choosing his mate even before he was born.

The conniving couple, created a major hurdle for the love birds,
By playing the hypnotized tribe, like a fiddle.
Making it impossible for the righteous, Dhairya to follow his heart.

Acknowledging the qualities of Dhairya, which came across to be a curse rather than blessings, to those who never practiced morality a single day of their life....
The tricksters were confident,
Either he would choose to be celibate for the rest of his life,
Or walk away with his love, never to return.

Getting Gayatri out of her way was indeed a victory for Lobhika,
Since she had felt threatened by Gayatri's presence even before they met.
But, driving Dhairya away for good,
Was a huge relief to the lost souls;
Considering Dhairya was the only one,
Carrying the burden of his brother's betrayal.

CHAPTER 7

According to the life experiences they had gathered so far,
Gayatri, Mantra and Dhairya each carried a different baggage…
In hopes of shedding some load along the way!

Cherishing each moment spent together without any distractions,
Dhairya took a detour in order to introduce Mantra to the *'Well of Divinity!'*
A divine space Gayatri was no stranger to!

This magical well, situated in the center of the spellbinding *Temple of Spirits,*
Was where their forefathers went to call upon the souls of their ancestors…
In order to seek guidance.

Fighting his fear of the dark, he had struggled to set foot in there as a child.
Yet, one day, he crossed the threshold into a realm known to be governed by spirits;
All to impress his mentor, Bhram, who had dared him to do so.

A few seasons later,
Driven insane by his idol's hypocrisies and the delusions of his tribe…
Dhairya embraced the unknown;
Frequenting this sacred space, to seek solace in its sanctity!
Feeling miserably lost and conflicted, that day,
Dhairya barged into this unparalleled universe in desperation,
Intending to rediscover himself, by diving into the well of divine life;
Oblivious to the surprise which awaited him, just around the corner!

Although he had faced his demons in the dark, he still feared falling. Therefore, letting go was proving to be a challenge. Yet, he eagerly accepted this challenge anxious to understand the purpose of his existence!

Focusing on his mission, in order to gain insight into the bigger vision…
Dhairya crossed a hallway where ancient, mythical statues flaunted multiple eyes;
Creating an illusion of being watched at all times.
Instead of chasing fireflies, like he always did in that eerie passage, to distract himself from his fears, young Dhairya headed straight to the *Well of Divinity,* to take that much awaited leap of faith.

Nervous of diving in head first…
As he kept retracting, over and over, away from the wobbly ledge,
An unusual laughter disrupted his composure.
Making him instantly wonder,
'Were the tales of the temple being haunted, actually true?!?'

Scanning the darkness with grave caution,

Dhairya, held on to a sturdy aerial root entwined with fragrant Rangoon Creepers for dear life, while sounds of flapping wings abruptly echoed in his sharp ears; Forcing him to lose his balance.

He had felt the presence of entities in the solitude of this sacred space before; But, he always entertained that scary thought by regarding them to be friendly, enlightened spirits watching over his actions!
Yet, what he experienced in that very moment…
Wasn't an ordinary occurrence by any means.
There was indeed, some difference, in the tranquillity of this mysterious temple!
Therefore he hastily mumbled prays to the *Divine Spirits,* requesting them to keep him safe from harm's way.

"Don't be afraid my child…"
A soft, hypnotic voice tamed the beast within him, by putting him in a trance!
"I am your creator…
I am your protector…
It is me, who you seek!"
Proclaimed the Divine Goddess, lifting Dhairya's spirit by the calmness in her tone.

"Close your eyes…
Open your hearing…
Loosen your stiff mortal being…"

Taking the mystery Goddess' wish to be his command,
Gluing his eyes shut, Dhairya devoutly followed her further instructions.

"Focus on your breath…
Connect, with the divine within you, by inhaling deeply!
For I am the one to take you places;
I am the one, to show you the way!!!"

Brimming with joy at the edge of the unstable ledge,
Happy to have finally made a celestial connection,
Dhairya let go of his anxiety by slowly releasing the enchanted roots.

No sooner did he give in,
He found himself free falling into thin air,
While a mysterious muse playfully rejoiced!

"Way down, to the bottom of this well of divinity!!!"

**"Of Divinity!!!
Of Divinity!!
Of Divinity!"**

Listening carefully, to every note created by the powerful words reverberating from the stone walls like enchanted music, rigorously piercing his soul…
Dhairya smiled from ear to ear!!!
For he now knew, he had finally found what he had been aimlessly searching for!

Making a huge splash in the serene waters,
Sinking deeper and deeper into heavenly bliss,
Spellbound at the sight of his sassy soul mate, he happily lost himself into the abyss!

Bending over into darkness anticipating a response to her prank,
Her heart pounded when the ripples created by his fall settled in quickly.
Dreading the worst, with no sign of life beneath her,
The fearless prankster leaped into the dark hole…
Making huge waves of her own.

Diving in deeper than she ever had, only one prayer occupied her soul,
**"Please don't let my mischief cost him his life.
Please don't let my mischief cost him his life.
Please don't let my mischief cost him his life…"**

Picking up on her anxious vibrations,
Mystical plankton in the holy well, lit her way!
Giving her much more than the clarity she ever needed!

Pockets of sparkling air bubbles quickly sought her attention,
Drawing her closer to the one she desperately prayed to save!

Rapidly moving towards what she dreaded was a sinking body,
Little Gayatri, lost herself in his blissful smile and soulful eyes!

Eyes which released all tension at the glimpse of an Angel!
And, a smile, which widened with her presence by his side!

Setting the mood for eternal love to bloom,
The enchanting spirits twinkled like floating stars;
Creating a perfect ambience for ethereal romance, underwater!

Locking eyes for the very first time,
The young langurs lost their hearts forever…
To the magnificence of Love, in *The Well of Divinity!*

It had been a few years since the lovebirds had set foot into their love nest…

Their expeditions, adventures and arising obstacles…
Had led them away from their sacred space for so long,
That they couldn't recognise where they stood.

The once celebrated temple where often echoed songs of his soul mate…
Seemed to have been abandoned for eternity,
Since trees had extended their roots wildly through its cracks and crevices…
Embracing all the magic which the arrogant had chosen to forget.

Mesmerized by an unusually massive plant at the entrance flaunting flowers her size,
Mantra was instantly bewitched by its enchanting beauty.
And, her tiny feet were drawn, closer and closer towards an enigma!

Following the footprints of their precious, then taking charge and leading the way,
Gayatri and Dhairya where eager to transcend into their unparalleled universe, yet again!

"Wow! This is breathtakingly beautiful!"
Mantra's little spirit was exuberant.

"**What is this place, Pa!?!**
Is this what you intended for me to see?!?"

Mantra's curiosity knew no bounds as she admired the mysterious statues, casting intriguing shadows, in the spooky hallway.

"**This is where your Ma rescued me all those years ago.**"
"**Ago… Ago… Ago…**"
Dhairya's high pitch bounced back brightening his being, while old memories made him blush!

"**Yes that's right!**"
Gayatri, cleared Mantra's confusion, since the little soul considered her Pa to be the bravest in the kingdom.

"**I rescued your Pa from drowning, because, he had lost his mind!**"
She chuckled, recollecting the surreal moment…,
When she lost herself in her beloved's eyes, underwater!

"**Your Ma is being modest,**" Dhairya humbly admitted,
"**She saved my troubled soul that day…**
By forcing me to let go!
Let go of all my fears…
Let go of all my anxiety…
Let go of all my ignorance!"
Pointing at the supernatural well which was now hidden under a dome of mystical roots, engulfed with colourful flowering vines, Dhairya revelled in its glory, thanking the playful Spirits for facilitating an *eternal union!*

Intentionally making Gayatri's soft cheek flush by singing her praises, he proudly proclaimed,
"**This is where it all began!**
This is where I was blessed!
Blessed, by Goddess Gayatri!!!"

Flattered by the devotion he always displayed, Gayatri simply batted her long golden lashes, and moved along to explore the neglected holy grounds. Within

the first few steps that she took in the dark, instantly draped in cobwebs, Gayatri wondered in her head,
'When was the last time anyone set foot in there, besides its residents?!?'

"It's been too long, you cheeky monkey!"
Dropping a fig on Gayatri's head, which now flaunted a crown of web,
A huge bat with a big belly made itself comfortable in a spooky corner.

"Raksha, is that you!?!"
Gayatri was elated to hear a familiar voice.

"Who else would bestow upon you your favourite fruit, silly?!?"

Celebrating their long awaited reunion, Raksha hovered over Gayatri's head,
Enticing her bestie to join her in a game of tag, just like old times!
Leaping from a rock, to a branch, to a vine, to a root, while Gayatri tried to navigate through the changed playing field, Mantra was excited to follow her Ma. However, she was soon distracted by baby bats who engaged her in their own play.

Taking a moment to catch her breath after all that excitement, Gayatri parked herself on her favourite spot at the tip of the temple, where Raksha took the opportunity to let out her bottled frustrations.

"Why did you disappear without saying goodbye???
You forgot all about me after you found him;
Didn't you?"
She passionately complained.

"Raksha, you know that's not true. I've missed you too,
Very much you know!"
Gayatri spoke gently in all honesty.

"I expected more from you Gayu... I expected more from you!
Don't you see what's happened??? Don't you ever regret your choice?!?
You rescued his butt, but he brought you nothing but trouble..."

Interrupting Gayatri even before she could begin to defend her love, Raksha continued venting.

"Hmmm, hmm… Not now.

Please don't go making excuses for him.

Not now!

I've heard the tales being told in the jungle.

And each time I hear those despicable rumours dragging your name to mud,

I feel responsible for your situation…"

Her buttony black eyes dropped a tear.

"Had I not dared you to scare him shitless, I would still have my best buddy by my side."

Raksha frowned.

"I'm sorry Raksha, I really am…

Sorry for all the pain I've caused you.

Because, I know you hold me accountable for our beloved's tears…,"

Dhairya, who couldn't resist eavesdropping on the ladies, intervened.

"I blame myself too, for all the pain I've caused your bestie…

But, I also count my blessings every day, keeping you in my prayers!

You are the Cupid that brought us together!

For that, I am eternally grateful to you!

I hope, I am worthy of your forgiveness someday…

Whenever you are ready…

There is no rush!"

Dhairya meant every word he said while trying in vain to cheer Raksha.

"Cheer up now; Please, I plead!

Causing you pain was never my intention…

Life just blew us away in another direction, with all its might.

Alas, here we are,

All together just like old times!

So, please forget about me.

Catch up with your bestie who has missed you by her side;

Or, above her head must I say!"

Dhairya's sincerity reflected in his nervousness, as he attempted to lighten up the mood while being unsure of how the feisty bat would react.

"Who am I kidding?"
The flapping of her wings rang a pleasant bell in Dhairya's ears.
"You lovebirds were born for each other!
I'm simply bitter because I lost a mate.
I was envious of Gayatri since she found her soulmate in a knucklehead like you,"
Raksha finally caved and smiled.
"Until Sunny the charmer, swept me off my feet and our little Suraksha was born…
I do understand the importance of family and protecting your loved ones,
Because, the endearing devil broke my heart and took off with another brat…"
She slowly unfolded her pain, sniggering.

"Life is not always fun and games…
Yet, together we can survive every storm!!!

What you have done for my soul sister,
I doubt if any other langur, in any kingdom, would do.
You have stood by her through thick and thin…
Taking upon your shoulders the burden, meant for her to carry.
You safe guarded her life, risking your own…
You are the hopeless romantic, Gayu dreamt of since she was a little girl!

So thank you, for making her dreams come true!
Thank you from the bottom of my heart!!!
Really, thank you!"
Kindness reflected in her tone, for the first time in the history of their interaction;
Clearly mending broken fences!

"Truth be told; I was awaiting your arrival!
Which is why I gathered all the figs I could find in the neighbouring land."
She astonished them by her revelation.

"How did you know we were coming?!?"
The couple was baffled, since only their trusted friends knew where the trio was heading.

Unsure of where to begin, Raksha got straight to the point,
"I know of your visions.
I know they give you nightmares..."
Raksha took Dhairya by surprise again.
Then, turned her attention to Gayatri.

"Gayu! Remember the random visions I had growing up?!?
I've learnt, to read into them now!

And, believe it or not,
We are connected in ways unfathomable to complex minds.
Because, our spirit is one!
One, 'coz we have shared the gifts;
Gifts we've each received in this sacred space!

Hence, I want you to be prepared;
Prepared for what is to come your way.
Because, I know where you are heading, and...

I will tell you all about it in the morning!
Now, let's go enjoy the feast we've prepared for you my darlings.
Right Suku! Come, lead the way!"
The wise bat diverted their conversation since the little ones rushed into their arms, craving delicacies carefully collected for the celebration, of a lifetime!

CHAPTER 8

Tantalizing their taste buds with fruity blessings beyond their expectations, Raksha proved to be a great host as she always had been. Breathing in the magical air of a space untouched by man, as old friends walked down the memory lane, the younglings exhausted themselves to bed.

Whispering sweet nothings into their ears, Raksha transported the sleepy heads soundly to yet another realm before escorting Dhairya and Gayatri to her favourite spot - a spot at the peak of the glorious temple where *Holy Spirits* came out to play under the stars.

Mesmerized by the mystical flowers glowing in the dark, a sweet scent revitalized their entire being, heightening all their senses.

"It is an exceptionally beautiful night! Isn't it?!?"
Giggled Dhairya, feeling a familiar ticklish sensation that had sent him squirming in the past.

"Yes indeed!"
Smiled Gayatri, counting her blessings as a gust of wind brushed lightly against her dimples, making the presence of spirits known.

This enchanting temple wasn't a place revered by the faint hearted.

Only a chosen few found themselves under the guidance of their *ancestors' spirits,* who aimed at nourishing their souls. Those who chose to remain oblivious to their true purpose of this lifetime, foolishly deemed it haunted. Haunted, so the generations to come would refrain from seeking the gift meant to be shared; the gift of eternal life, granted only to those who were willing to dedicate themselves selflessly to the higher force for eternity.

Recollecting the good old days, when believers worshipped their ancestors wholeheartedly, the protector of the mysteries expressed her concern as her voice trembled,

"While we free spirits sit here in awe of the supreme, those who are unable to tame the beast within them, selfishly plan and execute nothing but destruction.

Eager to indulge in illusions, the deluded are willing to sacrifice another because arrogance has blurred their vision. Which is why those who have been touched by the divine,

Find themselves on a mission!

A mission to ensure our survival, as we attempt to create a better world for our children. A world where, like our ancestors, we forget our petty differences and learn to live in harmony."

Raksha tried hard to choose her words wisely...
Yet, her anxiety got in the way of her tact as she blurted,
"But for you, that ship has sailed.
The ship has sadly sailed and sunk...
Sunk since you disregarded her voice.
The damage is done because the time has passed.
Now, all you can do...
Is simply head home, to pick up the pieces of what is left behind."

Dhairya's heart sank, as Raksha deciphered his dreams.

Seeing her beloved in tears beating himself up in silence,
Gayatri held him close, reassuring him, he wasn't to carry the burden alone.

Raksha, who had grown leaps and bounds since their last encounter,
Also leaned in to comfort the one, she had secretly wished ill upon in the past.
"Don't be too hard on yourself Dhairu!
The choices we make define our character.
And, you my brother, are a special soul.

Putting the needs of others, ahead of your own...
You have restored hope and saved lives,
Welcomed strangers into your home, making them your family!

Whereas, your spineless brother...,
Talked the talk, but miserably failed, to walk the walk;

Crushing the dreams of not only his tribe, but also the animal kingdom,
Who looked up to your ancestors for love, support and guidance.

He failed us all by giving into temptations, and unleashing a curse upon his
clan.
A curse your grandma knew, only the pure-hearted could lift.”

Hearing his grandmother being addressed in the past tense, his heart sank.
“I knew she needed me,” he mumbled.
“I knew she needed me by her side.
Instead, I ignored her calling because I was blinded by false pride.
I let ego cloud my judgement; I’m flawed.
I’m not the saviour you make me to be; I’m so very flawed…”
Dhairya could hold back his tears no more.

“**Look up, my love!**” Gayatri pointed at the rising moon.

“**Do you see her magnificence?!?**
I know she illuminates your being, bringing you immense peace!
Yet, some might say her aura is flawed.

Beauty lies in the eyes of the beholder, you say;
My love, you are the most humbly beautiful creature I have ever met.
Sharing and caring aren’t flaws.
Loving and giving aren’t faults.
This is how we are all meant to be…,”
Stroking the scar on his neck, she reminded him of his valour.

“**You had more than your hands full at that time,**
But now that you’ve come to understand the gravity of the situation you
overlooked,
Don’t let the guilt of what has transpired, weigh you down.
Realisations are important in life;
Followed by acknowledgement and acceptance…
So, we can pave the path towards self-growth.
But, if we undervalue our self, we are our own worst enemy.”

The wise one tossed his way the words he had once used to comfort her.

"These are your profound words of wisdom that got me through my dark days;
And, I've always pegged you to be the one who practices what he preaches!"
Gayatri pressed a nerve...

"Together we will mend!
Together we will heal!!!
This lifetime is a blessing, therefore, together we shall lift the curse.

We might perish from this body while doing so...
However, we will never give up on our calling!
We will be born again; because we believe!
Isn't that right, Raksha?!?"

"Yes! What's done is done.
Neither of us can change the past.
What we can do moving forward...,
Is embrace the divine, when she makes her presence known!

Dropping everything on our minds;
Paying close attention when she communicates...
We listen!
For we know she doesn't speak very often.

Don't be naive to disregard her voice,
Because, she is Sacred! She is Divine! She is Holy!
She is your gut! She is your intuition! She is your inner voice!

Yet, don't confuse her with your frivolous mind,
A frivolous mind whose sole purpose is to corrupt your thoughts,
Coaxing you to stray, from being true to yourself!

The Divine Goddess, who rests within us all,
Doesn't use trickery; she shows you the way...
For;"

"FOR SHE IS THE SOURCE, AND WE ARE HER CHANNEL!"
Dhairya and Gayatri completed Raksha's powerful words,
Amazed at where life had led them to...
Baring their hearts on their sleeves,
The trio stayed up all night in the company of old spirits, crying tears of gratitude and laughing away their pain, making the most of their time together, as if, it was their last gathering.

At the break of dawn after a good night's rest,
Mantra and Suraksha surprised the elders with a lavish spread of goodies for breakfast.
Just like their mothers had once bonded beyond all differences,
Mantra and Suraksha had blended into the roles of their mothers' past,
With utmost perfection!

Reluctant to cut their reunion short, as one tried hard to convince the others to stay a bit longer, the others insisted for them to tag along on their journey.
Parting from your loved ones isn't ever easy...
Therefore, Raksha was compelled to share a secret she had hidden for so long,
"As a kid, I had laughed when my grandma enlightened me of our history.
Being the protectors of this, magnificent yet mysterious, temple and all;
But, now I bear that responsibility, because I accept my calling with pride!
As much as I would love to join you in your quest to right the wrong,
I am on a mission of my own.
And, unless we do what we are meant to do in our lifetime,
How can we make an impact in this derelict world???"

Laying her cards out right, Raksha smiled.

Feeling fortunate to have received love in abundance,
Experiencing magic overnight,
And, inspired by her aunt's parting words...
Mantra broke away from the pack, excusing herself for a minute.

With Suku hovering over her head wanting to spend every last second with her new sister, the unadulterated minds, mounted the dazzling dome which acted as a shield around the *Well of Divinity.* Whispering little prayers through a tiny gap with utmost belief, while Mantra wished *'all the pure hearted success on their mission'* - a mission to rescue those in distress while rekindling love and reuniting lost souls - *Suku prayed for her bestie's wish to come true!*

Bearing gloominess as Gayatri, Mantra and Dhairya stepped out of the Magical Temple, heading into circumstances unknown…
The queen of protection who hadn't spilt all the beans yet, rejoiced!
Forcing everyone's heart to skip a beat.

"See you again my family!
If not in this lifetime, then, the next for sure!
Because we know that we are bound together for ETERNITY!!!"

CHAPTER 9

Although her words sounded promising for the long run…
There was a hint of despair in Raksha's parting note, relating to their near future.

A hint, the gifted ones had grasped on to immediately. Yet, not wanting to agonize the other, they headed towards their destination in utter silence. Praying that their counterparts weren't trying to fill in the blanks.

The more they dwelt on that notion, the denser the clouds of melancholy became. This was the first time, since they had commenced their journey, that the trail had failed to capture the essence of their silly jokes and hearty laughs.

At one point, unable to bear the thought of inflicting unreasonable pain to those who he treasured, Dhairya intentionally kept circling the wilderness, prolonging their journey…
Hoping they wouldn't notice. But, the brilliant minds, already had.

"Pa, this trail is wonderful!"
Mantra engaged her distracted father in a conversation.

"Yes it is…"
His smile showcased discomfort.

"These flowers are so beautiful!"
She stopped to invigorate her senses, gently sniffing on a Butt Moghra.
"I love the blend of fragrances, these delicate flowers exude!"

"Hmm, hmm…" he nodded.
The one who was usually eager to impart knowledge at every nook,
Seemed very out of character that morning.

"Wow! Look at this dwarf magnolia;
It's no dwarf at all!" She seemed excited.

"And these red flowers on this Cannon Ball tree are just magnificent! Shall we climb up there Pa!?!"
Mantra tested her father's presence while he mumbled, *"Not now."*

"If not now, then, when, Pa???"
She stood there like a statue adamant to break the monotony.
"When will you snap out of being a zombie? On the fourth or the fifth lap around this garden of the enchanted temple?!?"

Dhairya was stumped by Mantra's directness, but Gayatri simply smiled.

"Back there... They weren't Dwarf Magnolia...
It was the Divine Jasmine I pointed out to.
And this, this isn't the Cannon Ball tree I wish to climb;
It is the Needle wood tree from the tea family; also known as the Schima tree.
Am I right, Ma?
I know I am, because you have taught me well."

Dhairya found himself spiralling, still, unsure of what to say.

"It is alright, Pa. We don't have to keep going in circles, if you are unsure of the outcome of our mission."
Mantra rendered her parents speechless by her candour.

"I know it is hard for you to speak your mind when I am around.
Because, you feel the need to protect me. But, I am a big girl now!

Family is everything to you, and although I haven't met them yet,
I know, they will be pleased to see us, because our intentions are pure.
And, if they fail to embrace us, it will be their loss...
A loss they will regret, just like they regretted letting you go in the first place."
The conviction in her tone was astounding.

A night at the *Temple of Spirits,* had brought out a side of the little macaque which left her langur parents astonished. Little did they know of the magic Mantra had embraced in all purity, empowering her to look into the past - a past Dhairya had never been able to forget despite Gayatri's countless efforts.

"There is nothing worse than being betrayed by your own family...,
Who would know that better than us?!?"
Gayatri seated herself on the endless root of a peepal tree gesturing them to join her.

"It is their choices, which made them suffer a fate unimaginable to us.
That is not our burden to carry.
All we can do, is move forward instead of beating around the bush,
And, face the demons head on.

We might be devastated to see what remains of your clan,
Or, we might be pleasantly surprised by their inner growth.

The only way to know for sure is to witness the outcome with our own eyes,
Rather than letting assumptions, steer us away from our quest.
We are in this together, and no matter what comes our way,
We will welcome it with open arms. Won't we?!?"
Gayatri anticipated an answer from Dhairya who never seemed so lost before.

Chasing butterflies, Mantra smartly distanced herself from the adults,
Giving Dhairya the space to share freely.

"I doubt my decision to let Mantra follow us into the abyss...
You heard Raksha; uncertainty lies ahead.
I don't want her soul to be tainted by unruly actions of the naive.
This isn't her battle."

"Your right! This isn't her battle.
But, for how long can we shield our precious,
From the ugly truth of life and scorned relationships?

All she has experienced so far is unconditional love!
Love, we have bestowed upon her!

She needs to face the harsh realities of life too,
In order to understand the importance of right choices and wise decisions.

As much as we want our princess to be safe,
We have to mould her into a warrior,
If we want her to survive this cutthroat world after we are gone..."
Gayatri came straight to the point.

Understanding the depth of Gayatri's love for Mantra, the anxious langur took a deep breath and brushed off his insecurities, in order to keep his sanity intact.
"Yes, you are right. Yet again! What would I do without you my love?!?"

"You shall close your eyes and find me by your side...
Whenever you are conflicted my sweetheart!"
The love birds affectionately embraced each other not wanting to imagine life without the other.
Seeing her parents sharing a beautiful moment, Mantra bid farewell to her new friends, and squeezed herself between them smiling!
"I love you both so much! Now, let's go find more family to love!!!"

Without second guessing himself, like he had secretly done since they embarked upon this unsettling journey, Dhairya led the way without stalling this time. Their spirits were high and vision was clear. So, together, they covered long distances in a short span of time!
Until a particular stretch of broken landscape brought tears to Gayatri's eyes.

The colourful mountain ranges rich with minerals, that had evolved over millions of years, standing strong through volcanic eruptions and natural calamities, were now being torn down by the humans.
They had expected change in their minds.
But, this level of destruction was unfathomable to her.

Humans had crossed their boundaries, yet again...
Forcing the natives of the jungle to risk their lives while metal monsters with round rubber donuts for legs, disrupted the peace and serenity of the once tranquil space.

In the midst of the madness,
Gayatri's sharp ears heard moans and groans across the division created by the black mess, called tar. Dreading putting his family in harm's way, Dhairya

suggested they take the aerial route, and as they did so with caution, Mantra spotted a scrawny wolf entangled in the thorny bushes beyond the road.
"Pa, look down there. Someone needs our help."

Without questioning her judgement, Dhairya descended to lower grounds. Asking Mantra to stay put, Gayatri immediately started plucking on the wildly growing medicinal datura leaves, to attend to the one whose body was being drained out of blood.

As a youngster, Dhairya had escaped certain death with his wit when a ferocious beast with a million dollar smile, had tried to trick him into becoming his meal. As an adult, he was now attempting to save the same beast, without any prejudice.
"Please hurry. Please, help…"
Whimpered the once dreaded wolf.

"Hang in there Khatra. We will get you out of there!"
Dhairya gave hope to the one who had tortured many.

Unable to place the voice who had accurately identified his tangled body, Khatra wondered in agony, **"Have we met before?!? I don't recognise you…"**

"That's funny because I never forgot you, Khatru…!"
Dhairya addressed the victim by a nickname the wolf despised.

**"My eyesight is weak now, just like my other senses…
But if I recall right,
There was only one langur in the entire kingdom,
Who constantly, pushed my buttons…"**
His words were shaky just like his trembling body,
"Is it who I think it is?"

**"Yes, yes. It is me! But, this time, I am not alone!
So, don't you try any tricks on us, or I will bury you myself."**
A concerned parent, warned the wicked wolf.

**"Dhairu! I wondered what became of you;
Since you were banished from not just one, but two tribes…"**

Khatra giggled, quickly apologizing,
**"I'm sorry; old habits die hard! Can't help it; I am wired that way.
I am supposed to be the wicked wolf, am I not?"**

**"You are supposed to be who you want to be...
Not what others perceive you to be. Isn't that right, Ma?"**
Mantra smiled as she took baby steps closer to the one deemed a monster.

Confused at the sight of a macaque addressing a langur as a mother, Khatra laughed,
"Now, I can die in peace. Now that I have seen it all!"

**"Good. Keep your spirit high, because getting you out of this mess,
Isn't going to be easy..."**
Dhairya warned the wolf, trying to untangle his bleeding body from the thorny bushes.

"Uncle, how did you end up in this situation?" Mantra innocently inquired.

"Uncle! Uncle, huh!?!" Laughed Khatru uncontrollably...,
"Girl, I want to live! Don't force me to die laughing..."

He couldn't help himself but quiver in pain every time he laughed.
Yet, he continued laughing.

"Do you need our help or not??? Don't move."
Snapped Gayatri who was losing her patience with the obnoxious wolf.

"Oh feisty! Nice! Nice! Very nice!"
He tried to play it cool.
**"Now, I understand why Dhairu left and never came back...
He saw in you what his people failed to see...
Or did they?!?**

I think, they saw the fire I see.

Hmmmm...
It must have really threatened Lobhika, to have a fairer beauty as competition.
No wonder games were played!

She flaunted a langur body, but had the cunningness of us wolves for sure.
Damn! That creature! She was the epitome of wickedness."
He dwelt on the memories which caused him embarrassment and pleasure all at
once, until a stubborn thorn, sucked the air out of his being.

"What do you mean by 'she was the epitome of wickedness'?
Has Lobhika changed her ways now?
How is Bhram? Are they still together?"
Dhairya searched for answers.

"Hasn't the wind blown in your direction since you left???
Don't you know, what became of your blood?"
Khatru's voice trembled along with his body.

"Uncle Wolf, would Pa be asking you questions he already knew the answers
to?
We are on a mission to find our family...
Would you please be kind enough to point us in their direction?!?"
Mantra was eager.

"*Ha ha ha ha ha*! Family?!? *Ha ha ha ha ha*! You're kidding me right???
If that is what families do to each other?
Trust me child, you are better without one.

Even us wolves show our own mercy, but Lobhika...
She was ruthless!
I wonder how she would react, to this unusual family dynamics that you have
going on here. Can someone explain to me, why a macaque keeps calling a
langur, Papa?
Ha ha ha ha ha ha!"
Even in his suffering, Khatra couldn't help himself but be mean.

"Because, we are the parents she knows;
And, if you survive this ordeal, you are welcome to come meet our extended family.
I'm sure they would blow your mind, and you might just die laughing."
Gayatri sternly put an end to the mockery, while still tending to his wounds.

CHAPTER 10

Surviving an extremely excruciating ordeal while Dhairya carefully pulled out, every stubborn thorn from Khatra's bony body, Khatra, who was once the poster boy for the savages in the animal kingdom, dropped his fierce act displaying vulnerability, probably, for the first time in his life.

The one who took pride in the pain he inflicted upon others…

Cried tears of gratitude, laying as comfortably as he could on a bed of grass away from the roaring metal monsters wondering, *'how would he repay Dhairya for his selfless act?'*

**"I would put my hand in the lion's den if he was in trouble;
You were an easy save, Khatru!"**
Dhairya chuckled trying to lift up Khatra's broken spirit.

"Now, if you promise to not bite off our heads as soon as you regain some strength, we shall escort you to the river. I hope water still flows freely down there, because you need some nourishment my friend, and water is all there is on the menu…"
Owlishly, Dhairya reaffirmed the set boundaries.

"Yes it does…" Khatra let out a frustrated sigh.
**"But, we can no longer enjoy the water without being chased away.
And, I am clearly in no position to run."**
Dejection reflected in his demeanour.

**"Why do you look so sad, Uncle Wolf?
Don't worry, you will heal in no time. My Ma has magic in her touch!"**
Mantra affectionately stroked his ear proud to see her idol at work.

**"Child, why do you insist, on hurting me by making me laugh?
Stop calling me Uncle. I am no one's uncle."**
To whom meanness came naturally once, he now tried hard to put on a failing show.

"Night is falling upon us soon.
The two legged monstrous mammals,
Will be returning home to their families by the river.
They assume I am road kill; I'd like to keep it that way.
If they spot me now, they will undoubtedly hunt me down.
I might deserve that fate after all the games I've played,
But, you…," His prickled paws reached out to Mantra.

"I appreciate all your efforts to save me.
Therefore, I don't want to endanger your lives.
You have to move along to spread your love and share the light.
So move along. Move!
Before the beast inside of me decides to chew you for dinner.
Go. Go. Move along." Khatra tried his hardest to get them to leave.

"*He he he!* You are not as scary as you make yourself to be, Uncle Wolf!
My brother Capu does a better job."
Mantra teased the once dreaded wolf.
"If it makes you feel any better,
Capu is a fierce, yet, loving leopard; And yes, he is my brother!"

The smart one painted a clear picture. Yet, his limited mind, restricted Khatra from accepting the possibility of coexisting in harmony.
"Pa always says, *'Help those in need.'* And, you, Uncle,
You need all the help you can get to survive another day. So…"

"So, while I fetch you some water, and hopefully, find a carcass on the way,
Could you please enlighten the ladies as to why the humans want you dead?!?"
Dhairya sprung into action sternly laying a plan.

Always accustomed to have the last word, Khatru pushed Dhairya's buttons,
"Oh, so naive you are! Leaving your delicate darlings,
Alone with a ferocious beast like me. You fool!"

"Snap out of your delusion, old man!
I might look like a meek langur to your deluded eyes,

But, when I unleash my inner warrior goddess, you will regret having met us.
So, can we all get along without any drama,
Or shall I throw you back where we found you???"
Gayatri put an end to the egotistical maniac's assumptions secretly winking at
Dhairya, who quickly engineered a wooden flask.

"Alright, alright. You get going before I die thirsty.
I will keep the goddesses entertained!"
The wild wolf finally attempted to tame his wicked words.
While Dhairya nodded in agreement, and took off towards the river.

Giving the ones he mocked earlier his undivided attention,
Khatra tried to mask his fear with humour,
"My days are numbered, you see!
Or, given the state of me, shall I say hours...
There was a time when I was the most notorious wolf!
One, who gave chills to those, who simply heard of my existence.
But now, the tables have turned.

Ever since the ignorant inhabitants of the concrete jungle, have destroyed our
way of life, driving us away from our natural habitat...
We now struggle to survive." he groaned.

"I might boast of my desire to thrive still,
Yet, I secretly wish I'd perish in the wild, or what is left of it..." he seemed sad.

"I've remained stubborn all my life...
Disregarding the wisdom of the wise;
Because, I felt, my young blood knew better.
But now that I am old, and alone...,
And, I wish I would have listened, instead of acting on impulse."
Honesty shone in his confession.

"You asked me, how I got myself in this bloody situation...?
Well, I, who once terrorised weak souls of this jungle,
Am now spooked, by every shadow, cast around me...

Now, I understand the plight of helpless creatures;
Plight, when I took them by surprise for my guilty pleasures;
Because, I am no longer the hunter now...
Now, I am being hunted!

Hunted for preying on their cattle,
While they live in denial of driving away my meals.
They barge in whenever they want, wherever they want,
Flaunting guns and flames...
Forcing us out of hiding, to exploit us in every way possible."

The floodgates to his eyes were now open as he shared his horror...
"I wish now, my wounds do not heal; because then,
I'd be worthless to those who give me nightmares."

"Do not wish that."
The sensitive child stopped the sulking wolf right there.
"Never wish ill upon yourself or others.
Because, the Universe is always listening!
It is absorbing all the vibrations, the good and the bad.
Although it might seem like the reigns are in the hands of evil,
We cannot accept defeat."
Mantra enlightened him with her learnings.

"We might not be happy with the cards that have been dealt to us...
But, the only way you can flourish in life is,
If you utilize the given tools...,
To their optimum potential!
While aligning with like-minded souls, without any prejudice!
You are the bravest wolf I have ever met, and...,"

Unable to hear anymore Khatra interrupted Mantra,
"You can preach all you want,
But, when they are gunning for you, there is no mercy.
It's either give in, or lights out for good.

And, I rather die a free spirit, than be caged and tortured like the others, for my fur.

It's not only the furry critters who have met an unfortunate end in this land,
Your kind has been captured too.
They say, since you are their closest primate,
You are good specimens for experiments.
I don't understand what that exactly means;
But, I know for sure, none of us are safe until the so called civilized humans, are walking the face of this earth."
He chose his words wisely, dreading Gayatri's wrath.

"My Ma says no one is born evil.
Everyone bears a soul.
And, you are a perfect example, my wicked Uncle wolf!"
Mantra tried in vain to get him to smile.

"Yes, that's true!"
Gayatri was proud of her baby's views.
"We do not get to choose the arms that rock our cradle as a child...,
However, as we gain consciousness, it is our deeds that define our character.

You think of yourself to be alone when you most certainly are not.
We all have been forced to face demons and fight battles.
Battles, which we never imagined in our wildest of dreams.
Why???
Because, we were comfortable in our existence,
Living life the only way we were taught to live.

But with changing tides, we have to regroup and adapt.
Adapt, to the new dangers we face...
So that, we can safeguard what is truly precious!"
Fearing the future, Gayatri held Mantra close to her heart.

"These mammals you describe to be monstrous,
They might be facing demons of their own, for all we know.

Don't get me wrong,
There is no excuse for them being inconsiderate and inhumane,
But, to solve an issue, we have to get to the root of the problem.
There might be strange reasons for them to behave the way they do.

Maybe, they act out of fear...
Out of greed. Out of ego. Out of hatred. Out of vengeance.
Or, out of plain ignorance.

They consider themselves superior than us;
Yet, they do not understand the gravity of their actions.
Because, their minds are so limited...
Moving in a herd, doesn't always bring out the best in you,
Because then, you are confined in a box.

Yet, there comes a time in everyone's life...
When they have to face a mirror!
And, believe me, it's never easy to see,
What has become of the soul, trapped in that selfish body.

It takes a lot of courage to be true to oneself!
Therefore, we can't deem them all to be monsters..."
Gayatri paused, to catch her breath.

"Also, you must have gauged by now,
Not all situations and relationships in life are traditional!
And, not all wolves are wicked!
Because if they were...,
You would be chewing us for dinner right now, wouldn't you?!?"
Gayatri's compassion and rationalization comforted Khatra's scorned heart to an extent that he couldn't help himself but, apologize to Mantra, for his harsh remarks.

"Little angel! I'm so sorry, to have mocked you before...
My restricted mind refused to see your aura, up until now.
All because I was blinded by false belief.

A belief, that only those of the same kind, belong together...,
And, anything else is taboo.

Your Ma is right! She is so very right!
Not all relationships and situations are traditional,
And, not all wolves are born wicked!"

A first meaningful tear, trickled down his cheek,
As he gazed at the darkening skies,
Grateful for crossing paths with not just an angel in disguise, but two!

CHAPTER 11

With night falling upon them quickly,
The parched wolf anxiously awaited Dhairya's return,
While Mantra and Gayatri did their best to divert Khatru's mind off his pain.

On his way to fetch water,
Dhairya tried to make sense of what Khatru had said about Lobhika,
'Was she to blame for all their nightmares?'

Dhairya was never the one to make assumptions.
He had learnt this lesson early on in life, at the expense o. ...
brother, who he had once put on a pedestal. The thought of the temp... ...
mayhem, had crossed his mind in the past. Yet, he had brushed off that judgement,
knowing other dangers dangled over them like a double edged sword - dangers,
which he couldn't predict nor rule out, until he got to where he needed to be and
saw, what he needed to see.

Although he aimed to empty his mind of all the chaos…
His thoughts kept drifting towards darkness...
Forcing him to stop, and take a moment, to catch his breath.

Shutting his eyes, he prayed to see the light…

Attempting to mute the voices in his head…,
He focused on the sounds of the jungle.

Yet, surprisingly, he heard none.

The silence was crippling.
Yet, he dug deep and inhaled, to the best of his ability…
Then, he exhaled, when he felt he was ready.
By the time he finished his third fulfilling breath, he felt light as a feather,
And the music created by the free flowing water nearby, lifted his spirits!

Instantly engulfed by multiple emotions of varied magnitude,
Dhairya recollected the good old days when the river banks were their playground,
and getting there each time, was just another adventure! Picking up his pace, he
giggled like a little boy, and the next minute, tears trickled down his cheek. He
was finally where he wanted to be. *Home!*
Home, in the Valley of Hope!

A valley, which the folklore described as the birthplace, of the chosen ones!
Chosen ones;
*Because, they were blessed to be born at the hour, when the soothing rays of the
slumbering sun made the entire valley glitter like gold, and that very night, the
magnificence of the full moon reflected in the river, sparkling like a diamond!*

...t just born in the valley like the chosen few…
...parents took pride in mentioning, that,
...boy was born in 'the magical moment!'

Dhairya had never let the timing of his birth, get to his head.
He had brushed this story, as he had many other tales,
Because, he couldn't understand, what was being told…
Nonetheless, the way things were unfolding in his life,
He was forced to consider the folklore to be the prophecy,
Their ancestors staunchly believed in.

Because, now, he had learnt to acknowledge their spirits!

He wasn't perfect, but he was everything the prophecies predicted.
And if this were really true,
He wished, he had known the others who were touched by that magic moment too.
Feeling invigorated, just by the thought of not being alone on his mission,
Dhairya drifted into the past, hoping to find some clarity.

'*Those were the carefree days!*' he thought to himself smiling,
When, they explored every patch of the luscious jungle,
Without having to look over their shoulder…
Unless, it was feeding time for the predators!

Those were fun filled days of basking in the glory of the mighty sun,
After the cold agonizing baths he always dreaded.
He had forever cherished,
His favourite moments of heavenly bliss at the highest peak in their kingdom,
Where cottony clouds caressed his scrawny body;
Nourishing his restless soul!

Many memories were created in this paradise;
Which sheltered numerous species of birds, insects, animals and reptiles!

It was always hard to get away with any mischief,
Especially by the river banks,

Because there were eyes everywhere, and a background score for everything!
The only way one could go unnoticed,
Was if they sought the expertise of the master of camouflage,
Miss Gitty the chameleon!
Besides the regular bickering and banter between friends, families and seasonal clashes of the clans, for the most of it, they had all learnt to live in harmony.
Almost every day was a picnic for those who knew how to live life,
And, every night screened a movie with the stars for those who weren't afraid.

Things were wild! Things were real!
Yet, life was blooming everywhere!
There was once, magic in the air of his motherland…
The land, which was now left totally deserted.

'Where is everyone hiding?'
He thought to himself as he bent over to fill the makeshift bamboo flask with water,
While his eyes scanned the trees across the river, anticipating some action.

Disheartened at the sight of the emptiness, Dhairya's emotions ran high.
Which is when, a voice within reassured him, *'He would find his answers in time!'*

Yet, darkness crept upon him simultaneously, creating various doubts.

As much as he craved hope, conflict consumed his being causing despair.
He struggled not to let negativity overpower his faith.
But, the reality of it all was bewildering.
So, calling upon the souls of his ancestors with his eyes glued shut,
He prayed wholeheartedly, to seek direction!

And, within seconds, a calming voice commanded his attention.

"Have you lost your way, boy?!?" Wondered the concerned spirit.

"It seems I have, oh holy one!"
Dhairya confessed in all honesty tempted to open his eyes.
Yet, he resisted afraid of losing the connection.

"Please show me what I need to see...
Lead me to where I need to be!
I am, the son of this valley.
I seek those, who shared the same spellbinding blanket as me!
Kindly guide my way, since precious time is slipping away...
And, I have an important task at hand."

Dhairya gleefully awaited a glorious response from his ancestors,
Who, he was told, *'Were always listening!'*

"Oh really?!? I find that hard to believe!"
Sarcasm oozed out of those words, baffling the believer.

"What is it that you find hard to believe???
The fact that I am the son of this Valley of Hope,
Or, that I have an important task at hand?
Or, simply, that I am lost?
Which one is it?!?
Do enlighten me on your views.
Because, I've heard you see beyond, what we mortals can even begin to imagine."
Frustrated Dhairya demanded an answer.

"You are joking right!?!?"
Mockery was all Dhairya could hear in that tone.
Yet, he held his composure determined to hear more.

"You say you are lost. You state you are on a mission.
You also realise time is of the essence,
Still, you stand here with hands joined, and eyes glued shut.
Wonderful!!!

Open your eyes fool, and look around you...
How else, will you find your way and fulfil your mission?
Come on now, we don't have all day.
Tick tock, tick tock!"

Taking a moment to let the words of wisdom sink in, Dhairya slowly opened his eyes.
Only to find an imperial eagle-owl double his size, staring him down.

"Finally!" Rejoiced the regal entity in dismay.

But the anxious langur lost himself again in Vaani's deep blue eyes, chanting…
"She, who bears the tenacity of a fearless eagle…
And, the insight of an owl!
Looks upon us in our darkest hour guiding us to the light…
Provided we can see!"

To him, this was indeed a miracle!
For she who was rumoured to be a myth,
Had now mysteriously graced him with her presence.

Delighted to encounter this supreme being who not only embodied characteristics but also the features, of two different species, Dhairya couldn't help but lose himself in her uniqueness, over and over again.

"Snap out of it Mr. Langur.
Didn't your mama ever tell you it is rude to stare?"
Vaani, attempted to school the one who displayed boyish behaviour.

"Now, listen to me boy.
You are not only way out of your league here,
You are most certainly out of your zone.
I haven't spotted your kind around here since the senseless massacre last summer."
Her sapphire eyes turned blood red reflecting angst; Shaking him to the core.

"Massacre???" He wanted to cry.

"Yes, massacre…"
The feathery horns on her mesmerizing head absorbed all tension,
Making his head spin.

"It was the wedding season,
Homo sapiens clad in colourful attire and glittering jewellery, were storming the ancient temples in the vicinity from different parts of the land... To perform their 'sacred' rituals.

The serenity of our space was disrupted by the constant chaos and commotion,
While two legged mammals huddled to reach deadlines.
The wind constantly carried the fragrance of orange and yellow Genda flowers.
The occasional aroma of special lunches drew in monkeys from all around the kingdom.

The shy langurs never strayed.
But, the notorious ones;
They paraded the temple creating havoc and causing destruction,
While the queen bee admired the objects of her fascination from a distance.
She had him tightly wrapped around her fingers.
Hence, her every unruly wish always became his command."
The creature of mystic frowned while Dhairya couldn't help but wonder,
'Was it Lobhika she spoke about?'

"Such a pity it was. Such a shame...
One moment they were all celebrating;
The next minute, many families were scrambling for dear life.

Giving the ruthless sapiens what belonged to them would have averted the dark clouds which now engulf this forest. But, no; They chose to cover up their stupidity, or her greed shall I say...
By risking it all.
All that bloodshed, to protect her, who made a deal with the devil...
How brainwashed were they?"
Sadness reflected in her tone, slowly turning the ruby eyes, pale yellow.

"This isn't the place you might have once known...
The Valley of Hope, no longer exists.
It has now turned into the Valley of Despair.

Get away from here, son.
Get away before you get consumed by the darkness just like the rest."

He who was on a mission, couldn't begin to imagine the horror and suffering of his people. Therefore, words barely made it past his lips...
"It is Lobhika you talk about, right?!?
The one who had them tightly wrapped around her fingers?
I know it is her. Isn't it?"

He shook his head in dismay.

"I should have exposed her when I had the chance.
Instead, I let her manipulate me to walk out on my family.
I wish, I had the courage to stand up to the one I blindly worshipped back then.

I am Dhairya, the spineless langur, who kept running away from confrontations, rather than trying to make things right."
The brave heart bawled like a little child.

"I failed my family miserably. I lost the ones I loved...
My grandmother sought my help in my dreams.
But, I deemed them to be nightmares.
I could have saved them, I could have saved them all..."
He broke down completely.

"If you are the same Dhairya I've heard stories of,
Who your scars tell me, you are!
You are not the coward you make yourself to be.
You made the choices you made...
Because, you knew there was no reasoning with the ones blinded by false belief.

You are a free spirit, who refused to be caged!
You are humble! You are kind!
You put the wellbeing of others before your own.

Therefore, you are so harsh on yourself...
Unlike, the others who are ever ready to point fingers at everybody else;
Rather than accepting responsibility for their own actions.

You need to understand, precious soul...
You cannot save the ones, who do not want to be saved.

We all have a conscience; nobody is born without one.
So, don't blame yourself for what you think you could or could not have done,
Or, what u did and did not do.
You are special, my boy! Very special!
You just don't know that yet..."
The wondrous Vaani, comforted the pure hearted, by wrapping her dreamy brown and white dotted wings around the grief struck Dhairya.

Transporting him back in time...
To where he wanted to be and see what he needed to see!

CHAPTER 12

He yearned to reunite with his estranged family...
Miraculously, he found himself amongst them!

He had anticipated this reunion for a long time now...
Yet, he freaked unable to identify with his surroundings.

Something, had drastically changed.
The paradise he once called home had now lost its charm.
The peepal, the mango, the mahogany,
All trees had vanished, leaving traces of eradication behind.
The soil was coarse; their land was dry.
With hundreds of birds evicted from their homes,
There was no music left in the air.
Lives that still remained, sadly, brought nothing to life.
A sense of kinship and camaraderie was clearly missing...
The harmonious energy in the Valley of Hope had shifted tremendously,
Transmitting nothing but hostile vibes, within the tribe.

Just like him, his buddies had aged.
But, sadly, it didn't seem like they had all grown.
The bullies were now openly tormenting the meek,
While the rest, went along their business ignoring the plight of the traumatised.
The kind of behaviour which was never tolerated before,
Seemed to have become, a daily occurrence.

'Where was Dadima in all of this?' He wondered,
'How could she have let all this happen?'

Instantly fearing the well-being of his cherished grandmother,
His mind raced to her favourite spot in the Valley of Hope!

Where,
Besides bestowing blessings in abundance…
The Enchanting Goddess of Eternal Life,
Forever bedazzled her worshippers by her bewitching beauty!

She not only dug her rustic roots deeper and deeper into glorious grounds,
But also, spread her arms out wider and wider into mystical air,
Allowing herself the freedom to free fall into the wilderness!
The wilderness longing to be graced by her divine touch.
Slowly yet steadily, auguring the inevitable connection!
Spreading love furthermore!

For over centuries,
The beguiling Banyan conceived multiple mighty trunks,
By simply running wild through her briskly blossoming branches!
Occasionally, taming her madness, to give shape to her already enthralling self!

That was Dadima's temple!
That was her shrine!
That is where she went to seek guidance, whenever things got out of hand!

'In the arms of the Big Banyan, is where I might find her in these times of distress…'
Dhairya thought to himself eager to unfold the mysteries.

Yet, transcending to her divinity proved to be a challenge.
Because, he was constantly reminded of his nightmares.
The signs he had ignored; those visions he had dismissed,
His noncompliance gave him the jitters not knowing what to expect when he got there.
Yet, he found it in himself to battle all demons,
And, instantaneously, his gloomy spirit basked in the glory of her existence!

Unlike his nightmares, she hadn't turned into ashes.
However, Yet what remained of her, was very tragic.
Her dazzling sturdy roots which once supported their madness,
Had turned into shreds…
Her once significant stature, could now fit in a frame.

He apprehended the worst when he set out on this journey,
But, what he witnessed was far more devastating.
The once celebrated Banyan wasn't a safe haven anymore.
Hooligans had tainted the sanctity of her sacred space,
Forcing young parents away from the ruckus in order to protect their younglings.

So much had gone wrong, in such little time,
Making it dawn upon him,
That time was of the essence!
And, the more he dwelled in the past, his present was swiftly fleeting.

Inhaling deeply to regain his balance,
Dhairya let his eyes rest while his ears took him places...
Scanning through numerous voices both familiar and unfamiliar,
He stumbled upon a voice, which, often came to haunt him.

"I am stuffing myself! Gaining weight! Sacrificing my beauty!
All so your seed inside me can flourish. But, look at you...
You who constantly talks about taking me to the moon,
Plucking me some stars;
You can't even gather the courage to get me a stupid necklace.

You call yourself my loving and devoted husband?!?
Is our child going to inherit cowardice from you?!?!?
Answer me!"
Lobhika emotionally blackmailed Bhram, who seemed as smitten as he was before.

"My love, haven't I gotten you everything you have desired?!?
Look at this scarf...
Remember that afternoon!?!
You pointed at this green scarf and I immediately;
Immediately nicked it off that little girl in the village for you.

And then, a week later, when you saw a bride in the temple with this, red one,
You only had to mention, how much you loved the golden embroidery!
Didn't I draped you in silk myself that night?!? Didn't I?!?

These accessories... These decorations...
You so elegantly display in this love nest;
Your one look was enough for your wish to be my command!
Haven't I always got you what you've desired?"
Bhram attempted in vain to cheer his better half,
Who, for reasons unknown to him, was lately bitter.

"Ok then. You know what my heart desires!
So, quit wasting time, and go get me that diamond studded necklace!"
She demanded vainly.

"I would. You know I would!
But, you understand how risky this business is, don't you?!?
The last time we set foot in that village, a lot of blood was shed...

They've upped their security since.
Besides, the chief's daughter is getting married soon.
They will surely be on high alert right now. Give me a few days, please!
I will get you a better necklace than the one the mad man's wife was wearing.
I promise!"
Bhram pleaded to his wife who wasn't willing to budge.

"Oh, forget it!
I should have listened to my mother instead of following my heart.
She warned me that you weren't good enough for me...
She is right! She is always right!

You are not as brave as you say you are.
You definitely don't love me as much as you claim you do.
You care too much of what your grandmother has to say, don't you?
How will you ever keep me happy?!?

I'm such a fool.
Oh God! I'm such a fool!"
Lobhika put up a show crying crocodile tears while playing him like a fiddle.

"Don't be upset, my love. This uncalled for anxiety can't be good for our baby."
Bhram expressed his concern.

"Oh for God's sake! Please, drop the act. What do you care?"
Lobhika knew exactly, how to push his buttons.

"I do care! I care a lot, my darling!
Why do you always question my love for you?
You know, I would do anything for you. Don't you?!?!?"
He tickled her playfully.

"Alright then! Go get me that necklace!!!
And while you are at it, surprise me with something else!
Something equally special!!!"
The selfish beauty sealed a sinful deal, with a passionate kiss.

Then, revealing her true colours,
She implied he rally his troops along the way, displaying her lack of faith in him.
Gesturing him to move along, not much love reflected in her actions...
But, blinded by love, Bhram clearly failed to see her shady shades.

As much as Dhairya felt betrayed by his childhood idol,
He still cared enough not let Bhram risk his life.
Therefore, wanting to talk sense into his older brother,
He attempted to grab onto Bhram's shoulder several times,
Only to come to a realization that...
He was merely a spectator looking into the past.

Approaching his gang of thieves, the love struck Romeo quickly filled them in on his mission, and hurried back to the one he dreaded to let out of sight.
Unruly acts, not kept secret anymore;
His posies, openly bragged about the necklace they were commissioned to steal.

Fearing his tribe's wellbeing, the ever attentive Dhyan, rushed his limp legs in anguish towards the esteemed matriarch, to warn her of a disaster waiting to strike.

Following his childhood friend's wobbly footsteps, across barren fields and bone dried bushes, Dhairya was in dismay of the entire situation...
A distance which the daredevils covered within a minute years ago,
Now proved gruesome, for the incapacitated Dhyan.

Wondering what circumstances might have led him to this unfortunate fate,
Dhairya, was proud of his friend's commitment, given,
He didn't take a moment to breathe;
Knowing, there was not a second to spare.

Striding up the rundown steps of the crumbling ruins with the support of his muscular arms, Dhyan called his godmother in desperation...
"Dadima, Dadima! Where are you, Dadima?
You have to make him stop. The fool is going to get us all killed."

"*Shhhhhhhhh*. Keep your voice down...
Dadima has finally fallen asleep!"
A vaguely familiar voice whispered from inside.

"It is only Dadima who can stop this madness, please hear me out.
We have to get her to the Big Banyan right away.
Otherwise, we are all going to suffer the same fate, as his father.
Please wake Dadima. Please, listen to me..."
He begged for her to act promptly.

"This better be good.
You know, she hasn't slept a wink since Dheer has passed.
What is the matter with you???" Furiously shushing Dhyan for his intrusion, a ghost from Dhairya's past, stormed out of the stone walls.

It was none other, than the mother, whom he had chosen to forget.

Protecting himself from the anxiety of constant separation...
As a child, Dhairya had trained his thoughts to forget that Titli ever existed.
Yet, here she was, after all those years of neglect,
Mourning, the death of her husband...
While caring for the one, she forever despised.

Titli, had rightly earned the title of a butterfly, for she could never stay put.
She was never content, no matter where she went.
And, the company she sought, bored her easily.
Her frivolous mind was always on a prowl for greener pastures.
She constantly accused her husband of using children as a tool, to cage her free spirit.
Even the birth of her sons wasn't enough to tie her down.
Hence, running away from motherly duties came to her naturally.

Although Dhairya missed his mother tremendously in her absence…
Her presence, always made him uncomfortable.
It was like meeting a stranger each time she appeared.
Little did he understand then, that, she was running,
Not from the ones who loved and adored her…
She was escaping the demons in her head, which unrelentingly kept haunting her.

Dejected by her recurring nightmares, Dadima, who kept herself, from slipping into another realm, heard every word being whispered outside.
Struggling to carry the feather weight of her withering self,
The highly regarded langur made a shaky appearance, shocking Dhairya to the core.

Unable to control himself at the sight of her shrunken state,
His concerned spirit rushed by her side, desperate to comfort her.

"If it wasn't for me, none of this would have happened."
Dadima's saddened eyes, looked through his broken spirit,
Making him wonder if she felt his presence.

"Instead of punishing him for his wrong doings,
I repeatedly overlooked his shortcomings.
I was so naive to think it was just a passing phase of rebellion,"
Mocking her stupidity, she reached out to Titli for support.

"It is easier for one to admit their mistakes;
It is way harder to acknowledge that they've been fooled.

I fell into her trap. I got sucked into his lies. I allowed them to chase him away. I abandoned the one who had the courage, to protect us from this turpitude.

I should have stopped that madness then. I could have convinced him to stay...

**I could have! I should have! But, what's the point now???
Now, it is too late."**

Her once thunderous voice, which turned mischief mongers into statues, could now be barely heard.

Never in his wildest of dreams had Dhairya imagined,
That the one who raised him to be the valiant langur that he was,
Lived in denial most of her life.

He who carried the image of a strong, stern and unbiased charismatic leader in his mind, found it hard to accept her sincere apology. Painful memories of the past flooded his entity, recollecting the dark night when he was forced to leave his tribe...
All because, he wished to follow his heart!?!

'If she overlooked Bhram's imperfections, why wouldn't she accept my loyalty?'
He questioned her love and affection for a split second;
Then, quickly reminded himself that she loved them both equally.

'If so, then why the discrimination?' He debated...

His anxiety ran lose. Yet, he summed up the courage to look past her flaws. Because, in all honesty, although her words and actions hadn't aligned in the past, her desperate soul was indeed seeking the grandson she let go.
Helplessly invisible to the one who yearned his arrival...
Dhairya earnestly called upon the souls of their ancestors to give her the strength she needed, in order to put an end to the insanity which was to follow.

With the support of the angels who stood by her side, the Matriarch displayed her fighting spirit as they hobbled towards Lobhika's den. Standing at the foothills of the mountain which shadowed Dadima's once serene temple, Titli called out to Bhram numerous times. But, he chose to ignore the cries of his grieving mother.

"Bhram! I thought you were hopelessly blinded by love;
Now, has that cat got your tongue too?"
Dadima dug deep to make her presence known, but her words also fell on deaf ears.

"I know you can hear us, Bhram!
Please, my boy, please don't go back to the village.
Don't trespass onto their land, for you know, you are playing with fire.
Bhram? Why don't you answer us?!? Have you stopped listening???"
Titli's pleas echoed throughout the Valley of Hope, inviting all souls to her council.

Drowning in his delusions, the black sheep disregarded her concern,
Infuriating the mother who had recently lost her son to her grandson's antics.

"Stop swindling yourself son."
Dadima roared in fury.
"Who are you trying to deceive?!?
You were a disgrace to your father when he was breathing;
And, now that my son is gone,
You shamelessly go about destroying his legacy?
Who do you think you are???"
The astute langur challenged a buffoon's ego.

"Look at her!
There is no life left in those bones.Yet, she screams on top of her lungs!"
Influenced by Lobhika, the brainwashed Bhram ridiculed the one who rocked his cradle.

"Who am I you ask???" sinking to lower depths, he laughed.
"Who am I?!? Who am I?!?!?" he mockingly repeated.

"I will tell you who I am, you fossilized monkey!" he charged at the elders hoping to intimidate the crowd, while his entourage cheered him on.

"I am the one who you must bow down to!
I am the one whose feet you must touch!
For, I am the one who will let you live, another day in Paradise!"
Intending to impress his lady love who looked down upon him from higher grounds, Bhram crossed all his boundaries enraging Dhairya who powerlessly watched the events of the past unfold.

"Bhram! This is Dadima you speak to. Show some respect!"
Dhyan intervened defending the honour of an adulated soul.

"Oh! I know who, she is, alright!!!
But, it seems like you are the one who has forgotten;
Step back, you cripple, before I break your remaining limbs."
The deluded langur reminded Dhyan of the unfortunate afternoon when, upon Lobhika's orders, Bhram's goons ruthlessly broke his hind legs for interfering in their delirium.

"You are going to lead us all to our graves, you ungrateful beast;
Just like the way you did your father.
His blood is on your hands. And, you shall never be forgiven."
Wept Titli cursing her first born who, she feared, was already doomed.

"Oh, mother!!! Don't cry. I know you love me. I know you do…"
His childish tone almost melted a mother's heart.
But, his theatrics left her speechless.
"You love me, so much; So much, that you constantly abandoned me!!!
I cried for you to stay, but you always got away.
If it wasn't for Lobhika's love, I would have died lonely a long time ago…"
He pointed her failures deflecting from his own actions.

"It was his choice to take the bullet for me. I never asked him to.
The old man lived a fool and died a fool.
It is those villagers who are responsible for his death, not me.
So, don't you blame me for your loss, you vagabond!"
Bhram senselessly insulted his mother, for he was eluding reality.

"Stop! Stop right there, Bhram.
I hear the words coming out of your mouth,
But, I very well know they are not yours!"
The fearless primate touched a nerve.

"You, Bhram.... You were such a brilliant young boy.
A boy who genuinely cared!
Not only for your own but also those who needed support.
You were kind, and compassionate.
That is the grandson whose memories I hold on to.
One who would never hurt a fly,
This; this Bhram who stands before me dripping in arrogance;
This is a langur living a lie!"
Dadima urged him to reflect into his soul.

"The drapes of denial are clouding your judgement right now;
And, malicious monkeys are pulling your strings.
You were destined for greatness, my boy..."
Her shrivel body gasped for breath.

"You hold the fate of this tribe in your hands, Bhram!
Please don't steer away from your responsibility.
I bow before you, begging you not to throw it all away.
Please don't throw it all away..."
Dadima's feeble body dropped at his feet, displaying her vulnerability.

"Oh grandma, I am sorry... Please forgive me! I am so, so sorry."
Bhram's apology took everyone by surprise as he helped the revered back on her feet.

"I promise, to be the apple of your eye!" Holding her close, he consoled her.
"I promise to do right by this tribe!" he acknowledged, his audience.

"I promise to risk my life to protect you all!!!"
Witnessing a miracle, the entire clan was exuberant!
Until, their glimmer of hope turned into despair.

"Is this, what you were all waiting to hear?!?!?"
Shoving her reverence back on the ground, he guffawed;
Exposing himself to be the monstrous marionette he had become.
Aggravating Dhairya, who could do nothing but watch his elder brother,
Dishonour the one he loved.

"Listen carefully, you low lives…" his pitch was ear-shattering.
"If you dare to disrespect the love of my life,
The mother of my unborn child,
I will bury each and every one of you with my bare hands.
Is that understood???"
He screamed defying every onlooker, while his goons rallied around him
encouraging the fool by chanting senselessly.
"Yes! Is that understood? Is that understood???"

"With one leg in the grave, she thinks she can still have her way!
Isn't she funny?"
Bhram had a hearty laugh along with his posies, exaggerating his performance, by
kneeling before her.

"Now stop whining and bestow blessings upon your favourite grandson!
For, I embark upon an important mission…
A mission, to fulfil my darling's every desire!!!"
Blowing kisses to his wicked mate who thoroughly enjoyed every moment of
disrespect, the nincompoop summed up his atrocious act.

She, who had put her life on the line on numerous occasions to keep her tribe
from harm's way, repeated history by lovingly placing her fragile hand on his
head.

"Go my child! Go, fulfil your fantasy!
Go embrace the Gods of death, who await you impatiently!
For he whose hands are coloured in blood,
Will never, ever, have a happy ending."
Her dimmed eyes, sparkled bright, scaring the degenerate who acted in disdain.

"Your father, took a bullet meant for you...
Yet, you ungrateful creature show no remorse.
This is how deluded you have become, Bhram!
This is how deluded you have become.

You killed my son in instalments and in increments,
And still, you stand before me in denial.
You are deluded to the extent that you are unaware,
Of the burden of blasphemy, piling up on your broad shoulders..."
Bewildering the brainwashed who shrugged her to be crazy,
The prudent langur shed light on his ignorance.

"You stabbed him in the back, the day you plotted against your brother.
You punched him in the gut, every time you disobeyed.
You ripped his heart out of his chest...,
When you laid hands on what didn't belong to you.
And, by the time you started to openly gloat of your atrocities,
My son, was a dead man walking..."
Dadima painted a painful picture.

"Although my son suffered a slow painful death at your hands,
I pray for yours to be quick!
Quick, because you are condemned for abomination son,
And, most definitely, there is no escaping your curse.
So, go on, my child...
Go, gamble with our lives.
Go on! Don't let the reality of life affect your illusions.

Our wellbeing means nothing to you,
As compared to the deluded love you carry in your heart.
I only wish she loved you too.
But, it's too late for those dreams now.
I simply wish your soul transcends into another life with ease,
Because, your suffering Bhram, is inevitable!"
Giving Bhram her last assessment, Dadima kissed her grandson's forehead with
compassion. Then, without any discomfort or assistance, she headed straight

into the arms of the *Enchanting Tree of Eternal Life*, to hopefully, perish in peace.

Dreading that moment ever since Dadima took ill, Titli, who forever battled her own demons, broke down into tears. Blaming herself for their family's downfall, she begged her mother-in-law for forgiveness. Giving the ailing langur with a heart of gold, an opportunity to comfort a mother who was soon to lose her son.

"I know of the weight, you carry upon your chest, my child.
Now, I want you to understand…,
You did, what you did, because you thought it was the only way;
The only way you could protect your tribe from your insanity.
It is them… Each one of them who chose to become who they are.
That is not your cross to carry."
Dadima affectionately wiped Titli's tears.

"You have repented enough;
Enough to wash away the stigma of abandoning your family.
In the past few weeks, you have done for me,
More than I'd expect my own daughter to do! So, don't fret!
Your spirit is distort, but your soul is awakened!
You have big shoes to fill after I'm gone!
So, gather yourself together and do what is right by this tribe.
Do it with the help of my ever gracious Godson!"
Conveying her last wish to Dhyan, Dadima looked relieved.

Feeling at home under the shade of the withering Big Banyan,
Dadima addressed her tribe who were still walking in her footsteps…

"Forgive me, my tribe…
For I might be solely responsible, for the nightmares you suffer.
I have failed each and every one of you miserably…
Failed you by keeping mum, for as long as I have.
For my trespasses, please do show me mercy.

I wish I had the courage, to do right by you, when there was still hope;
Alas, I am a mere mortal; so very flawed.

I won't add to the list of my failures, by straying you while I count my last breaths.
I admit to my flaws. I admit to my shortcomings.
I pray to our ancestors, to help me heal...
Heal me for my soul is wounded!

My humble message to you, all my darlings...
Please, do not repeat my mistakes.
Do not allow cunning minds, to pollute your soul and manipulate your spirit.
Do not fall in the same trap as me. Do not be fooled, like I did.

My time has come!
And, in the arms of this Goddess, I pray, I find peace as I move on...
Don't be saddened by my departure.
My mortal body, is, going to perish!
That is the price we have to pay for bearing the burden of flesh.

However, I will forever rest in your hearts!
Because, you are a piece of me, and I am a part of you!
We shall meet again in the next life. Hopefully, by then, I will be wiser...
We will all, be wiser!"
The esteemed matriarch, who lived a wholesome life until the mistakes she made killed her softly, cheerfully crawled deeper into the bosom of her Goddess, seeking solace.

Masking his fears, Bhram attempted to have the last word...
But it was too late.
No one, was listening.

Her tribe, had gathered around the beguiling Banyan...,
Paying their respects to the one whose glorious life,
Flashed before their eyes, bringing them immense joy in a dire situation.

Among them, those awakened enough to believe in the higher power,
Were honoured, by a heavenly moment in the withering *Valley of Hope!*
When, her sovereign soul radiated divine light upon them,
As she swiftly, transcended into an unparalleled universe…
Detaching from her earthly existence.

CHAPTER 13

"*I***s that all you needed to see?"**
Vaani unwrapped Dhairya from her wondrous wings,
When, dreading the brutality to follow, he opened his eyes in helplessness.

"Precious time has passed...
There is nothing, I can do to change the outcome.

I ignored my calling...
Now, I can't help, but blame myself, for the loss of my loved ones."
He wept, uncontrollably.

"So, that's it, huh? You will carry this burden wherever you go?"
The regal entity, shrewdly, expressed her disappointment.

"Giving up is so easy...
Withstanding a storm,
Now, that is the true challenge!

I thought that you bore a heart of gold, and the courage of a warrior!
I never imagined you to ignore the harsh reality of life,
Instead of embracing its lessons!

I know it is hard for you to accept the fate of your family;
Nevertheless, I also know you have it in you to finish what you started."
Vaani coaxed him to get back in there.

"Nothing is set in stone. Everybody has choices!
They could have averted their demise,
But, their lack of faith in themselves...,
Is what led them to suffer the monstrosities.

Now, it is your turn to make a choice.
Either, give in to the nightmares,
Or, get an insight into their delusions. Like I have been doing for eternity!"
Triggering the desired effect, the far sighted creature pushed his buttons.

"So what is it going to be?!?" her spellbinding tiger eyes stared him down.

Soaking in, the Goddess' sentiments along with her coded words of wisdom...
Dhairya wiped his tears, obediently, stepping into her angelic wings again.
Extremely grateful, to have this surreal encounter!

Unlike the dreadful scene of bloodshed, he'd visualized,
This time, he found himself outside an ancient mansion beaming with luminous lights.

There,
Half a dozen elegantly decorated elephants were chained to metal beams,
While handsome horses happily munched on fodder inside the stables.
Keeping an eye on them, were at least a dozen two legged impressively dressed primates carrying swords and rifles while pacing up and down.

Instantly reminded of Lobhika's tainted desires,
Dhairya's anxious spirit reckoned it to be the Mad Man's mansion, where prominent Homo Sapiens were clearly gathered to celebrate a special occasion.

Keeping an eye out for his lost brother while invisible to mortal eyes…
Dhairya brushed shoulders with royalty closely admiring their rich, colourful silk and velvet attires loaded with extravagant jewellery.

With richness, oozing throughout the stellar space, Dhairya thought that it was impossible to identify the one diamond studded necklace in question. Yet, he wandered, hoping for a miracle.

Everybody seemed happy, at least, on the surface…
People were laughing, singing, dancing and making merry.
In the midst of all that noise, his extra sensitive ears gravitated towards a concerned mother seeking guidance from her cheerful husband.
"How are we going to fulfil all their wishes???
Their demands never seem to end…"

"Don't you worry about these matters, my darling! That is my department!
You focus on keeping our royal guests entertained!
No one should feel neglected. Absolutely no one!
After all, it is our only daughter's wedding!"
Curling his long bushy moustache, the Chief requested his wife to keep her spirits high.

Locking the room loaded with precious items meant for the groom's family,
The excited father of the bride shoved the key in his khadi pant pocket,
Ordering his men who guarded the treasures to not leave their post.

Dhairya, was just starting to piece the puzzle together,
When a few other conversations caught his attention,

Making him realise, beneath the facade of cordial behaviour,
There lay tons of unspoken animosity.

"Oh, what a beautiful bride you are blessed with, Ranima!
And this grand reception, Wow!
Looks like Chief Mangal has let money flow like water!"
A gaudily overdressed stout lady, buttered the Queen.

"Yes! Isn't she stunning?!? They are absolutely a match made in heaven!"
Ranima, seemed very pleased gloating.

"As for the chief, we made it very clear...
If his daughter is to marry the Prince,
He has to give us gifts worth her weight in gold!
As you can see,
The wise father fulfilled all our demands without any fuss!"

"Oh your highness,
It is a shame you turned down our proposal then…"
Holding her oversized belly, the fat lady laughed like a hyena.
Subtly flaunting her diamond studded necklace in the greedy queen's face.

"You do realise,
You would have acquired much more wealth from us, don't you?
Given, how healthy our daughter is and all!"

"Oh, oh; stop it Dharti!"
Ranima let out a nervous giggle.

"You know I was joking right?!?
We are a modern civilization, against the age old tradition of dowry!
Everyone knows that. Everyone!!!"
The stepmother of the groom faked morality. Yet, she secretly sulked over lost treasures.

"The…, The Prince was madly in love.
How could we ignore our only son's desire? Tell me.

She is a charismatic beauty! She belongs to a valiant and sane family! What more could we ask for?!?"

The conniving queen insulted the Mad Man's wife.
And, moved along to take a dig at someone else.

Embracing the unknown, had heightened Dhairya's senses…
Giving him the uncanny ability to look into people's souls…,
Shedding light, onto their buried darkness.

Scanning through the crowd carefully, he now noticed many smiling faces masking their true emotions. Overall, egos were in play while testosterone flared across the lavishly decorated *pendal*. Almost everyone surrounding them seemed to have a secret agenda.
Instead of showering blessings on the happy couple about to tie a knot,
Mingling with high profile guests was their obvious 'priority'.

Clearly, there were many who envied the Chief's daughter for marrying into royalty.
Then there were those who despised the royal family for their double standards.
And, others, they wished they wore the crown jewel or fit some fancy shoes.
Only a handful of pure hearted souls, were genuinely present, to celebrate the union of two lovebirds coming together from different walks of life.

Feeling the lack of meaningful love at such a joyous occasion…,
Dhairya was forced to wonder,
'What was the point of a big fat wedding?!?'

Offended by the self-proclaimed queen,
Of a dynasty destroyed by Mughal invaders over a century ago,
Dharti, who was known to stir trouble wherever she went,
Was out to seek vengeance.
It wasn't just the pitiful dialogue which had touched a nerve,
Having their proposal rejected, had also weighed heavy on her family's ego.
Since then, the Mad Man, originally named Bojh, was thirsting for royal blood.

Bojh had earned the title of 'The Mad Man,' ever since he had savagely unleashed his wrath on the poor villagers for not obeying his orders. Proud to be feared, his antics had escalated to an extent that no one wanted to be in his bad books.

Contemplating on how to create a rift between the soon to be in laws, Dharti's wicked mind had spewed multiple options. But, the meanest machine in town chose the one act which, in her mind, guaranteed severed ties and broken bonds for good.

In the land of staunch believers of ancient traditions and forced rituals, Dharti, slyly, snuck away from the ceremony with the intention of framing the Chief's wife, whose charisma she forever envied.
Hoping to kill two birds with one stone...,
The cunning woman, successfully distracted the Chief's men guarding the treasure by mimicking monkey calls, and sending them on a wild goose chase.
When the coast was clear...
Using her hairpin, she unlocked the heavy lock like a pro.

Overwhelmed at the sight of silver platters covered in gold and precious objects,
She was so tempted to steal. Yet, seeing the bigger picture in play, she resisted.
Smugly, the deranged woman hid her diamond studded necklace among the jewels meant for the Queen, unaware she was being watched.
Covering her tracks, or so she thought...
She carefully placed the lock back in position, then, took off towards a nearby hallway.

Setting a stage for deception,
Dharti, who usually struggled to carry the weight of her obesity,
Cautiously collapsed at the end of the mind blowing hallway,
Pretending, to be rendered unconscious.
But, with all eyes on the Prince and soon to be princess, her ploy went unnoticed.

Desperate to get anyone's attention at that point, she pulled herself up with the support of a marble pillar and tried again differently. This time, she charged into an exquisitely tall brass oil lamp lighting up the end of the corridor like a mad elephant. Misjudging the might of the metal, she truly managed to knock herself out of consciousness upon impact. An impact, which indeed attracted her desired attention when a few flying sparks set the purple silk drapes ablaze, igniting a full-fledged fire.

A team assigned to promptly fix any unforeseen problems at the royal wedding, jumped into action dragging Dharti away from the flames while other guards and guests hastily worked on containing the fire. Specializing in shamelessly taking advantage of any situation, the Mad Man who always preceded his reputation, overindulged at the bar trying to numb his pain clueless of the chaos caused by his wife - a wife whom he had secretly grown to despise.

Splashing ice water on Dharti's face, their robust daughter Tara,
Leaned over her mother, begging Dharti to open her eyes.
Arriving to her senses at a scene better than she'd imagined,
The drama queen made a slow comeback holding her throbbing head.

"Where am I?!?
My head hurts. Why? Why is there blood???
What happened to me???" She played the crowd, just like Lobhika would.

"Did I collapse on my own?!? Or, did someone render me unconscious???
Why am I bleeding? I'm bleeding..." she cried.

"I can't think straight...
Where is my husband? Oh my God!
Where is my diamond necklace?!?!?"
She sharply drew everyone's attention to her bare neck.

"How can this be happening??? How can I be robbed at a royal wedding?!?!?
Help me... Help me up, now!"
She screamed hysterically.

"Help me look for that necklace. Help!
Help, before my great great great grandmother comes out of her grave to
haunt us.
I can't afford to lose our family heirloom. I can't.
I'm supposed to hand it down to my daughter when she gets married."
Unaware of the made up history, Tara who watched her mother run, probably for the first time in her life, was baffled.

"Come on, Tara's Dad, help me find that God forsaken necklace,
BEFORE EVERYONE HERE IS BURDENED WITH OUR CURSE!"

Emphasizing her last words, she aimed to instil fear amongst the traditionally blinded, who still believed in black magic and family curses.

Hiding behind a bottle unlike ever before, the Mad Man let his wife fill in his shoes while he simply enjoyed the show. Speaking in tongues, Dharti made a mess of herself by pulling her oversized hair piece out, and tossing it into another burning lamp. Starting yet another fire and pretending to be possessed, she continued her tantrums.

Deceiving the shocked audience, she yelled,
"Cursed are those who go about their business in times of one's distress.
I have been invoked by unholy hands. Come forth, and I shall show you mercy.
But, if you hide,
I shall call upon the dark forces to rip out all your hearts."

Giving a brilliant performance, the conniving woman provoked the priest to support her insanity. Interrupting the royal nuptials, a learned Brahmin urged his king to solve the situation at hand before the auspicious night turned into a bloodbath.

Paying heed to his guru's advice, the king roared,
"Nobody leaves here unless I say so. Is that understood?
I shall execute the thief with my own hands after the nuptials are completed.
Now, Guruji, can you please deal with the devil inside this woman,
While Panditji continues the ceremony?!?"
The king wanted that evening to move along unfettered.

Displeased by his words, Dharti snapped out of her act. But, not before taking a few heavy hits of brooms and whiffs of stinking leather footwear; An ancient remedy of exorcism followed in their land!
Back to her regular self, she focused on her 'missing' necklace starting another drama.

"Rajaji! By the time the rituals are over, my great great great grandmother's necklace will have disappeared for good." She cried crocodile tears.

"I can't let that happen. I can't let that happen.
Otherwise, each and every one present here will be damned by her spirit!"
The manipulator tried manipulating the King.

"So, what do you suggest we do?" Ranima screamed in frustration.
"Shall we frisk the guests to make you happy?" The Queen, who could care less about the necklace, mocked.

"Oh no! You go carry on with the ceremony your highness.
I will get your men to strip everyone down." Dharti was spiteful.

With emotions flaring high between the selfish queen and a drama queen, the royal families who had travelled for days to attend a grand event were mortified.

"What? Rajaji, we didn't keep our lives on hold to be mistreated by this crazy woman." Screamed a Diva.

"Let's not start with the name calling, we all know who is capable of what here…" Dharti snapped.

"Whoever had the gall to lay hands on me, might not be stupid enough to hold onto my necklace. Therefore, let's search every inch of the premises together. Or, I will turn this place upside down myself!"
The crazed woman on a fatal mission wouldn't give up.

Breaking up the barrage of allegations being thrown around despicably, a silver headed, refined lady, who once wore the prestigious crown herself, took centre stage.

"Let us not forget why we assemble here today…
We are here, simply to bestow our blessings upon these two young souls,
Who vow to spend this lifetime together! And, if we do it right,
My grandson will cherish his princess from now, until eternity!
So, let's prioritize our actions shall we?!?"
The former queen eloquently dictated the terms.

Seeing the crowd nod heads to her reverence, Dharti crossed all boundaries by interrupting her holiness who, in return, lost her cool.
"Woman, if you continue to disrespect your hosts your head will be in the gallows before the thief loses his limbs. Have I made myself clear?" her prudence was impeccable.

"Rajaji, Rajaji!
There is a gang of ferocious langurs prowling around the mansion.
They are the same monkey thieves who've been stealing from temples and villages.
I suggest, we follow them." a guard interrupted the session.

"Nice! Now, blame it on the shy langurs!" Dharti slow clapped in disgust.
"What are diamonds worth to them?!?
And, if that is even a possibility, then mustn't we check on the royal dowry???
The Chief has put his blood sweat and tears in accumulating this wealth,
So, his daughter gets a royal husband.
I'm concerned about my family heirloom alright…
But, I'm not so selfish, that I wouldn't hear a concerned mother's heartbeat."

Convincingly making her problem their problem, Dharti consoled the Chief's wife even though, up until that point, neither of them was concerned.

Ranima, who had faced enough embarrassment for a lifetime, was very nervous to look her husband in the eye. Because, the king had sternly warned his self-indulgent queen not to accept a dime.

"There is nothing as the royal dowry anymore.
Your king has sworn to eradicate this despicable tradition.
So, why would we make demands?!? God has given us in abundance!!!
Then, why would we ask for material possessions??? Why?"
Ranima attempted to save face turning the tables on Dharti.

"You are jealous that it is not your daughter wearing Naina's shoes.
It was a mistake on my part to invite your insane family on this joyous occasion.
Forgive me, Rajaji… I should have listened to you."

The insatiable Queen had made demands on behalf of the king, putting the Chief's family through a lot of anxiety. Now, totally denying her actions, she left the parents of the bride genuinely disturbed.

Seizing this opportunity, Dharti hit back hard screaming in disgust, **"Enough of your slander, Ranima! If there is nothing to hide... Why don't we go check the room which is being guarded by not just one but three three men in the Chief's house?"**
Dharti stomped towards the treasure room enticing everyone to follow her.

Afraid of being exposed for who she really was, Ranima urged Rajaji to stop that madness. But, he was in no mood to show her mercy. Humbly requesting Chief Mangal to open the huge wooden door, the king asked his guards to step aside. With Ranima giving him a killer look and Rajaji eager to get this drama over with, The Chief was in a dilemma as he slowly reached for the key.

With her nerves getting the best of her...
The Chief's wife snatched the key from her husband's hand, then, unlocking the door she flung it open, only to break down in tears.

"Oh my God! We've been robbed..."
She collapsed crying, dreading the outcome of her daughter's happiness.

"What???" The greedy queen had to see it for herself. So did Dharti.

"How is that possible?!? We had three guards guarding these doors..."
Ranima seemed confused, while Dharti was shocked to find her necklace, indeed, stolen.

"Yes, how is this possible?!? Did you leave your post again?"
Dharti couldn't help but interrogate the guards.

"What do you mean again?!? Did you see them leave before?"
The Chief's sharp wife caught Dharti's every word.

"What?!? No, wait... What?!?"
Dharti realised she had put her foot in her mouth.

Quickly trying to recover from the goof up, she blamed the guards,
"Oh yes, yes… You see…
Just before the thief rendered me unconscious, I heard some weird noises
coming from this direction. When I peeked in this corridor, I didn't see
anyone here. Now my necklace is gone, along with the many precious stones
laying in that silver platter."

"How do you know what's missing?" Ranima was on her case,
"Have you set foot in here before?!?"

Blatantly challenging the queen and caught up in her own lies, Dharti implied it
was Ranima who had bragged about the precious stones just a while ago.

"Don't fabricate stories you conniving woman!
Yes I did take a dig at you earlier,
However, I never mentioned what the gifts were.
So, how do u know there were precious stones in this platter.
You most certainly have something to do with all this, don't you?!?"

Instead of owning up to the mess she had made of the auspicious night, Dharti
desperately played with words to redeem herself when Tara finally snapped.

"Ma, stop! Please stop this show right now!
Ever since I was a little child, I've heard you talk the talk.
But, not once have you lived up to your words.
You say it is a sin to lie! Yet, you lie through your teeth every day.
You instil the fear of the Gods in all of us;
Yet, you don't confess your own sins.

I am ashamed to call you my parents.
You are the perfect example of what not to be.
You both scheme and plot against those who speak their mind,
Because you are threatened by their righteousness.
Confess, mother… Admit your sins… Tell them what you intended to do.
If not, I will!"

"How dare you talk to your mother like that?"

Finally, the Mad Man's voice was heard as he charged to strike his daughter in rage. Which is when the Chief who had heard enough, grabbed a guard's gun, and shoved it in the deranged man's chest,

"If you lay, even a finger on this young lady, I will blow you into pieces."

"Come here, child..." The Chief's wife pulled Tara, away from her fuming parents.

"Tell us what you know. Don't be afraid.
We will not harm your parents. You have my word!
However, I will make sure...
You, don't have to live with the burden of their sins anymore.

With our Naina gone,
We will miss our daughter dearly!
I know you are special! I see you bear a heart of gold!
We will be proud to have you in our lives,
If you are willing to accept us, that is!

Don't let your misguided parents scare you.
Tell us everything that you know. I vow to protect you! I do!"
A concerned mother encouraged a hurting child to do the right thing.

Tired of living a lie, Tara looked at her mother with hopeful eyes...
As if, signalling her to speak the truth...
But, delusional Dharti, didn't seem to care.

"Ma, please tell them what you intended to do."
Dharti and Bojh, looked away, ignoring their daughter's plea.

"Alright then, I choose to break free of the shackles you both have bound me in ever since I was a child. If you do not care to make things right, I will! Rajaji, I not only saw my mother enter this room, I also saw her exit in a hurry."

"Oh, you wicked little girl! After all that we have done for you, you throw us under the bus to impress these degenerates." Dharti lost her bearings.

Unable to tolerate their king and queen being insulted,
The loyal guards pulled out their swords on the schemer.

"You are playing with fire, Dharti!
If you had anything to do with this, now is the time to own up."
Her husband changed his tone bewildering the anxious audience.
But his arrogant wife, didn't budge.

"Ma, I heard your conversation with Ranima earlier...
I followed you to comfort you.
Because, I thought you were hurt by her words...
But then, I saw the games you played with the guards,
Tricking them to abandon their post by faking monkey calls.
Great job!
I saw how easily you let yourself into this locked room,
As if you have done it a million times before..." Tara was ashamed.

"When you tactfully placed the lock back, like it had never been opened...
I noticed, your precious necklace wasn't around your neck.
I understood then, you were up to some mischief...
Moments later, I watched your drama unfold.

I always knew, never to cross you because of your temper.
Today, I witnessed the depths you would fall to to have your way.
Your diamond studded necklace is our family heirloom?!?
You want to hand it to me when I get married?
Really?!?
That piece of jewellery you never let me touch...
That necklace, you cherish more than me...
I know, you stole from your dying sister!!!"
The crowd was flabbergasted, and Dharti was shocked at the revelation.

"Yes mother, I was there. I saw what you did... Then, and even now.

Since your recovering sister, mysteriously passed overnight...
You have kept me away from my cousins.

You have done nothing, but tried to plant seeds of hatred in my heart against them.
What were you planning to do this time???

Frame these nice people and break my best friend's heart?
That's all you both have been dreaming of, haven't you?!?
Ever since you got the invitation.

Naina and Shravan love each other, Ma.
No piece of jewellery is going to stop their union.
If I wasn't born from your womb,
Maybe, I'd be fortunate enough to be loved by someone…"

Embarrassed of her parents' antics all her life, Tara finally got the courage to speak her mind. Yet, she controlled her tears, turning her attention to her best friend.

"No matter how flawed they are, I've always hoped that they will change.
But, who am I kidding? They will never change,
Even if it is necessary for them to save their souls.

They forever live in denial, and always choose not to accept their shortcomings.
So, all I can do now to maintain my sanity is,
Enforce change in my life, so their actions do not weigh me down.

I had no choice when I came into this world,
That was my cross to carry.
But now, that I have a sister like you in my life.
I choose to break free of all their barriers!
And, make sure no one ruins your special night!"

Touched by her bestie's words, Naina wrapped her arms around Tara, who tried hard to stay strong. But, as soon as the bride's parents displayed affection, towards the heartbroken child…
Tara wept inconsolably, apologizing for her mother's blunders.

CHAPTER 14

Breaking free, from the bondage of obligations and immorality, Tara embraced her new family undaunted of the repercussions in the future. While her diabolic parents, were immediately confined in a spacious room with guards manning the door.

The ceremony commenced,
Binding Prince Shravan and Naina in the sacred union of marriage!

Engulfed with mixed emotions, Naina's parents held on to their daughter until the very last minute humbly requesting the Prince to safeguard their daughter's honour with his life. Assuring them of her well-being, Shravan once again bowed before the elders. Then, he thanked all the guests for their presence. With a pressing matter at hand, the reception was cut short. And, in the company of their close friends and family, the newlyweds got ready to celebrate a new chapter of their life.

Under strict orders of the intemperate Queen, everyone was secretly frisked. Their belongings checked multiple times. To ensure not a single item of royal dowry left the Chief's mansion.

Consoling his weeping bride, the love struck groom escorted Naina to the most ostentatious elephant, while their cheerful crew mounted the grandly groomed horses with elegance. Bidding farewell to the onlookers as fireworks lit the sky, unaware of the monstrosity to follow, the cheerful party headed into the forest with *mother moon* guiding their way!

As soon as their children were out of sight,
Ranima vouched to slay those who dared to steal from her family.
When Bojh and Dharti were summoned in front of an impromptu court,
The villainous couple pleaded for their lives,
Begging the King to show them mercy.
Throwing each other under the bus, they accused the other of scheming.
However, both swore not to have stolen from their gracious hosts.
To tame the gluttonous beast within Ranima, Dharti, who now feared for her life, promised to gift the queen her diamond studded necklace whenever it was found.

After each pocket was emptied and every corner of the huge mansion turned upside down, Ranima screamed in fury,
"Bring forth the guards who dared to disobey the Chief's orders!"

Seeing them bound in chains meant for prisoners, Rajaji ordered for his trusted soldiers to be immediately unchained. Grateful to be given an opportunity to defend themselves, Bheema, whose family had served the King for generations, admitted to his actions,

"Rajaji, you have to believe us. It is the monkey's we should be chasing down. We had heard only stories of the erratic langurs of this region. But, this evening, we saw them obtrude into our space.
This lady thinks it was her who distracted us,
But, the truth is that we were already alerted of their presence."
The brave heart confessed in all honesty.

"Yes, Rajaji. Bheema speaks the truth!
If the Chief's cousin hadn't stopped us from shooting the troublemakers, I would have their heads on spikes right now." Laxman, the oldest of the three guards, bowed before his king.

"Yes, brother, he is right!
I've been vigilant so that the volatile monkeys who cause mayhem,
Wouldn't disrupt my beloved Naina's wedding.
You know, she has dreamt of this day ever since she was a little girl!
I couldn't taint her dreams by going on a killing spree all at once..."
Dangal, Chief Mangal's shady cousin, accepted his role.

"Our hands were tied then. But, with your blessings we promise to hunt each and every one of those thieves and recover every item that is stolen from your majesty."
Bowing before the king, his guards were adamant to rectify the damage.

With no other option in mind,
Rajaji ordered his men to saddle up and make things right.
Seeing the king's men strap bullet belts around their hips,
While loading every rifle with precision as if they were going to war,
Dhairya found himself shouting on top of his lungs,

"It was one of your own who dared to steal from you.
He has a duplicate key to that room. Check his pockets. Check his pockets."
But, no one could hear his restless spirit.

What he had failed to see was,
Bhram's best buddy, and the biggest, brawniest bully in the langur kingdom,
Swarth, was casing the Chief's mansion days before the wedding.

He had been secretly serenading Lobhika, for many seasons now.
And, the power hungry diva, who fondly played with fire,
Had successfully charmed that selfish animal into her web of deceit.

On a solo impromptu visit, a night before the wedding,
Swarth had stumbled upon a duo planning a robbery.
It was none other than the Chief's jealous cousin Dangal,
Being coaxed to steal some jewels by his dishonourable wife.

Sitting on a huge flowering mango tree overlooking the marvellous mansion,
Dadima's last words constantly echoed in Bhram's ears,
"You are condemned for abomination. There is no escaping your curse.
You are condemned for abomination. There is no escaping your curse.
You are condemned for abomination. There is no escaping your curse."

Masking his fears with false bravado,
The oblivious langur ordered his hooligans to take charge while he cautiously maintained his distance from those who couldn't help but draw attention. When the clueless gang catapulted helter skelter wondering where to begin, Swarth stealthily separated himself from the crew intending to follow his mark, Dangal.

After Dharti foiled his plan with her antics, Dangal had tossed the red velvet bag loaded with jewellery over the back wall of the mansion hoping to retrieve it later. But Swarth, who was on his tail constantly, had immediately backtracked and whisked the treasure from the bushes while the guards chased his troupe. Signalling everyone to disperse, Swarth handed over the precious goods to Bhram. But, not before tucking away the diamond necklace his temptress so desired.

In a world full of deception,
Dreading the worst,
Dhairya's spirit tried in vain to get to where his brainwashed brother was.

Just about then, the lights at the beaming mansion abruptly disappeared,
As if announcing that the celebration was over.
Men with fire torches stormed out of the magnificent mansion,
Heading towards the Valley of Hope,
With the intention of torching up the thieving langurs' hideout.

Trembling like a leaf,
Witnessing the mob get bigger and bigger as frustrated villagers who'd been burnt
by the notorious langurs, also joined forces with the Chief and King, Dhairya
struggled to find ways to avoid the massacre. Anxious to change the outcome of
what seemed inevitable, he hit a brick wall.
Acknowledging the fact that there was nothing he could do to change what had
already transpired, he sought solace in his flowing tears.

Although it was gut wrenching to witness the horror to come,
His broken spirit kept up the pace going back to the Big Banyan, where not so
long ago his beloved grandma's saddened soul transcended into another realm,
leaving her sickened flesh behind to perish.

Finding the surroundings almost deserted, Dhairya was somewhat relieved.

After Dadima's impactful exit from this life...
Under the guidance of Titli and Dhyan, her disciples who honoured the matriarch
and treasured their families, broke away from lost souls who they knew, would
cause nothing but harm. The other langurs who wanted to leave, yet, failed to
gather courage to take that first crucial step, were soon to run helter skelter,
scrambling for their lives...
All because they caved to the forced obligations, of their misguided tribe.

With the troops and villagers closing in on them,
Dhairya couldn't help himself but get sucked into an unholy space;
A space which reeked of Lobhika's treachery.

Seeing Swarth standing too close to his brother's wife,
Dhairya was furious at first, but soon saw through their trickery.

**"Hurry up, my princess! The king's men are just around the corner.
Let's leave this God forsaken place this very instant!"**
The brazen bully affectionately rubbed her belly.

"No, not without the necklace you promised to put around my neck!"
The stubborn langur, consumed with greed, pushed him away.

"Your heart's desire is safely tucked away in the jungle!
Because, I couldn't risk them finding it on me.
I promised you the day would come very soon, didn't I?!?
Now, we don't have to worry about the coward who irks you...
The angry humans will make sure none of them run around these jungles
anymore.
Let's head to our private paradise; you, me and our baby!
Let's go before Bhram sees us together."
He tried hard to convince Lobhika to elope.

Breathing the suffocating air of betrayal,
Dhairya's tumultuous emotions took him back to his childhood,
When everything was simple. Everything was easy!
All you had to do was embrace the wisdom of the elders.

Witnessing the masterminds flee into the dark night,
He wondered, '*Where had it all gone wrong?*'

Nothing was as it seemed.
There were lies and deceit around every corner, around every nook.
And now, to make matters worse, bullets were roaring through thin air,
Setting the bone dried bushes around him into flames.

The humans were known to be merciless when enraged.
They'd been on high alert since the last raid.
Now, they were looking for any excuse to put an end to the monkey business.
Therefore, tracking down the langurs wasn't hard for them.
The difficult part was to differentiate the good ones from the nasty lot.
But, instead of focusing solely on the culprits,
They conveniently labelled everyone to be a nuisance.

Losing material wealth meant more to them,
Than the innocent lives they were about to take in the pursuit of some perpetrators.
Making it a mission to destroy anything they felt threatened by,
They were known to demonize themselves in the name of protecting their families.
Hence, they added themselves to the list of most cruel predators.

Under the command of the Queen,
Whose sole purpose of this lifetime was to gather wealth gluttonously...
Younglings and expectant mothers from various species were rounded up and forced into sacks and cages, while they cried in horror seeing their loved ones drop dead like flies.

Their priorities had shifted along the way,
Recovering stolen jewellery wasn't the only task in mind anymore. Trading helpless souls to different parties with varied agendas in return for stacks of money, had now taken precedence.

It had taken forever for life to flourish,
Now, in a split second, everything was meeting the dust.
All because some langurs crossed boundaries they shouldn't have crossed.
Took something they shouldn't have taken.

Pointing fingers came naturally to everyone.
But, acknowledging their nightmarish actions,
Always proved to be a challenge.

Blinded by senseless rage, villagers lost their minds as they thoughtlessly began burning down the few trees left in that patch of the valley. When a concerned nature lover intervened to stop that madness, The Mad Man handed him a flaming torch,
Mocking him to do the honours.
Once he refused to be a part of that insanity,
Everyone present tried manipulating him, in the name of brotherhood.
When he didn't budge, they reminded him of the King's wrath,
Forcing him to set the last standing tree on fire.

With the wild flames engulfing the already withering *Eternal Tree of Life,*
Her devotees fled the scene fearing a curse to fall upon them. While the haters stayed back to senselessly massacre every monkey that caught their eye.

Unable to see clearly, since deadly smoke clouded the Valley of Hope turning it into a Valley of Despair, the sound of rolling stones in the midst of that chaos made Dhairya's weary heart sink into abyss.

Bheema was standing over Bhram's badly bruised body ready to slay the thief,
While Laxman collected every piece of bling in sight.
Shattered, watching his older brother take his last breath, Dhairya again wondered
if Bhram knew, 'He had been betrayed by the one he risked everything for!'

With that thought in mind weighing heavy on his soul,
He also witnessed his nightmare swiftly unfolded in front of his eyes,
His favourite Banyan rapidly turn into ashes,
Leaving nothing but the cries of the tormented in its wake,
Weakening Dhairya's spirit by the second.

Although he wasn't present in flesh, he was being torched by the flames of his past,
Leaving him with a flesh wound in spite of his absent body.
Indicating his struggle, to let go, of what had transpired.

Unable to hang in there any longer asphyxiating in hell,
He forced himself out of that horror,
Falling on the rocky riverbed drenched in sweat and tears.

"I should have stopped, after the first time!
At least then I would know who to hold accountable.
Now, seeing everything that I saw, I don't know who to blame.
Dadima? Bhram? Lobhika? Swarth?
The greedy queen? The angry king?
The Chief? His cousin? The villagers?
Myself? Who do I blame???"
In agony, he pleaded to the Majestic being from an unparalleled universe,
To give him some clarity.

"Don't you get it, child?!?
This isn't your battle to fight.
Incomplete knowledge and blind faith is often 'the reason' for one's downfall.
Is it absolutely necessary to find someone to blame?"
The prudent soul attempted to give the broken hearted an insight into his
perceptions.

Staring into Vaani's enchanting eyes like a lost child,
Yearning to seek solace in her words of wisdom, Dhairya whispered,

"Enlighten me mother, for I have lost myself into this nightmare.
My spirit is shattered, after the devastation I've seen.
What happened to those young souls in captivity?
If I was there, when I was needed to be...
Could I have averted this tribulation?
Did I fail my tribe miserably???"

Embracing his quivering existence, the Goddess at work shed light into the darkness which was suffocating the one who feared nothing, up until that moment.

"Your tribe was doomed, since the stage was set...,
Simply because, their soul had lost its course.
There wasn't any harmony among the humans to begin with.
Therefore, they were all very eager to point fingers.

Since everyone was fending for themselves,
They lacked compassion, and chose, not to understand.

Playing judge, jury and executioner,
Comes naturally to those who are deluded...
Simply because they lose the ability to differentiate, right from wrong.
Love from hate.
Evil from divine.
Reality from illusion!

But you, my boy! You are nothing like them.
You are a pure soul! A soul who is true to his calling!

You left your tribe,
Because there was no reasoning with those who chose to ignore the light.
You embraced life with open arms!
You saved those in plight!
You care too much to harm a soul.

No wonder, my boy, you hurtso much the way you do!"
Vaani, the Divine Oracle, worked her magic on his burnt flesh,
Making his wound disappear, without a trace.

"Pinning the nightmare you suffer on any soul,
Including your own, is you hampering your own growth,
By allowing baggage of the past to weigh you down.

That, my boy, mustn't be you!

Learn from what you have been blessed to see.
This agony might blur your vision right now.
But, there is a reason you were where you were then,
And why you are where you are now!"
The mythical mother lovingly stroked her mortal son's back.

"Now you have a better understanding of the dangers, which surround us.
But realise, there is never just one creature to hold responsible.
The chain of events contributed by multiple souls...,
Has led us to this path of destruction and devastation.

Always remember,
One spark is enough to ignite a fire,
And, a slight breeze to spread it wild.
Therefore, it is of utmost importance,
You gain clarity in your vision,
And, an insight into your soul.

You are the chosen one. Believe me, you are!
Because only those who are true to their calling are graced with my presence!
And, those who have the courage to withstand any storm, are let into my
wings!"
While diligently absorbing the intelligence being imparted upon him, Vaani's
glorious white spotted, horned feathers abruptly summoned his attention.

As if receiving a signal being transmitted from outer space,
Her antennas intensely elongated, and her emotions instantly flared high.

With her spellbinding eyes suddenly changing colours erratically,
The supreme being stood tall casting her surreal shadow upon him,
Urging him to get back to where he belonged.

Stepping away from him as she launched herself like a rocket into the darkening sky, Dhairya who was in awe of his Oracle couldn't help but wonder...
If his mortal eyes, had just caught a glimpse, into her eternal nightmare?

CHAPTER 15

After a powerful yet surreal encounter with the Goddess herself, Dhairya took a moment to let Vaani's words sink into his soul.

It wasn't his fault he realised after all...
Still, the harshness of reality was hard to fathom.
In a world full of unpredictable predators,
He wondered, *If his outlook on life will ever be the same again?*

Finding goodness in any soul came to him naturally in the past,
Now, would he be able to trust, his instincts again?

Disoriented by the bizarre brush with life, death and nightmares…
What was supposed to be a sublime gift from the supreme, suddenly felt like a curse.

Forgetting for a brief moment what had brought him to the river,
The makeshift bamboo flask, stuck between rocks, drew his attention,
Instantly reminding him of Gayatri and Mantra,
Whom he had left in the company of an, injured yet wicked, wolf.

Quickly filling the flask to its brim,
A concerned husband and a worried father,
Hurried back to his family fearing their wellbeing.

His visions had felt like nightmares…
And, now that he had travelled back in time to witness the horror,
His patience was running out, and distress had consumed his being.
The one who always looked on the bright side of life in spite of everything he went through, suddenly found himself drawn to unfathomable darkness.

Unlike any other time when he would be thoughtful not to spill a drop of much needed water, Dhairya couldn't care less. His mind had started playing tricks on him, and his desperation to reconnect with his family, had surpassed the need of the one in plight.

Finding his way back to the spot where he had left them,
Dhairya was relieved to hear his little Mantra's cheerful voice.

**"So, that was how my parents met, Uncle Wolf!
Now, it's your turn! Tell us your love story!"** she clapped.

**"Yes Khatru, it's your turn now. Stay with us!
Dhairya will be here any minute now. Please, don't close your eyes…"**
Gayatri was persuading his withering spirit to hold on.

"Pa is here! Pa is here!" happy to see her hero, Mantra gave him a tight hug.

"Hurry! Pass me the water."
Dhairya sensed urgency in Gayatri's actions as she lunged towards the flask.
"Here, open your mouth. This should help quench your thirst."

With barely a few drops touching Khatra's bone dried tongue,
Dhairya's head drooped in shame realising, he had failed his mission...
All because, he was engrossed with the demons of his past.

While he added to his misery beating himself up furthermore, a carcass of an indistinguishable animal fell from the open skies above landing right at his feet.

"Ma! What is that, Ma? What is that?" Mantra panicked.

"It is a blessing, from above!"
She who had refrained from expressing her disappointment for insufficient water,
Was elated to find a source of energy for the ailing wolf drop in front of their eyes.

**"Here Khatru. Smell this meat!
This is a gift from the Gods because it isn't your time to perish!"**
Gayatri teased the wolf who, despite his flaws, bore a good heart.

Although his severely wounded body had fallen totally numb,
The agonized wolf's spirit lifted when the aroma of fresh meat tantalized his senses.
Any other day, he would chew into any flesh irrespective of who had hunted the meal.
But, nothing about that evening was normal.
As eager as he was to take a big bite,
Something inside him stopped him from doing so.

The one who was known to be ungrateful, on his deathbed, shed tears.

"I am not worthy, of this blessing..." He struggled to speak.

"You put your lives on the line, to save a horrible creature like me.
For that, I am eternally grateful!
Still, I am a wicked wolf...
I don't deserve your compassion."
Accepting defeat from life Khatru seemed eager to embrace his death.

Bewildered still, by the chain of events leading to that point…
Dhairya's wandering eyes caught a glimpse of the wondrous entity,
Who had helped transport him into the past.
Understanding very well, the enchanting Oracle was aware of his tumultuous
emotions, he took that as a sign, for him to overcome his anxiety.
With a whole new world of revelations awakening his senses,
He took it upon himself to shed light onto Khatru's want to wither away.

"Who are we, to question the higher power?!?
Who are we to arrogantly disregard their blessings?

For you to dismiss a meal served to you on a platter,
Depicts you have no desire to live.
Therefore, you need to understand this;
If it wasn't your time to survive,
We would have never crossed paths!
However, since this connection is made…
We, most definitely, feel responsible for your wellbeing.

You could have easily chosen to harm my family in my absence.
But, you didn't!
You could have conveniently administered your selfish tactics,
Yet, you didn't!

Instead, you reflected into your soul,
And, opened doors for love to seep in!" Dhairya consoled the disheartened wolf.

"There is always, a bigger picture to admire!
Yet, our limited minds, force us to self-destruct.
Because knowingly or unknowingly, we might have already accepted defeat.

So, listen up, my old friend,
If it is your time to go,
You will go no matter what we do to make you stay.
But, by acknowledging the blessings bestowed from above,
At least you can move on with a full belly!
Or else, your hungry soul will haunt every spirit who walks this trail!"
Dhairya attempted to cheer the wolf while secretly thanking Vaani for rectifying his error.

"Yes Khatru, your Dhairu is right." Gayatri stepped in to convince him some more.

"You might think that you don't deserve our compassion,
Still, it isn't up to us to deprive you from what you need.
You might have done something right; which is why we were guided to you.
Maybe, the Universe is telling you that your time here on earth is not done.
Maybe, it's asking you to open your heart and repent for your sins,
Before you move along into another dimension.

Not everyone is lucky to receive a chance like this in life.
You might want your suffering to end,
But, if this agony is written in your stars,
Then, that is what you will have to endure whether you like it or not!

So, make it easy on yourself and us, your new family!
Please, bite into this gift from the Gods!"
Gayatri, sharply yet lovingly, spoke her mind.

"Yes, uncle wolf. Please eat your food...
If you stubbornly choose to ignore all the signs,
Our energy invested in you will be wasted.

Pa says, 'By overcoming the hurdles of this life,
We pave a path for a better future, be it in this lifetime or the next...
As long as we have willingly served our time!'
So what is it going to be?"

Mantra stared at the transformed beast until he finally took a bite holding back his tears wondering all along, 'What *have I done to receive this kindness?'*
'Why is it that I deserve their love?'

Using banana leaves as a blanket to protect the patient from an unusually chilly night,
The unconventional family took turns tending to Khatru's wounds besides constantly checking if the heavily damaged wolf was still breathing.

At the break of dawn,
To their surprise,
The one who they feared wouldn't make it through the night,
Was now showing signs of swift recovery!

'Was it the medicinal datura leaves, or the meaty blessing from above?'
They each contemplated. Whatever it was, it was, indeed, a miracle!
And, for that, they couldn't help but look above and beyond with gratitude.

With Mantra happy to keep her new uncle entertained,
Gayatri pulled Dhairya aside asking him of his whereabouts the previous evening.

Unsure of where to begin, he reminded himself of the power of the Goddess, who stood beside him through thick and thin. Starting from the surreal encounter with an enchanting creature that took him under her wing, he went on to narrate the entire journey just as he experienced it.

Attempting to mask his angst, he let her know by the end of it all,
There was nothing, left for them in the Valley of Hope.

"What about your estranged mother?"
Gayatri pricked his wound knowing he wouldn't want to address that situation.
"Wouldn't you want to know, if she survived the vicious attack???
And, Lobhika?!? Aren't you curious to know what happened of her and Swarth?"
She enticed him to dig deeper.

"No I don't. I don't want to know what became of Lobhika.
Because, from what I have learnt,
She will certainly receive what is coming to her in some way, shape and form.

It is not up to me to chase her down and make her suffer,
Because then, I will be tainting my hands with bad blood.
If I seek vengeance, I will be draining my energy;
My energy which needs to be utilized where it really matters.

Her suffering is inevitable.
I'm just saddened by the chain of events which transpired.
I am in shock to have witnessed that degree of monstrosity.

Yet, I've understood, it isn't my cross to carry.
I say so with conviction because I've seen...,
I've seen, Dadima's soul transcend into the unparalleled space!
And if I'm right,
She must have joined the souls of our ancestors at the Temple of Spirits.
But, not before she has graduated from the Dome of Healing.

Because, from what I witnessed...,
Her concerned soul bears the burden of her tormented tribe."
In all honesty, he expressed himself embracing Vaani's wisdom.

"I get that, and I pray her soul forgives her spirit soon enough, so Dadima can move into another phase. But, what about Titli? Don't you want to reconnect with your mother?!?"
Gayatri wished for her beloved to tie all the loose ends.

"Honestly, in the past, I forced myself to forget she existed;
But, after seeing her caring for Dadima in her times of distress,
My heart truly melted!
She gave me hope to think that nobody is set in their ways.
There is scope for betterment as long as you acknowledge your demons.

I'm not worried about her wellbeing,

Because, she is stronger than I ever gave her credit for.
Although I've never admitted, I've often felt,
I get my fighting spirit and urge to thrive from her.
She is indeed a fighter! She is a survivor!"

Finally, acknowledging Titli's contribution in his life, Dhairya's spirit was now at ease.

"Besides, she has Dhyan by her side!
Although they have butt heads in the past, they surely do make a good team!
I wish to cross paths with her someday;
But, I intend to let nature take its course and the Universe show us the way.
After everything that I have experienced in a short amount of time,
I believe that when the forces align our union, the meeting will occur!"

Trying to give Gayatri an insight into his experience,
Dhairya surprised himself, given how open he had become to sharing.

A meeting with an Oracle,
Had changed Dhairya's perspective on life, death and suffering overnight.
Although his journey into the past had shaken him to the core,
He had come to realize,
He was blessed in ways more than he could begin to imagine!

The connection he had established in the pursuit of his nightmares...
Was, indeed, Priceless!

To lighten their load of fending for Khatru,
Vaani kept dropping gifts like clockwork for a fortnight,
Gifts meant to heal not only his wounded flesh,
But, also awaken his lazy spirit;
Because, from what Dhairya could tell,
The once wicked wolf who flaunted a notorious reputation,
Was turning into a happy, witty and virtuous carnivore.
Affirming his new found belief that *'nothing is set in stone!'*

CHAPTER 16

When the meaty blessings stopped appearing from above,
     The wolf surprised himself by not letting hunger,
Tempt him to drool over the little macaque for his fix of protein;
Which is when he knew that the beast within him had succumbed to those fatal injuries,
Eliminating Khatra forever, and making room for the improved Khatru!

Khatru now expressed gratitude every night before he slipped into sound sleep;
And, with the first rays of the rising sun caressing his hollowed cheeks,
He never forgot to thank his angels for the gift of a wholesome life!

Successfully protecting the wolf from being targeted by certain villagers in that vicinity, his new family was astonished to see his growth. Besides the beast transforming into a loving creature, he now flaunted a new look, bearing spots on his fur-less skin.
Spots, which had resulted due to the brutal piercings from thorny bushes.
Spots which now left him with a new identity.

Encouraging Khatru for a new beginning,
Gayatri insisted that he join their unconventional tribe,
Emphasising that he'd fit in perfectly!

Having lived a lonely life, the wolf was overwhelmed at first;
But, soon, he accepted her gracious invitation shedding tears of joy.

Considering the tall mountains and steep valleys they had to cross to get back home, Dhairya and Mantra happily began rigorous training sessions to strengthen Khatru's weakened limbs, so he could cover long distances without any physical limitations.
Setting aside his ego and stubborn nature,
Khatru, dedicatedly, followed the instructions of those younger than him,
Because, he was beginning to look at life in a different light.

It wasn't all about him and his selfish needs anymore,
Their love and compassion had opened the gates to emotions,
He thought he was incapable of feeling!

Once they were all satisfied, in his ability to embark upon a journey to greater heights,
They took off to where they needed to be;
But, not before Dhairya suggested that they pray for the restless souls and abandoned spirits, struggling to move on in the Valley of Hope. Because, secretly, he had still been battling the nightmares of their past.

"May the Almighty give you the courage to acknowledge your shortcomings,
For, there is a place for every soul in heaven,
Provided, you accept the part you have played in this lifetime.

Together, we pray to the forces of this Universe to show you mercy!
To give you the tools you may need, to be the best version, of your good self that you can be!"

With only best wishes and hopeful thoughts,
The foursome bowed before mother nature,
Waited for the coast to be cleared of metal monsters,
Then, crossed the asphalt once again.

"Aren't we heading in the wrong direction?!?
Weren't we supposed to check in on Dadima and the rest of your family?"
Questioned Mantra who had patiently awaited Khatru's recovery,
Anticipating every single day for that 'family reunion' to take place soon.

"Yes indeed! We were," Gayatri picked Mantra in her arms.

"But, they no longer live where we thought they did...
The first evening we got here,
Your Pa looked for them on his way to fetch water.
He found out, they have moved into another place very far from here."
Protecting Mantra from nightmares, Gayatri chose her words wisely,
"Since Khatru needs a lot of tender love and care now,
We are going back home to our tribe who miss us dearly."

Sensing disappointment in Mantra's eyes,
Khatru, who had grown to adore her, jumped with enthusiasm!
"Yes please! Let's go get me more love! Love feels good!"

"I wanted to feel loved too...I wanted to meet Dadima too.
Shouldn't we be going in search of your tribe?"
Disheartened, Mantra looked at her Pa for answers.

"Yes, my love! We would have, if I knew where to look...
With all the dangers of mankind hovering over our heads,
I need more time to figure out how to reach them.
When the time is right, our union will happen.
Until then, we have to focus on the wellbeing of your new uncle.
And, it is your responsibility to introduce him to his new tribe.
Are you up for the challenge?!?"
Dhairya comforted Mantra by giving her something to look forward to.

Although she sensed that they weren't telling her the full story,
Excited to reunite with her friends, Mantra's cheerful spirit sang songs of friendship, and occasionally told Khatru the tales of their little expeditions.
Slowly yet steadily, they had crossed Gayatri's place of birth from a distance, and were now climbing the same mountain which was being bombed by humans to extract minerals.
Everything was going smoothly until the smell of fresh blood distracted Khatru...
Whose animal instincts, hadn't completely gone away.

"I smell danger on the other side;
I don't think this is the best route for us to take."
Instead of craving fresh meat, Khatru whispered in Dhairya's ears...
Concerned for their safety.

"What is it, uncle wolf?!? Why do you look so worried?
Does someone need our help?!?" Mantra innocently inquired.

Under the pretence of picking exotic flowers,
Gayatri smartly lured the sensitive child away from the elders.

"Whose scent is it that you pick up?" the valiant langur got straight to the point.

"It is a mixture of different scents...,
Peacocks, deer, wild boars, bears, most certainly, bears...
Both, dead and suffering."
Sniffing into thin air he whispered in dismay.
"There is also a pungent aroma of human blood,
In the mix of a female leopard and a bunch of elephants.

I hear faint heartbeats of different babies...,
I smell... I smell, your kind too!" The once dreaded wolf looked horrified.

"Let me go check on what is happening on the other side."
Dhairya anxiously volunteered.

"No, no. I don't think it is safe out there.
Don't you hear the metal monsters with rubber legs?
The humans ride on them along with deadly weapons.
It would be foolish of you to endanger our lives trying to be a hero.
Think about Mantra..."
Khatru made a valid point. Yet, Dhairya wanted to know what was going on.

"Don't worry about me. I will get a better view from above.
They won't even know I'm there. Trust me!
You stay close to the ladies and guard them with your life."
Entrusting the lives of his loved ones into the hands of the former beast,
Not once, did Dhairya's mind question if the wolf might be playing tricks.

Zooming up to the tallest tree, Dhairya looked down to find Mantra waving at
him while Khatru and Gayatri seemed to be engaged in a serious conversation.
Unable to get an insight of what was happening in the valley below them,
Dhairya suddenly noticed a massive truck pull up beneath him.

Within seconds, it was clear to the one who had witnessed monstrosity at its peak,
As to what was going on. In the name of mining for rich minerals,
Some vicious humans were trafficking not only younglings,
But also were rounding up wild animals they'd just killed for their horns, tusks
and skins.

"Hey! Be careful while loading them in the truck.
Our previous shipment was rejected because you people worked in haste.
Remember, they are no good to our employers if they've been too damaged.

As for the ones alive,
Make sure they are well sedated so they don't harm anyone else.

**Dose them enough so they don't wake up before we cross the border.
We don't want them alarming the rangers now, do we?"**
Leaning over his comrade whose guts had been clawed by the feisty leopard, the
merciless leader slashed the man's throat putting him out of his misery.

"No one is going to miss this troublemaker," the killer grinned.
*"Make sure you bury him deep into the jungle so that his remains don't lead anyone
to us. Now hurry! Hurry before someone catches us in the act, and more blood is shed."*
The heartless hunter put his crew to work overtime, signalling for more 'mining
trucks' to pull in.

Dhairya had caught a glimpse into another nightmare, occurring in broad
daylight.
By now, he had learnt to choose his battles wisely.
Understanding that he was no match to the evil which lingered below him,
His family's safety was his obvious priority.
Hence, instead of playing a hero right there and then like old times,
He chose to be wise, and live to fight another day.

Descending quickly to safer grounds,
Dhairya kept his cool, not wanting to spook Mantra in any way.

"The path we took to get here has been destroyed by miners…"
He who had never lied in his life, found it hard to fabricate fiction.

"Really? Those humans! Everything they touch meets the dust." Khatru played
along.

**"It seems impossible to cross this region without drawing attention. *We have
to think of a safer way.*"** The concerned father looked at his better half for her
input.

"Alright then," thinking of a best laid plan, Gayatri's eyes shone bright.
**"Why don't we take a little detour and prolong our family expedition!
Let's introduce Mantra to the Dome of Healing, shall we?"**

"Yay! The Dome of Healing! Sounds exciting!!!"
Mantra was ecstatic, to explore a new place.

Recollecting, fascinating yet inconsistent, stories about the mysterious dome where no living soul had dared to visit, the adults were unsure of what they were getting themselves into. Yet, with no other option in mind, Khatru seconded Gayatri's idea while Dhairya understood her sentiments behind that suggestion.

Gayatri, who loved and adored her langur, wanted him to heal his spirit after all the heartache, betrayal and bloodshed he had witnessed. Although she had her doubts about whether they would even find the stellar world of supernatural, where only the ones who crossed onto another phase were invited, she listened carefully to the Goddess within her to prompt the way.
Ready to expect the unexpected, Gayatri prepped Mantra not to be spooked by anything out of the ordinary that she might encounter.

Instead of bombarding them with questions as to what it could be like,
Mantra was simply elated to seek new adventures on their extended journey!

Keeping up their spirits as they all followed in Gayatri's footsteps,
Each one of them had different expectations of what they might see...
Discussing possibilities of talking trees, flying monkeys and giant flies, they enjoyed letting their imagination run wild! Until a tricky climb to the top of a rocky hill commanded their full attention.

Successfully making it to the top without any casualties,
The descend, seemingly trickier, forced them to concentrate harder,
Making them take every step, with caution.
Because, that slippery slope, led them deeper and deeper...
Into the never ending treacherous Valley of Doom.

Contemplating if they were terribly lost,
They decided to take a break and figure out if they had taken the right route.

While Khatru stretched his fatigued limbs on a giant golden boulder,
Which looked like a tiny rock when they began,

Mantra was in awe of the illusions created by colourful rope like roots,
Which seemed to have suddenly fallen from the sky.
Spotting outlandish formations of rocks and trees playing tricks on his mind...
Dhairya was certain, they were heading in the right direction!

Gayatri felt the same, when her naked eyes, caught glimpses of oddly shaped
flowers sparkling in broad daylight.
Inhaling the unadulterated air, she held her breath until anomalous sensations
flowed smoothly through her veins rejuvenating her existence; while sharpening
all senses and making her aware, of pure water flowing under her dry feet!

"Are you ready to unfold the mysteries of a mystical land?!?"
Gayatri seemed euphoric!

"The mysterious Dome of Healing is closer than I thought!
It's just a matter of entering the right portal into another dimension now!"
Glowing like she had never glowed before, Gayatri encouraged everyone to take
a deep breath before they were wowed by the wonders, of this paranormal world.

Unlike those who effortlessly connected with the divine within them, with each
breath that they took, Khatru found it difficult to inhale the magic they felt.
Instead of instantly seeking guidance from his family, he focused on what he was
doing wrong, struggling to keep up. When came the time to take a leap of faith
over the mesmerising turquoise waters flowing gently below them, Khatru froze
standing still like a statute at the edge of the cliff.

Not wanting to disappoint his little angel who cheered him on to jump,
The wolf gathered all the courage he had and made it across the river in a flawless
leap,
Restoring faith in his abilities.

Successfully overcoming what he thought to be the biggest hurdle so far,
Khatru was anxious to see where the invisible road would lead them to.
Cautiously stepping onto what they guessed to be the 'Unsturdy Redemption
Bridge,'
Their spirits were exhilarated witnessing spectacular fluorescent creepers,
Appearing out of thin air, to solidify their path.

Once on the other side, Gayatri, Mantra and Dhairya seemed to float with great ease towards the unknown. But, Khatru, who had his doubts, suddenly struggled to carry the weight of his scrawny self as soon as he stepped on enchanted grounds. Hurting more and more as he attempted to move forward,
He was reminded of the tales told about a bewitching bridge...
A bridge, which separated reality from fantasy.

Rumors were those who overstayed their welcome,
Didn't live to paint a picture of their travels.

Everything about this situation was asking him to back track.
As soon as he did, he regained his composure!
In order to reconfirm his newly discovered theory,
He gathered courage to set foot on the magical land again.
But, this time, not only did he feel an enormous weight of his bones,
His head was sent spiralling by the rapidly changing landscape.

"I don't think I am destined to experience this magic...
The likes of me are, most certainly, not welcome here."
Khatru blurted out loud catching those moving effortlessly, off guard.

"What makes you say that?"
Wondered Dhairya who had grown to love the wolf.

Getting back on the bridge which now rocked him senseless, Khatru spoke his mind,
"You know the amount of baggage I am carrying with me, don't you?!?
You also know what this sacred space symbolizes...
Maybe, it's just not my time.
I mean, come on,
I am surprised to stumble upon this unparalleled world with such ease.
This only goes to show that you my friends, are the chosen ones!
Chosen to explore a space where I might be lucky to end up, even after I die."

"What baggage are you talking about, uncle wolf? We always travel light!"
Oblivious to the facts of his past, Mantra tried to cheer him up.

"My little angel! Your innocence woos my heart!

But, I am not who you think I am.

I've been a monster up until I met you.

I have been cursed by too many tormented spirits, to be able to live a life of bliss.

I have to repent for all my sins, before this dream, becomes a possibility for me.

Trust me when I say, the list of my sins is very, very long...

Therefore, more than anything right now,

It's time for me, to break away from you,

And, do some soul searching!" He found it hard to look Mantra in the eye.

Giving his words a thought, the smart one came up with a plan.

"So why don't we all take a little rest for now!

You go park yourself back on that orange rock. Or, is it golden?!?

Never mind that; go and ask for forgiveness!

There is no need to rush yourself.

We have all the time in the world to wait.

We shall wait until you have made peace,

With every last one of your demons!" Mantra seemed proud of her brilliant idea.

"Yes! And, while you are at it,

Say a little prayer to acknowledge those...,

Who you might have forgotten to add to your list.

Because, as you rightly mentioned, it is a very, very long list!"

Gayatri wanted to make sure, if this was his time for contrition, he did it right!

"My lovely ladies aren't joking!"

Showcasing his acrobatic skills Dhairya landed on his feet, standing tall on the transparent links which supported their connection to the unprecedented creation.

"So please, allow us to escort you back to the golden boulder, or is it orange?

It is hard to tell, isn't it Mantra, with everything around us changing colours so swiftly?!?

Never mind that. You know which one I mean right?

The one, where you seemed to be so comfortably at peace!"

Dhairya walked his buddy across the invisible bridge and stood by his side at the edge of the cliff, so that the anxious wolf wouldn't panic noticing the calm turquoise waters, turn into wild rapids below them. Displaying darker and darker shades of blues, the river turned grey, and then, black as if testing the one who already had jitters.

Overcoming that hurdle successfully, Khatru made everyone proud!
Walking on shaky grounds, he held onto Dhairya...,
Who in return, encouraged Khatru to mount the marvellous rock and be still.

"We are here, waiting patiently, for you to make things right!" Mantra assured him swinging from a red root to a pink vine and then to a purple branch above his head, **"Just remember to clear your mind first!"**

"Then, listen; listen to the music in the air!
Let the symphony guide you away from your nightmare!" Gayatri's tone was musical.
"Don't let your demons overpower the goodness!
Be true to yourself, and rise towards greatness!"

"Yes my friend! If you focus on the obvious...,
You might just tend to overlook the wound, which needs nurturing.
So, please do dig deep. Go back to where it all began!

Then, separating your blessings from your curses,
Understand your true purpose in this lifetime!

Once you've done that, it will be a lot easier to be remorseful of your actions, which clearly, never matched your original vibrations!"
A good friend and guru encouraged his pal towards the path of redemption,
Because, he wanted Khatru not to deprive himself from self-healing.

CHAPTER 17

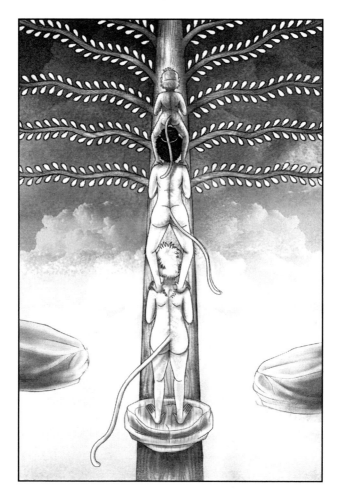

Always finding ways to keep themselves entertained…
While Khatru, contributed to the mystical waters,
Allowing tears of repentance to flow in abundance,
The thrill seekers explored every nook of the magical landscape, in awe!

Reacquainting themselves with the bedazzling roots of mystery dangling above their heads, they had ample time to contemplate, '*How they came to be?*'

Closely inspecting the igneous rocks they sat on...,
Dhairya came to a conclusion that,
They were conceived, during an ancient volcanic eruption!
But, before his thoughts could make way through his lips and into their ears,
Endearing colours, invisible to mere mortal eyes, caught their attention.
Causing ripples, in the treacherous Valley of Doom!

In spite of the intimidatingly rough portrayal of its looks,
The crust of this land comforted their existence,
Unlike the distressed world they had, somehow, managed to leave behind.
Although alien to this sovereign state, their mysterious host had been very kind!
She had many layers to her just like an onion!
Besides the terror that she was...
Tenderness dripped under her tough skin!

To test their willingness, to embark upon a life altering adventure...
The Queen of that kingdom played pranks, startling her guests.

Out of thin air,
Popped delicate, diaphanous flowers,
Varying in textures and colour schemes!
There were sheer shapes in the midst of glassy teal!
Where some flaunted a fiery silk base,
Few feathery flowers looked like they were made of steel!

Rather than wasting time rationalizing and reasoning...
All exhilarated, they graciously admired her creation,
Simply going with the flow!
Enthralled by the mysteries of the supernatural world,
They made a pact to stay close!
But, with too many options presenting themselves, confusion arose.

Mantra was invited to play catch by gelatinous bouncy pebbles, the size of her fist!
An unusually large butterfly with purplish green wings,
Caught Gayatri's attention in the mist!
Seeing his soul mates in euphoria, Dhairya was blissful!

Yet, as soon as he noticed them drifting in opposite directions, he found himself rattled.

Following in each other's footsteps came naturally to them;
Therefore, adjusting to separate desires proved to be a challenge.
Afraid of being detached from his Goddesses in uncharted territory,
Anxiety hit him hard!
Taking a moment to analyse his feelings,
He understood where the hurdle lay.

It was his selfish urge to have them joined to his hips, which caused him to stress.
He knew, they were their individual entities bringing glory to his life; yet,
Accustomed to explore everything together, he found it hard to let them be.

Consciously accepting his contribution in their lives,
He commanded his thoughts not to become an obstacle in their path.
No sooner did he acknowledge his flaw out loud,
He received an invitation of his own, guiding him towards an enigma.

Holding onto their jaws from dropping onto glorious grounds,
Each had infinite 'wow moments' of their own.
Regrouping, to share their joy of being present in paradise!
They found it impossible to describe, what they'd seen.

Surprisingly, all thoughts seemed to lead to the most intriguing tree;
A tree that they wished for the other to see!
Still, from where they each stood,
Neither of them could relate to the ultimate point of attraction.
The object of fascination, was the same. Yet,
Their fingers pointed in totally different directions.

Captivated by the illusionist at work,
Mantra subtly signalled her parents to her side!
Although they wanted her to see what they saw, right then,
The delighted parents indulged in their daughter's request.

Sharing the same space as her, they realized,
She had already spotted what they intended for her to see.
But, the flimsy rock they stood on wouldn't let them be.
Instead of spoiling the fun by asking her to hop onto the sturdier molten rock of their choice, Dhairya suggested his ladies to climb onto his shoulder, for he could then maintain their balance with ease. Doing what his heart desired, the unconventional family rose to greater heights, building a monkey tower harmoniously!

That tower was meant to be, because from where they originally stood,
Their eyes didn't do justice to the marvel that she was!

'How weren't they able to spot her before?' the intrigued parents wondered.
"Because, you weren't on the same page!" a passing wind answered!

Her never ending, bronzish golden trunk was as striking as the tigers eye!
Her slender red branches spread systematically across the sky!
Her opalish leaves shimmered like water drops!
And, blue blood ran freely throughout her veins!

One moment she was there,
But, as soon as either of their focus shifted, she was gone.
Then she appeared when she pleased, and vanished again with a passing breeze!

Emerging again, she sprinkled some seeds...,
Watering them lovingly with the moisture in her leaves.
With every last drop consumed, she disappeared,
Only to create another optical illusion, when she reappeared!
Bringing life back to the barren craters which lay bored by her side,
She hypnotized her audience with an impactful eruption from the darkened soil.

The extinct volcanoes were now active, oozing out lava like never before.
Getting sucked into an imaginary tube...,
The enchanting entities arising, seemed eager to stand tall!
Because, they knew that they had mortal spectators watching their every move.

Blossoming together with her doppelgangers up to a mighty height…
She wrapped her arms around herself leaving them with a mind boggling sight!
Riveted by the mirage of four tiger eyed pillars staring them down,
Their applause echoed throughout the valley,
Instantly saddening Dhairya who missed his tribe dearly.

Yes, he had moved on, to build a better life for himself…
But, bearing the burden, for his beloved grandma…
He wished, to reconnect with her soul, in this magical realm.

Humbled by his allegiance with his ancestor's soul,
The prolific pillars moved enough to give him a glimpse of what was to come.
Standing as two separate halves of one big puzzle, as they rose,
The swiftly heating Sun tested his devotion, just before he saw a sign.
Embodied as one, they stood tall for long.
But, as soon as his thoughts drifted towards pain…
The rock shook, forcing them all to fall.

Instantly checking for any bruises,
Gayatri and Dhairya apologized to Mantra in one voice.
Insisting not to sweat, she sparkled when she said,
"I'm a big girl now! Don't worry about me!
Let's get back up there to see what we are meant to see!"

Taking a hint from the raging sun who insinuated something else,
Gayatri suggested they have a little picnic,
In order to shield themselves from the swirling heat wave.
Excited by the thought of food, their tummies growled like never before.
And, just on cue, fruity blessings arrived from a secret store!

Quickly arranging a lavish spread gifted by the courteous Queen,
They munched on blessed berries and nibbled on delicious nuts!

Expressing her desire to stay there forever,
Mantra was curious to know if the *Valley of Hope* looked the same!

Caught off guard by the inquisitions which didn't seem to stop, Gayatri gave Dhairya a chance to let Mantra in on his secrets, by pretending to take a nap.

Unsure as to how to address a disastrous episode,
Dhairya babbled, to mask his discomposure.
Ensnared by the vision he failed to receive,
He diverted Mantra's curiosity to a beguiling tree of his past.

Capturing the essence of her Majesty, *The Tree of Eternal Life,* on a large muddy canvas, Dhairya relived his childhood memories with unspoken grief.

Absolutely certain, her parents refrained from sharing a heart-breaking story.
Inspired by the magnificent, mobile tree she had seen moments ago,
The thoughtful child eased his pain.
Significantly placing shiny stones and withered leaves around his masterpiece,
She gave it a life of its own!
Pleased, to see a glimmer of hope in his eyes and a smile on his face,
Mantra carefully completed her project, decorating every inch of that space.

Once they were satisfied with what they had achieved,
Mantra flung a gummy mud ball on his head, ambushing him from behind.
Swinging like a pro, from the heavenly roots which seemed to have squeezed themselves through the tough mountain rocks, she forced him to chase her among multi-coloured vines and purple branches, of another divine bark!

Goofing around some more, he playfully wondered if she was ready to learn awesome aerial tricks taught to him by his favourite grandma. Having waited for that moment to arrive since she took her first swing as a toddler, Mantra attentively observed his every move. When asked to perform her part, the natural learner, flawlessly repeated the difficult tricks with sass, making Dhairya a very proud father!

Sitting still like a statue for hours in the scorching heat,
Khatru was also humbled by the Mighty Sun.
Yet, he didn't allow any source of distraction to disrupt, his act of contrition.
As if melted by his pure intention, the ball of fire tamed its rays.
And, a huge gust of wind tried soothing the wolf's barbecuing flesh.

Sensing a shift in the atmosphere, at once, Gayatri invited the daring duo to huddle up on a translucent boulder, sticking up like a big sparkling diamond in the rough. To observe a phenomenon, they most certainly would never witness again.

Waiting all along for them to take their seats,
The setting sun unevenly splashed the sky,
With various shades of blue, green, yellow, orange, red, purple and pink.
Assisting the artist to blend his palette to perfection,
Enormous cottony clouds gracefully moved across the space...
Giving the priceless painting a soul!

It was indeed the most spectacular piece of art created by the Gods,
Who, clearly, didn't feel the need to rush their creation!

Admiring the bright pictures in motion for hours, the theme changed...
As soon as the bewitching Blood Moon made her presence known!
Besides the slippery slope shimmering away to glory,
The red spots on Khatru's body also glittered like precious stones!

Forever feeling connected to the mysteries of the moon for reasons unthinkable,
Absolutely content with his hours of atonement, Khatru slowly opened his eyes,
Simply to find her reflecting into him, touched by his dedication.
Grateful for that meeting when it was most needed,
The wolf howled into the glorious night...
Paying tribute to his Queen!

Thrilled, to see her dejected uncle rejoice, Mantra's exuberance invigorated his spirit, forcing him to lend a ear to her unpolished howls. Intending to exercise her vocal cords, Khatru, who struggled to breathe that magical air earlier during the day, filled his lungs effortlessly howling again. Listening closely to his powerful vibrations becoming one with the universe, Mantra's sparkling spirit howled again and again and again...
Enticing her parents to instantly join their band!

Nothing about that union was normal from the usual perspective; yet,

Together, they created an inconceivable symphony conducted by the enthralling
moon.
Inspiring every soul listening, to celebrate her charisma!

With the forces of the cosmos joining in to serenade the benevolent,
A sudden shower of shooting stars dazzled its spectators,
Instantly gratifying their existence!

Seizing the auspicious occasion to secretly transmit tools, needed for a triumphant
transition, beyond conception...
The fallen stars slowly turned to dust. Lighting up not only the sky, but also
creating fireworks, within each soul watching!

Making an impression which would never be erased, the curtains dropped on cue
when flickering lights across the Valley of Doom, zombified every lingering spirit.
It was time, for all to travel the distance to get to where they belonged...
In the company of those who were already separated from flesh,
The fascinating four proceeded to explore the paranormal world; full of zest!

In spite of the invisible entities casting eerie shadows around them,
Undeterred, they followed the light!
Dangerously leaning over the cliff,
In order to gauge the unpredictable river beneath...
The adventurers were amused to catch their reflection,
In what was now crystal clear water!

Intending to distract the mortals from their mission,
Wondrous creatures, of the ineffable underground world...
Tried in vain, to lure them in by turning their fabulous fins into elongated limbs.
Transforming into ostentatiously glowing mermaids dancing in synchronicity,
The vicarious beasts performed with intensity,
Enticing the onlookers to leap into their arms.

Their tactics were successful in the past,
Consuming those who didn't know where they were going.
This lot, was determined to reach their goal!
Therefore, there was no way they were swaying.

Shining her light upon the free spirits to give them a better sight,
The Blood Moon enhanced their vision,
Giving them the sanity, for all temptations to fight!

With clarity in mind, as to which way to go;
They avoided falling into the waters of deception,
Disappointing the diabolic mermaids, but, winning the Goddess' heart!

As a sign of good faith, a Sorcerous shooed away the demons, putting an end to their farce. Assuring her tribe a safe passage, she showed them what they needed to see!

Projecting herself in the crystal clear water,
She transported Khatru to his happiest times!

He'd spotted her magnificence brimming to its full potential for the first time;
While he was still attached to his mother's udder!
Besides his radiant aura and the depth in his deep blue eyes,
His purity, instantly put him under her radar!
Although she kept an eye on him at all times,
Every 29 days, she was flattered to see his devotion towards her.

She never failed to hear his heart race,
As he cut through the dense forest excited for a secret rendezvous!
Striding to the top of a tiny hill,
Overlooking the river flowing through the Valley of Hope,
The impatient wolf practiced patience…
Eagerly waiting to be graced by her presence!

Mostly, he would sit in silence; fixated on the flow.
Innovating ways to tease him…
When she would finally sparkle like a diamond in the water,
Consumed with glee, he would rise to serenade his only love!
Howling away to glory!!!

Mantra was a happy child! Everything made her happy!
Picking one particular moment seemed impossible.

So, the sorceress gave her a flashback of them all!
Realising within seconds, her happiness reflected because of her Mother!
The Goddess at work smiled!

Gayatri and Dhairya, were destined to meet!
They lived a wholesome life ever since they made a big splash.
Although their hearts had melted too many times,
And, tears of gratitude always flowed freely,
The highlight was their union! *One, which they never forgot.*

Observing the colourful plankton below perfectly follow the rhythm,
Gayatri blushed,
Recollecting her union with Dhairya, under unusual circumstances as these!
Reminded of the exact same moment at that very second,
Her soul mate gently planted a kiss, on her already flushed cheek.

Each one of them saw exactly what they needed to see.
Reaffirming, their mission!

Instead of lurking over their shoulders,
The converted Khatru decided to give the lovebirds some privacy.
Without second guessing himself this time,
He leaped across to the other side, unfazed, pleasantly surprising them all!
Applauding his bravado, countless fireflies guided his way towards the Redemption Bridge, cheering him on!

Determined to vindicate himself, as he stepped onto the dreamy ropes,
His eternal love shone upon him, rejuvenating his senses furthermore!
Already acquainted by his spirit, the fluorescent creepers welcomed him grandly by reconstructing a glowing bridge!
Eager to exonerate himself from the guilt of his past...
She felt his heart race, just like it had when he was thrilled to meet his Mother -
The Moon!

Waiting for his extended family to join him...
So, they could take that big step together!

Watching them dance their way across the dazzling Redemption Bridge, Khatru tapped his paws in delight!

Aligning together with their kindred spirit, at the end of all that jazz...
Their bodies stood still, while their spirits slowly levitated into another spectre!

CHAPTER 18

P uzzled by their sudden disembodiment…
Floating in thin air, Mantra innocently asked,
"Does this mean we are dead now?!?"

"No, silly. We are simply fortunate;
Fortunate to have an outer body experience right now!"

Gayatri pointed at their physical state waving at their spirits.
"This isn't a world we are conditioned to live in.
The land of new beginnings is here!
A land where mortals cannot enter…
Carrying the weight, of their flesh and bones!"

"So, how were we able to walk here this afternoon?!?"
Mantra's restless spirit sought answers.

"Because, it might have not been the magical moment, to make this precious meeting!" Dhairya took a wild guess.

"It most certainly wasn't!
If it was, I would be standing along with your bodies,
Bidding your spirits a safe trip, wouldn't I?"
Khatru chuckled, taking pride in his progress!

"I wonder what we are thinking right now! I mean, them;
Oh my Lord! This is so confusing!" Mantra exclaimed.

"We are all in the same boat!" giggled Khatru's spirit, **"Isn't this bananas?!?"**

"Thanks, uncle wolf.
Now, I have to figure out where the boat with the bananas is?"
Her sassy spirit rolled her eyes in bewilderment.

"Oh, Mantra! It is just an expression!
An expression to describe the bizarre situation we find ourselves in."
Gayatri's hearty laugh elevated the vibes of the supernatural kingdom.

"Come on now, Chop, chop!
Let's not wile away our valuable time here,
Racking the minds we should have left behind."
Dhairya's spirit was eager to reconnect with Dadima.

"Since there is no reasonable explanation, for the wonders we've been exposed to…

Let us keep faith in the creator, to usher us towards the mysteries meant for us to probe. Because, if it wasn't our time to be here, we wouldn't be floating in mid-air having this conversation, would we?"
Owlishly, a father enlightened his child.

Taking another moment to wave back at their flesh and bones, Mantra's inquisitive spirit took charge heading straight towards an array of trees flickering in the dark. Her fascinated spirit flared astonished by the remarkable special effects, meant only for their eyes!
Time was of the essence, she knew. So, she tried to soak it all in.
Unsure of where to go after a certain point, since everything looked the same,
She glided from right to left and left to right, before reaching out to her Mother.

Sucked into bewilderment, they individually waited to receive a sign,
Which is when, out of nowhere,
Appeared a peculiar phosphorescent dragonfly hovering around them...
Flapping its beautiful, shimmery violet wings, it stood still before their eyes.

Excited to make a new friend, Mantra elegantly extended her arm,
Inviting the extraordinary helicopter to land on her palm!
Then, blushed at her silliness, comprehending what she was about to do!

"Follow me!" *the* radiant insect whispered.
Gleaming even more when she giggled.

"Thank you for leading the way! Is someone expecting us?!?"
Dhairya struck a conversation charmed to meet their chaperone

"Yes! Of course!"
His reflection beamed in her free styling sand duney eyes.

"And, who might that be?" Khatru was curious.

**"The gatekeeper of this kingdom!
The gardener of these woods!
The educator of the ignorant!**

I, personally, call them 'Iilliteraties.'
Educated, illiterate beings, you know!
Those who think they know everything,
But, actually, they know almost next to nothing!"
An orangish yellow dragonfly with silverish green blades, enlightened him in jubilation.

Seeing her better half lose himself in excitement, his counterpart, completed what he was meant to say loud and clear this time, "And, the healer of broken souls! Chop, chop! Move along!"

"Chop, chop! She says! Chop chop!"
Hearing the same expression used by her father moments ago,
Mantra giggled to glory.
"Really?!? All these people! Sorry, spirits, or souls, must I say???
Are awaiting our arrival. That's awesome!" The confused wolf seemed thrilled.

Finding his enthusiasm extremely funny, the soul mates chortled in harmony,
"They are All in One, and One in All!"

Seeing big question marks on their faces, the dainty dragonflies laughed,
"You are not our typical guests, I'm sure you've understood that by now!"

"Yes!" this time, the four awestruck spirits harmonised!

"In the centuries of our service to the High Priestess,
We've never seen her make exceptions.
You, special souls are indeed 'The Chosen Ones!'"
Perplexed by their jaw drop, Param's bronze eyes failed to flutter.

"Wait a minute! How old did you say you were?" Khatru was baffled.

Taking that opportunity to introduce themselves,
The bubbly violet winged insect cheerfully said,
"We haven't told you anything yet!
But, now would be the perfect time to enlighten you some more!

Hi! I'm Aatma! And, this is Param!
Together, we are the Ultimate Souls!
Living in an Everlasting World!
We've been in love since we set eyes on each other millions of years ago!"
The love struck soul mounted her marvellous mate,
Who was forever eager to share their eternal love story.

"After suffering the anxiety of separation,
Over and over and over again through different lifetimes…
When an opportunity to be bound together forever presented itself,
We happily chose to stay and serve the Goddess, Herself!

The same Goddess is eagerly awaiting your arrival.
Won't it be extremely rude on your part to make her wait?!?
So, if there are no more queries,
Shall we carry on?"
Turning his engine on, the fastest flying insect on any planet,
Hoped the new arrivals understood the essence of time.

In agreement with Param,
Dhairya took off after them in full speed asking his family to keep up.

Noticing Khatru get distracted along the way with unnatural activities occurring around them every step of the way, Mantra ceased the moment to say,
"Chop, chop, Uncle! Chop chop!"
Instantly bringing a smile on all their concentrated faces.

Gliding into the unknown further and farther, the mortal spirits stayed close to the Ultimate Souls so they wouldn't lose their only guide. Unaware that they were travelling almost at the speed of light in mid-air, suddenly, their spirits got sucked to lower grounds - grounds invisible to their restricted eyes. Blinded by the sudden darkness that consumed them, they tried to grab onto each other, but were unable to make contact. Asking them not to fret, Aatma exuded more radiance lighting their path with her phosphorescent effects. Illuminating their descending spirits!

Leading them lower and lower, towards what looked like an entrance to an erosional cave, the lovebirds expressed their excitement!

"Our mission is accomplished! At least, for now!
Here on, it is solely up to you.
Up To you, to explore whatever direction you might choose.

Consider this your test!
If you knock on the right doors, and, push the correct buttons,
Her Grace will bless you with her presence!
If not,
At least, you will consider yourself fortunate enough to get this far!"
Blowing kisses their way, Param and Aatma winked,
Then, circled around their newest most extraordinary tribe members in haste.

Sparking light into the blinding darkness by their speedy rotations,
They instantaneously bumped into each other, uniting as one divine entity!
Making the mortal minds spin by giving them a taste of what was to come.
Covertly conducting their operation, they combusted, right before their disciples'
eyes. Abruptly vanishing out of sight!

Gleefully thanking their angels along with the souls of all their ancestors,
The mortal spirits crawled into the tiny opening underground,
Looking forward to an eternal union of their own!
Although, the tunnel was pitch dark and the space restricted,
Their being was lit, and their hearts were absolutely open.

Slithering through the wriggled trail without squirming for a second,
The overjoyed troopers were hopeful to make it past this maze.
But, suddenly, smashing into an invisible wall,
Little Mantra, who'd taken charge of the expedition,
Sought guidance from her elders wondering what to do next!

"There must be a trigger in here somewhere.
A trigger, that might open the door to another dimension..."
Said Khatru, trying in vain to prove his theory.

"Didn't they say 'knock on the right doors and push the correct buttons'?"
Having concentrated on Param's and Aatma's advices, Mantra struggled to find a
door.

"I can't seem to make contact with these surroundings Pa...
What am I doing wrong?" She expressed her frustration.

Taking a moment to reflect on their Chaperone's words, Dhairya explained,
"It is not the surrounding you must connect with...
The secret trigger you are looking for lies within us all!

Although we are given a destination...,
It is up to us, how we cover that distance.

Either, we can blindly follow what we've heard,
Or, we can understand the true meaning of that message!"
Dhairya hinted, they dig deep.

"When we have reached a crossroad...,
Or in this matter, a dead end...
There is only one way to proceed - inward!"
Sharing the same views as her soul mate, Gayatri gave them another clue.

Without once doubting their wisdom, Khatru and Mantra paid close attention. Humbly asking her beloved to lead the way, Gayatri requested the confused spirits, to follow the sound of Dhairya's voice.

Putting forth their intentions,
They emptied their frivolous minds.
Focusing all their energy into the Divine,
They prayed to the source silently, until Dhairya broke the silence.

"Even though all of us came into existence at different times,
We were meant to embark on this particular journey, together!
Everything we have seen and experienced so far,
Lead us to where we desire to be. Because,
They are, ALL IN ONE and ONE IN ALL!
ONE IN ALL and ALL IN ONE!"

Inhaling deeply, Dhairya repeated the Ultimate Soul's words,
Gradually giving it a profound twist of his own!

"Together we unite, when we are grounded!
Together we remain, when we are stable!
Together we align, when we are one with the force!"
Expanding his astounding aura he bestowed light, enlightening his tribe furthermore.

"Becoming one with the source is the vision!
Putting in the required work is our mission!
It is essential to seek the divine right now...
Because, Dark Days and Nightmarish Nights,
Aren't so far away.

We are running out of time. Therefore, we must hurry.
Irrespective of our differences, we need to seek one goal.
Dissolving as one entity, we need to stay sublimed!
Only then, there will be no reason to worry!"
Acknowledging the urgency, Dhairya passionately went to a greater extent rekindling hope!

"We do not have to search elsewhere to make that difference,
Because, we have all that it takes to make wonders happen!

BALANCE is the secret!
COURAGE and CHARISMA are essential!
FOCUS, DEDICATION and PERSEVERANCE are the key!
APPRECIATION, GRATIFICATION and COMPASSION will lead us places!
These are our TOOLS!

With these qualities embedded in our souls,
We can conquer greatest heights and unlock even invisible doors!
Yet, realise,
It is necessary to remain centred at all times!

Because, where goodness is in store,
Ego and arrogance are lurking around the corner...
Waiting eagerly to seep in and pollute our existence.

Intending to distract us from our mission.
Simply to hamper our progress and self-growth!"

With every dedicated breath that circled their spirits,
And, each heartfelt word which left his mouth…
The one anxiously awaiting their arrival tapped onto his *eternal devotion*!

Persevering to unblock their personal clogs using tools at their disposal,
His disciples' dedication and determination dazzled the Queen!

It was time!
Time, because now they were prepared!
Prepared, to take the world by storm!
Without a fear; without any doubt!

Running freely through their veins, she manifested their desire!
Elevating their scrunched spirits beyond the restrictions of the dark cave,
She tested them again, examining further…
To see, if they were absolutely willing, to let go.
Willing to accept the gifts and blessings,
Which, upon them, she was about to bestow!

Free of the imaginary barriers and boundaries…
They weren't constricted anymore!
Rising higher than they had ever dreamt of,
Everyone was ready, to embrace her magic!
Yet, only when they expressed their impulse to be one in her arms…
Did the gates to her kingdom open, and, a magical ball appeared!

Focusing all their energy on the transparent globe bearing watery fluids,
They wished for it to be the portal they had been desperately seeking.

Collectively, sending pure vibrations into space,
Which, in return, got sucked into the globe…
They witnessed HER wizardry first hand, when slowly, yet, swiftly, the contents
of the simmering orb drastically changed colours!

The first colour, instantly painted a picture of Aatma's wondrous wings!
Then, as indigo replaced violet...
The fragrance of that beautiful flower invigorated their senses...,
Leaving the scent behind to linger!

Then, the mighty ocean, took over the sphere,
Forcing waves of turquoise waters to create a clear blue sky!

Suddenly, boiling to a brink of explosion,
The blisters inside the globule popped green, yellow and orange bubbles,
Bringing Param's exotic appearance to mind!
Captivating them furthermore by blending every single colour that appeared
before them to perfection, the undercover magician blew them away when, inside
the orbiting ball of mystic, the *Blood Moon* emerged; bringing them to tears!

The enthralling object of sorcery mystified their space,
Emitting icy white smoke...
Blurring their vision some more!

Seeking clarity, as they rubbed their eyes,
The mystical sphere rotated around its imaginary axis...
Summoning the smoke back where it belonged!

Making their heads spin faster and faster with every expeditious rotation,
The smouldering sphere convoked all the fog, all the mist...
And, spun with agility.
Yet, in its speed, reflected its might!

*Unable to keep up with its own madness, now revolving, faster than the speed of
light, the globule dropped onto the enchanted ground shattering itself into a gazillion
pieces!*

Stunned by that occurrence, yet, disappointed by its fall,
Just when Mantra was to express her sentiments,
The magical substance rose to the auspicious occasion!

Synthesizing itself into a rickety blob of vortex!
Swirling around the speechless spectators,
The Alchemist wrapped up her show,
By blinding their mortal spirits…
In the purest flash of light!

CHAPTER 19

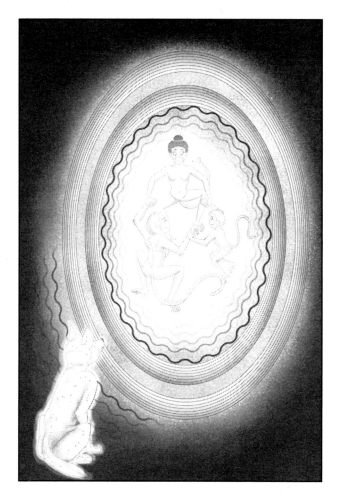

Disoriented by the sudden burst of energy penetrating their souls…
Their spirits failed to witness the magic unfolding before their eyes.

A Spectrum of Rainbow had met its end imbibing in its glory...
Opening a Portal into the sacred realm!
Facilitating a safe passage for an ultimate union to occur!

Quivering in harmony, they received Divine blessings!
Accepting them graciously, they united with the Eternal Light!
Euphoric by the warmest welcome ever, the elders rejoiced in tears!
And, Mantra, unrestricted, she shared her enthusiasm,
Clapping while jumping with joy!
"Wow! It's a rainbow, Ma! It's a double rainbow!!!"

Instantly gratified, the delighted soul glided towards her dream,
Like a Celestial Body, one with the cosmos!
Gently strumming its radiance with her delicate fingers,
Gracefully swaying, to the tunes of an empyrean creation,
Mantra serenaded the Empress she was about to meet!

Hypnotized by the softness in the heavenly notes,
Gayatri rejoiced in ecstasy! Appreciative of the miracle too!!!
Uniting on the dance floor with her darling daughter,
The Goddess lost herself in a sacred space, simply to be found!
Found, by the one who worshipped her for the Divine-Self that she was!

His intentions were godly; her aura was remarkable!
Their thoughts were pure, therefore everything seemed possible!
Ever willing to put himself in jeopardy for the sake of his tribe,
His actions reflected nothing but a passionate drive!

Passion for living a life meant to live!
Drive to selflessly give when he's meant to give!
Accepting every challenge with a smile was his brilliance!
Acknowledging his flaws without resisting was his innocence!
Realizing his potential,
Dhairya, the brave heart dove into the force,
Willingly submitting to the unknown! Leaving absolutely, *no room for doubt!*

Although fighting a battle of his own,
Khatru was fortunate to witness this cosmic connection!
Eager to explore some more...,
He joined their circle of love seeking further direction!

Bound together in the band of colours he dropped his inhibitions completely,
Twirling in harmony with the free spirits!
He celebrated his queen devoutly!

In sync with their vibrations…
The glorious illusion of light imploded!
Initiating her devotees into a stellar space,
Meant only for the divine!
Soaking them in its radiance, the rainbow aggrandized their vibes,
Instantly invigorating their spirits!
Glorifying the fact that, *'Their journey into the future had truly just begun!'*

Dissolving in her divination!
All in one and one in all!
They graciously received each sign and every gift,
Bestowed upon them by the supreme!
Full heartedly obtaining the keys to thee kingdom,
Her charismatic tribe, was now ready!

Ready to venture into the unparalleled world!
Where *divinity itself* was expecting them!

CHAPTER 20

Closely tailing the twin rainbows, farther and farther underground…
Wriggling through minute spaces meant only for ants,
Two langurs, a little macaque and a big wolf,
Embarked upon a voyage slithering in spirit!

Covering unimaginable distances under unorthodox circumstances,
Frantically, keeping up the frenetic pace all along not wanting to lose their guide,
The mortal spirits couldn't help themselves but take a moment to fathom,
Fathom, a world which had, literally, been turned upside down.

Defying gravity by all means possible…
Unfathomable heaps of garbage,
Floated as mountains of stink in the disturbingly gloomy sky.
Unable to bear the burden of its weight, once cottony clouds,
Now transformed, into disgustingly dirty sponges dripping bane below.
Boisterous bubbles of toxic gasses burst upon slight friction,
Triggering a deadlier mixture to combust, in the already deadly gas chamber.

Every ounce of its soil was soaked in obnoxiously filthy water bodies, flowing like
puss oozing out of rotting wounds, throughout their disgustingly dirty dwellings.
The decaying mutants of that Godforsaken planet,
Struggled to carry the weight of their oddly oversized heads and unevenly placed
extra limbs - limbs which were soaked in faeces.

Their backs were scalded. Their chests were scaled.
Their hair was harrowing, and, their squalid nails…,
They were senselessly being used as a venomous weapons.

There was no sign of a chirping bird or a purring animal,
Only ravaging rodents were out feasting in filth.

There was no pure air left to breathe; it was only poison.
Poison they had created themselves, by ignoring the plight of their planet.

Demented by the illusions of their superficial world,
They had laid their beds in hell...
Now, they were all simply laying in it!

Utterly distressed by the ways of the world they saw,
They instantly felt her pain.
That mother was suffocating in toxins;
That mother was drowning in venom;
That mother, was crying in distress.

With anxiety, frustration, sadness and restlessness kicking in all at once in that ungodly space, the earthlings looked for their spectrum of light in desperation to rescue them from this devilish place. Catching a glimpse of the disappearing light in what looked like a passage to a tunnel, Mantra mumbled, *"That way..."* trying her best not to evoke the demons of an already disturbed domain.

Catching up with their saviour and getting out of the hell hole,
They continued zooming while still in shock.

Crossing wretched colonies of weirdos and imbeciles,
Then, passing grim provinces with pernickety broods,
They counted their blessings in abundance for not being stuck with those forlorn souls, in these forbidding territories. Keeping up with their conductor, they moved in frenzy making sure no one stopped anywhere anymore. Because, getting to the Dome of Healing, was their only priority!
Everything else, was purely a distraction.

Staying on course, they followed their convoy without a blink,
Yet, somehow, the rainbows managed to slip out of sight again.

The space they hovered over now, was empty as a blank beige canvas...
Still, the energy of that land was calming to their souls.
After the many disturbingly different dimensions they had travelled through to get here, this was the most inviting by far!

Venturing in a bit more…
Fluffy white clouds lifted their already floating spirits,
Transporting Dhairya back in time to the tip of the highest peak in the Valley of Hope.
Where,
Cottony clouds once caressed his existence!
And, heavenly breeze always nourished his soul!

Eager to reconnect with his grandma,
Taking this to be a sign,
The brave heart suggested, they seek the rainbow.
Because, he was absolutely certain that they were on the right track.

Searching for their companion and guide who seemed to be playing hide and seek with them, the fascinating four spread out in all directions determined!

They looked over the clouds…
They looked under the clouds…
They looked around its borders…
They took a peek inside each sensational mass of fluff,
But, the double rainbow didn't want to be found.

Unable to trace the Siamese twins, a thought came to Gayatri's mind,
'Just like the magnolious dragonflies Param and Aatma,
The splendorous rainbows could be done playing their part.'
Now, it was for them to navigate through the clouds, holding on to its reins.

Instead of allowing uncertainty ruffle their so far exhilarated spirit,
They simply let the calming breeze,
Blow them in the direction they were meant to take.
At ease with their decision to be gone with the wind,
They, indeed, enjoyed their splendid ride!

Sensing her naive uncle about to bombard them with a million questions,
Mantra rolled her angelic eyes intending to keep the tranquillity intact.

Never able to stay quiet for long, the big wolf found it hard to resist his curiosity.
Yet, respecting the sentiments of the ones he'd grown to love, he bit his tongue.

No sooner did Khatru put his complex mind to rest and went with the flow,
They were all amazed by the surreal scene they saw.
The happy campers were being led straight into a heavenly hallway by a refreshingly
kind breeze, which, after a certain point, suddenly bid them *sayonara!*

Assuming their destination had arrived,
They were all so eager to make a grand entrance!
Zooming through the never ending passage, they anticipated another guide...
But, this distance too, they were meant to cover on their own.

While the majority felt privileged to be chosen for this journey,
Khatru kept his constantly arising doubts a secret.
Being tested at every turn, he held onto their faith...
Because it was only their love, which kept him going.

Reaching a dead end after yet another long commute,
This time, Mantra knew better!
They were obviously standing at the threshold of a realm they needed to enter!
Instead of wasting her energy trying to find an outside fix,
She lifted her hands above her head like a chalice,
Softly praying to the Queen, to fill her cup!

Giggling at her limited mind, she promptly corrected herself.
"Sorry, sorry,
Don't just fill it to the brim.
Please! Please! Please!
Make my cup overflow, with your eternal love!"

Proud of the wonderful soul they had for a daughter, Gayatri and Dhairya followed
her lead lifting their hands up in the air unable to contain their smile. Sending
out pure vibrations into her temple, the monkeys felt their fingertips tingle while
current passed through their spine.

But, the once lone wolf mimicking his gang missed out on the sensations,
Unaware, that his expectations, were overpowering his natural senses!

Touched by their commitment, the creator was tempted to let them in!
Yet, she refrained from doing so.
Focusing on their every breath,
The Queen of the Kingdom closely followed her tribe's pulse,
Deciding to test their dedication some more.

Unlike the bright magical light which disoriented them not so long ago,
An eerie shadow fell upon them examining their courage.
Staring into darkness with their eyes twinkling like stars,
They embraced its serenity, hoping to catch a glimpse into her world!
Not realising that instant, that their eyelids, were glued shut.

In the calming dark space where time stood still…
A microscopic, fiery dot appeared in the extreme right corner of their shut eyes,
Waiting patiently to be acknowledged by the blinded broods.
When they simultaneously opened their eyes fixating on the mystery,
The heavenly spot took its cue, to slowly move!

Before they could lose focus bundled in joy,
Their inner voice quickly suggested they follow its heartbeat.
Receiving the speck of spark still in sight with absolute adoration,
Without any apprehension; that is exactly what they did!

Delighted by their devotion,
The Divine gave them each a unique taste of what is to come,
By slowly expanding the miniscule macule into a big ball of soothing flames.
Feeling the warmth of their hearts, the Goddess melted furthermore!
Shifting the scene, from fire to water and then to sand,
The Almighty wondered, 'If they'd manage, to just be?'

Catching a glimpse into the cosmos they were instantly humbled!
Humbled by the incredible sight, unimaginable to mere mortal minds.

Gracefully absorbing the nurturing stillness of her bosom,
They hungered for more...
For they couldn't get enough of that mothering magic!

But, to get to where they needed to be...
Their goal had to be solidified.
Their vision unified!
All eyes had to meet as one, in order to see a trailer of the Universal Vision!
A vision, which would freak those who didn't keep faith, because,
'Trickery comes naturally, to anxious minds, possessed by demons.'

The one who bore infinite eyes,
Knew that these unusual spirits were no ordinary beings!
They were passionately persistent to reach their destination;
Because, to them, love meant everything!

Wooing their Goddess by not flinching a lash,
They simply focused, on their Divine Connection!

Aligning with her children,
Becoming one in sight!
The Goddess bridged all gaps, and connected all dots,
Anchoring the unconventional family in ways beyond reason.

Already in love, his spirit was in bliss!
And, the more magic he witnessed,
Dhairya couldn't help himself but acknowledged out loud, that,
"Nothing is ever a coincidence. Everything, is a sign!"

CHAPTER 21

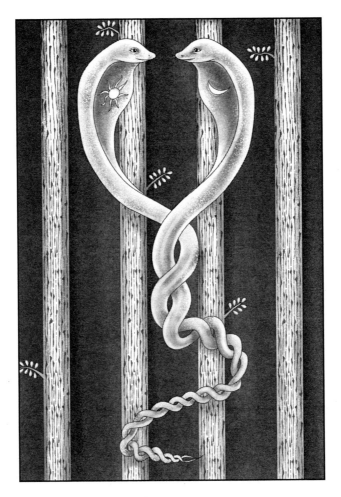

Uncovering the priceless secret, waiting to be tapped upon…
The calm space they occupied spun around them in great haste,
Invoking the Gods of thunder and lightning to come cause mayhem.
But, the ones who were determined not to be fooled, stood still,
Allowing the flurry of atoms to settle in its wake.

Happy with their commitment, the Goddess running the show,
Bestowed blessings upon them furthermore,
Making a wondrous wall of gold appear, turning darkness into light!

Doused in cosmic shimmer, while in awe of the wonders they saw,
The foursome glided towards the glorious gates of glitter as soon as it appeared,
Knocking one by one.

Jubilant to feel a pulse upon contact,
Each one of their spirits was consumed with glee!
The beguiling bailey and the glittering gates were alive,
Breathing the same air anomalously!

Watching their veins swerve and slither taking shapes never seen by mortal eyes,
They eagerly waited for an answer...
But, there was no response.

Understanding the relevance of timing,
Gayatri, Mantra and Dhairya admired the creator's imagination,
Feeling blessed to be standing in its presence!
Pleasing the Goddess with their patience some more,
The sorcerer surprised these sharp souls,
By inviting an eclectic bell to drop from the Universe...
As if opening another channel, to enter the sacred Dome.

Feeling the vibrations of the descending piece of art in their souls...
The monkeys were elated!
However, their newest family member displayed haste,
Proving he hadn't fully tamed his inner beast.
A beast who constantly kept Khatru on his toes,
Not allowing his mind to ever be at ease.

Consumed with emotions of various magnitude,
His restlessness got the better of him, when,
Instead of retrieving the hidden message meant for them all,
Hasting to speed up the process, Khatru took the liberty of ringing the humongous,
majestic, mitre like holy bell.

No sooner did he force contact with the deep purple crystals hanging for its tongue,
Khatru was sent flying across the smouldering sky disappearing out of sight.

It wasn't his time to ring that glorious bell just yet.
It wasn't for him to rush.
Even though he had made it past the inconceivable,
He wasn't nearly ready.
His channels were only just opening;
Therefore, keeping his impulses in check,
Was clearly an additional obstacle he had brought upon himself.

Patience was a virtue!
Unconditional dedication and devotion was the secret!
There was never any room for doubt.
No reason, to question Her pace.

Dropping to the holy grounds after a whirlwind of realizations,
His spirit felt the impact of the great thud.
Rushing by his side to make sure he was alright, his tribe felt his pain.
Seeing stars orbiting his thick head, he wondered, '*What just happened?*'
"*Are we already inside?*" annoyed he questioned.

Furious by his actions…
The once vivacious glittering gates,
Integrated themselves within the wondrous wall of gold creating a rift in its frame,
Bringing to life the protectors of her kingdom, who disguised themselves extremely well.

"Nobody enters her space unless they are invited!"
Grunted a bronze pillar stepping out of the golden facade.

"Nobody enters Her space, unless they are prepared!"
Softly spoke a second pillar taking her spot next to her soul.

"Unless She is your only priority, She is out of your reach!"
Raising his tone, a third pillar emerged fabricating a shift on the screen.

"She must be your only desire!
Not an object to your mortal fascination."
Sternly stating the obvious, a fourth pillar united with her triplets standing oh so tall!

"If you intend to cross this threshold,
It is all or nothing!
There is no meeting halfway."
Speaking in unison, the four fabulous columns showcased their true selves, elevating the mortal spirits already levitated souls, so, they could look them in the eye.

Little Mantra who had lost her heart the very instant, their eyes first locked back in the alluring valley, now blushed as his extraordinary brown eyes penetrated her exultant soul.

Thawed, by the love exuding from the sight that stared her down,
Gayatri was thrilled, to finally make his ethereal connection!

Captivated by the purity of her almond eyes,
Dhairya's gratitude flowed through his own!
Overjoyed for the opportunity to redeem himself from a test he failed earlier on,
The determined langur was adamant not to lose focus this time.

Instead of focusing on the eye aligned with him,
He who had backtracked in order to vindicate himself in the Valley of Doom,
Was the only one startled to see two sets of gigantic tiger eyes staring him down.

Slipping away from her spell just for a second,
Mantra pacified the wolf asking him not to worry.
Introducing him to a blast from their near past, she rapturously said,
"Don't sweat, Uncle! Don't be silly!
These are no monsters intending to gobble us down for dinner.
Look closely! They each have a life of their own!
These are the same trunks of magnificence,
Whose branches carry droplets for leaves!

**I described them to you on our way here!
Don't you remember?!?"**

Her words had reached Khatru's ears then,
But, had failed to register in his preoccupied brain.
Nothing about their experiences was normal ever since they had stepped over the hill that morning. *So what was he questioning now?* Mocking his stupid self, he tried to maintain his composure.
Exhilarated to be graced by beauty so drop dead gorgeous...
His fears and doubts, eventually, vanished without a trace!

Excited to be in the presence of Divinity, Khatru, once again, let his impatience make him fail his test. Anxious to move on to another dimension, he left his mesmerised tribe behind. Recklessly heading towards the slender columns of mystic.

Stopping him from crossing forbidden boundaries before Dhairya could react,
The double spectrum of splendour emerged once again from the mirage,
Seemingly tired of the wolf's antics this time.

"Stop right there. Don't you move!" Converting Khatru's restless spirit into a statue with sight, a spectre's tough voice echoed into the cosmos from inside the delicate rainbow, which was now losing its vibrancy.

"We still have our jobs to do. So, don't you rush naive one!" Holding her composure, the spectre inside the second fading spectrum, addressed him with poise while generating some scales.

Taking a bow before the four significant pillars of the sacred kingdom with grace, the twin ribbons of radiance got ready to perform an exotic ritual, unseen by mortals before.

Honouring the diaphanous quadruplets of devotion,
They bent themselves like two separate horseshoes,
Then, slowly, came together as one.
Grooving to the music created by the emerging mystical leaves,
The rainbows parted ways only to meet again, spiralling around their mate.

Bound together as one, a little prayer was said;
Then, casting a spell on the other...
Certain colours were exchanged, and a new canvas was spread.
Synthesizing themselves into the shades of their choice,
They stood still beside the other, like Khatru in his mould!

Each absorbing colours chosen for them,
One soaked in the darker shades, and the other, flaunted the lighter tones.
Eventually, showcasing themselves as individual entities,
They took on distinct personalities of their own!

Manifesting into two different globes,
One reddish brown, the other greenish blue,
They bounced graciously towards the Trees of Devotion,
Bursting their own bubbles upon impact!

Consuming the magnificent trunks of mystery in individual flavours,
Then, wrapping themselves around the entities they serenaded,
The artists, reduced the four pillars of the enchanted kingdom,
Into capacious columns of two!
Emitting dry smoke upon constant friction,
The once amazingly colourful spectrums of rainbow,
Transformed into two scaled chimneys rising endlessly towards the sky...

In anticipation of what was to come next,
They watched closely, every act, not wanting to miss a sign.
Shocked to see two colossal cobras...
Break through the barriers of smokestack, crumbling it to the floor,
Their mortal spirits were blown out of their limited minds!

The four trunks were visible again, and their individual eyes were lustrous;
Yet, the king and queen of snakes,
Commanded the spirits' undivided attention!
Coiling themselves before the grooving pillars of passion,
They slowly lifted their spectacularly defining hoods,
Higher than the animals had ever known them to rise!

Gently merging as one from the tip of their tails to the peak of their hips,
The scaly duo sprung tall reaching enigmatic heights!
Their upper halves slithered like two separate serpents;
Yet, they gracefully danced together as one!

The entire performance was enthralling!
But, if they weren't ready to witness this magic…
The mortal beings would have, most certainly, received a stroke!

Nothing simply existed for the sake of existing in that realm.
Every life had its significant purpose, and only unexpected was to be expected!

With music originating from the bedazzling bell of crystals,
Endearing tunes enticed the little macaque to take centre stage.
But, the bright soul tapped her feet where she stood not willing to swallow the bait.

Rendering their spectators speechless throughout their act of devotion,
The entangled Cobras released powerful energies through their glaring eyes…
Detaching from their entwined flesh, instantly igniting sparks,
The king cobra headed to the right, and his queen sprung to the left.

Yearning for more affection, the volant beings wrapped themselves around the other in desperation, anxious not to let go. Yet, they repelled circling the grand space at the speed of light infinite times, understanding the importance of the mission in their hand. Shedding their skin due to the force generated by their expeditious movements, they charged towards the four tantalizing trunks of eternal devotion, leaving the four mortals utterly stumped.

Parking themselves precisely in between the enthralling pillars of wonder,
Their scaly tones faded behind the rekindling colours of the ensuing rainbow…
Once again, dividing the four Trees of Devotion into two equal halves!

"What did you see then and what do you see now?"
A spectre tested their knowledge speaking from inside its tiny bright ball.

Raising her hand eager to answer, Mantra innocently blurted,
"At first, they looked like four separate ones…"
Using the enchanted air for a drawing board, she drew '1111'.

"But, now that you have taken the centre spots!"
Gayatri assisted Mantra in completing the image, 11:11.

"They become, eleven, eleven!" Glad to be his normal self again, or whatever
normal was in that realm, Khatru was most certain that he was right.

"Which ultimately means, One in All and All in One!"
Dhairya explained, in depth, so they wouldn't be misconstrued.

"That is absolutely what it was, and this is exactly what it has become!"
The spectres sparkled, thrilled to see the clarity their disciples sought.

"Persevering goodness as one individual entity…
Can often, prove to be a challenge!
Therefore, joining forces with the Source is of utmost importance,
Before you take on any mission.
For then, and only then,
Will you expand your horizon…
Along with the possibility of success,
In all your endeavours!"
In his indirectness, the double-sided spectre,
Directly handed Dhairya the keys to the kingdom!

In a short span of time,
In a space unknown to mankind,
Four mortal animal spirits witnessed two ribbons of rainbow,
Transform into colossal cobras!
Cobras that affectionately celebrated four dainty trees!
Trees, which now stood as two perfect 11's!

Receiving inconceivable knowledge on their quest to the Dome of Healing,
Dhairya, who was eager to make things right,

Now, understood the depth of their teachings.
Gathering his tribe who had certainly gotten wiser,
They glided towards the beguiling crystal bell one more time,
Intending to open the significant doors resembling the once mysterious, 11:11.

Forming a circle under its astounding rim...
Without a prompt, their hands attached,
Evoking their desire to be one with the Source!
Collectively channelling their vibrations towards that goal...
They reached out to its twinkling tongue,
Gently striking the clapper to its edge!

Creating friction upon impact, sparks flew haywire;
Still, her devotees did not flinch.
Soaking in the warmth of the crystals...
Their existence lit up from within, displaying an aura, oh so divine!
Exuding nothing but purity inside and out,
The magnetic amethyst crystals overhead,
Sprightly siphoned their extraordinary light!

Although instantly dizzy...
Getting their energies guzzled so quick, they did not waiver.
Unlike before, their mission to them had now become clearer.
It wasn't the obvious doors they'd originally tried to knock on,
Which would lead them to where they needed to be…
The way they were being led,
Was the only doorway to the Dome of Healing!
A doorway, which an ordinary soul could never see.

Stepping into their own radiance, synchronized still,
They gratefully let the powers of the Universe suck them in!
Becoming one with the mysteries of the cosmos,
They rose higher and higher,
Into the endless passage of the crystal bell…
Enjoying that moment to the fullest!
Because, Divinity Herself, was awaiting them!

The living, breathing golden pillars and the mystical trees of Devotion,
Were simply a mirage to many;
But, even as an enigma, they were indeed a reality in the sacred realm.

The bedazzling rainbow and the dainty cobras,
Were signs telling them to let go.

Let go of all the assumptions, all the presumptions and all the perceptions.
Because, by allowing oneself to fall into their own trap,
'How would anyone, attain clarity, anymore?!?'

CHAPTER 22

Once their vibrations matched their intentions,
The mortal spirits embarked upon yet another adventure!

Sucked into the marvels of the glorious bell,
Feeling weightless as a feather…
Holding onto the others tail, they remained connected,

When the wide passage got scanter.
Nothing was normal about the past few days in terms of mortal standards,
Yet, this courageous lot had discovered more than they could begin to imagine.

Thrilled to be a part of this extraordinary expedition,
Khatru's once wicked existence, was most certainly humbled!
And, Mantra's innocent soul couldn't stop counting her blessings!
Because, she knew she was the luckiest macaque alive,
To be gifted with such amazing parents.
As for Dhairya and Gayatri, their heart was stuck in their daughter.
Still, they encouraged the young child to explore the wonders of all worlds,
Hoping she'd be the one to bridge all gaps in the future!

The journey of mortal life brought about major complications;
But, in their sincere quest to the inexplicable Dome of Healing,
They overcame each obstacle with grace, bringing them even closer!

Detached from their physical flesh for now,
Gayatri, Mantra, Dhairya and Khatru were grateful to get as far as they did!
For, this wasn't a simple safari trekking through the paranormal world,
Where awakened mortals wished they would eventually go.
They were now a part of an elite tribe!
A tribe, eagerly awaiting them to slide through the dazzling door.

Enjoying the upward ride into glory,
Although their eyes failed to capture every astonishing detail at that speed,
Their souls absorbed every ray of brilliance along the way!
Reaching a crossroad amongst neatly placed crystals,
While the elders contemplated as to which direction to take,
Mantra, who was once afraid of looking down from great heights,
Didn't fumble when she excitedly pointed at the colourful trampoline under.

Soon transforming into a picturesque pond of colours,
The illusionist tempted the little soul to take a leap...
But, she controlled herself realizing that it was merely a mirage.
A mirage created by the double sided spectre to test, *how focused she was!?!.*

Turning her attention to her parents, she understood their intention.
Together, closing their eyes while opening their hearing,
They listened carefully, sorting through the various sounds of distraction.
With Godly beats catching their attention, they were now clear of their direction.
Without faltering, they followed the invigorating music, shooting up furthermore!

Crouching in a tight space at the peak of the magnificent bell,
Their smoky white spirits were suddenly soaked in the fountain of colours,
When the illusionary pond rose with all its force.
Grooming them for the most important meeting of their mortal lives,
The Siamese twins gave them each an incredible makeover,
Making them sparkle; making them shine; the stylists smiled,
Because, their guinea pigs were now ready; to meet the divine!

"Look at these souls so wonderfully beaming in brilliance!" One spectre said to the other transforming into a majestic mirror, allowing the curious spirits to catch their radiant reflections.

"Our work here, is almost done!" The spectress took pride in her creativity admiring the fabulous four, who were awestruck by their colourful selves.
"Yes indeed!" The spectre expressed his satisfaction upon closer inspection.

Preparing them for what was to come next,
His partner-in-crime announced with glee!
"Huddle together and buckle up now!
We are about to take off on a ride of a lifetime!
A rapturous ride, you won't soon forget!!!"

Excited to make the most awaited acquaintance, they did as they were told!
Perching on top of the fascinating fountains of mystic,
The enthralled passengers watched its radiance flare beneath them,
Gradually rocketing them through the tight space with great ease.
So far, it was the four commuters following their guide. Now, the roles were reversed since the rainbows were throttling its passengers away from all darkness, straight towards the light!

Unlike what they each imagined,

There were no doors to knock, or mysteries to solve...
As soon as they took off, they immediately landed.
Landed in a stellar space twinkling like stars!

Within the blink of an eye their escorts were gone, leaving them to fend for themselves in a place overcrowded with tormented souls.
Instantly noticing their absence, Mantra sulked;
Because, she had fallen in love with their quirks!
Not knowing what to do next, Khatru suggested they ask for directions...
Hearing those words leave his mouth, Mantra's lost smile returned!
And, Gayatri, she couldn't help herself but burst out laughing!

"Look around you Khatru! Besides us lost souls here, do you see anyone else standing still?!?" Dhairya tried hard not to giggle!

Wanting to have a few laughs of his own, Khatru wondered what was so funny...
Taking another look around him, he cracked up too spotting a flying bunny.

For the first time, since they left their bones back at the Redemption Bridge, they found themselves grounded, unable to fly. They were the only ones on their feet in that heavenly expanse. Because, to cruise through the Dome of Healing one most definitely had to be free, of mortal existence.

Shaking his thick head at the big blunder, Khatru loudly suggested they take a walk!
Upon which, a passing soul whispered that he tone down his volume...
Since a show, the departed souls were impatiently waiting for,
Was about to begin!

CHAPTER 23

W̶hile all the temporary resident souls in that kingdom,
    Came together in excitement forgetting all their heartache and pain!
The mortal spirits took their spots by an ensnaring pillar of wonder,
Eagerly waiting for the entertainment to begin!

With everyone overhead almost fighting for space to accommodate themselves,
little Mantra couldn't help but wonder, *'How come in a magical land as this, there
wasn't enough room for everyone to stay comfortably?'*

Those who had been there long enough to work their own magic,
Quickly gathered a level below the chaos, inviting their prestigious choir to
assemble into position while ordering the rest of the congregation to settle down.
Within no time, there was pin drop silence in the dome;
As a stunning seraphim elegantly made her presence known!
Singing melodious notes as the choir set the mood,
The Goddess captivated her audience with her angelic grooves!

With all eyes from above looking down at the dancing queen,
The mortal spirits were very self-conscious in the beginning,
Since they were the only odd ones standing on the floor.
But, soon, noticing all eyes fixated on the diva,
Their embarrassed souls found instant relief!

Was this, what all departed souls were impatiently waiting for?
They each wondered admiring every little move in disbelief.
Little did they know, that;
This was just an appetizer being presented before the actual dinner!

Struggling to contain their excitement they wisely fought their impulses. Folding
their hands behind their back, they somehow managed to control themselves
from applauding out of turn. The enchanting being resembling one of their own
was extremely beautiful! The monkey family had thought. But, when the entire
gathering bowed before an intriguing entity, who stooped in from greater heights
with its angelic wings spread wide replacing the dancing seraphim...
Dhairya, in his mind, tried hard to connect the dots.

Unable to lay his finger on who she might be,
He found himself wondering, '*if She was actually He.*'

This enthralling entity that stood taller than the graceful giraffe...
Flaunted distinctive looks from every angle,
Making it impossible to pinpoint as to what exactly it was.

When facing the front, the division was clear;
Its left half resembled a dainty dove, and the right side, a polished pigeon.

Confusion arose when it turned, because the sides seemed switched!
When one appeared, the other was hidden...
Because the backside of the pigeon was as white as the dove!
And, the dove's back was grey like the spotted pigeon!

The little chitter chatter they heard when the Goddess was performing,
Had now turned into deafening silence;
For this mythical creature commanded their undivided attention!
Wrapping itself in its own wing,
It painted a picture of two passionate birds locked in an embrace.

Seeing everyone's jaws dropped and the choir fumble,
The Divine Entity secretly smiled!
For this was the first time in the history of its existence,
It had showcased itself on that platform in front of the entire congregation.

This wasn't any ordinary appearance;
The timing was set long before Dhairya and his tribe set off on their mission.
As excited as they were to meet the Goddess they visualized...
The Ethereal Being was excited to meet them too!
Since their desire to connect, was mutual!!!

'Who was this Mysterious Entity?!?'
The mortals wondered, while watching the Enchanted perform a heavenly dance!

Joining its dual facet wings,
Then, stretching them gently above the crown of its head!
Absorbing every subtle vibration exuded in that room,
The magician's beatific radiance bedazzled the dead!
It's already endearing aura enhanced,
When rings of purple, indigo, blue, green, yellow, orange and red,
Systematically circled around its already enigmatic anatomy!

Slowly moving its conjoined wings from top to bottom...
Making past its divided forehead, eyes, beak and neck,
The Celestial Body stopped to take a deep breath!

Moving along, it paused at the exact spot where their hearts met!
Sliding further down to its core, it halted again,
Sucking in the magnetic energies some more!

Folding the fascinating feathers in an intricate form,
The Elysian Beauty held that pose…
Siphoning the light from the heavenly source,
Into the gap showcased by the magical mudra,
The exquisite soul took a twirl…
Solemnly drawing everyone's attention to its root chakra!
For, that was where it all began!

Keeping them grounded, while maintaining their balance was the purpose…
Once the first step was taken right,
The ascend towards the unparalleled world was made easy!
Forever binding them in eternal love!

There was so much for lost souls and mortal spirits to register in such little time…
That, just like the spiralling colours casting an incredible spell upon them,
Their menial existence was sent spinning.
Everyone present watched closely the exotic dance in awe of the Divine,
Ignorant to the fact that they had stumbled upon a cosmic jackpot!

The sacred soul's delicate feathers,
Had split in ways unimagined before, forming spectacular shapes.
Shapes, which had significant meanings!

Meanings, which were simple yet complex;
Complex since it was a test, 'for them to uncover the signs.'
Signs which were meant for self-healing!

Self-healing which was much needed in those times of distress,
Because her space was being stormed by millions of souls suffering.
Suffering which they had brought upon themselves,
By taking the invaluable gift of life, for granted.

Around every nook, in very corner, the living beings were faltering…
Exploiting each other, then choosing to live in denial,
Their physical existence was being ruined.
Because, in their arrogance they were causing not only others pain,
But, especially, their precious soul harm!

CHAPTER 24

Although it was his grandmother's wellbeing that had brought him here, Dhairya felt immense peace in that space when down his cheek, trickled a tear!

Gayatri smiled ear to ear realizing their destination was near!

Having wished to have her cup overflow with eternal love, Mantra melted with every step made special by the Supreme!

And, Khatru, he was simply amazed;
Amazed to witness wonders in the company of his wonderful family,
Who helped soothe his pain and keep his vision clear!

"Welcome, my children! Welcome!
I've been awaiting your arrival for eternity!"
The mysterious Sorcerous flew high up into the air, getting her V.I.P. visitors to notice, the distinguished dome they were seeking,
In a totally different light!

Fixated on the spectrum of colours spreading evenly, through every little feather of the Divine Soul, they were joyous to hear themselves being addressed by Divinity itself. Bowing before the God and Goddess living harmoniously in one body as one soul,
Their existence was humbled.

They had finally reached where they wanted to reach!
Now, unknowingly, they were receiving the tools they needed to receive!

"Dhairya, my boy; What took you so long?
Is it only Dadima who led you to me?
Or, were you secretly intending to visit me someday?!?"
Although the deific deity knew all the answers, some digging was done.

"My king! My Queen!
Forgive me, Oh Empyrean Soul!
I do not know how to call your name..."
The astute langur raised his joined palms above his head, just like the enigma had.

"It is not my name which is important,
It is the purity in your heart I seek; that matters!"

Entwining its wings around itself along with its dual coloured feet,
The beguiling bird displayed the wonders of the dynamic dome,
As it came spiralling down in style...
Then, perching on a flaming throne, it comfortably took a seat!

"**You are no ordinary souls! We hope you know that by now.**"
Its dovey wings caressed its pigeony shoulders.

"**You've crossed thresholds,**
Which no mortal has ever come close to crossing!
It is only when they transcend into another phase...
Do fortunate souls get to see us, for who we really are.

Those unfortunate,
Have to slog their behinds again and again and again in numerous lifetimes,
Until they have learnt all the lessons meant for them to learn.
Or else, their restless souls continue to wander into infinity,
In search of something, that has always been in their plain sight."
Speaking in code, the double sided spectre smiled, signalling the souls in their
kingdom to disperse with grace.

"**Tell me, little Mantra. Who do you think I am?**" Hearing her heartbeat, the
Sorcerous put the little macaque under the spotlight. Presenting her the mike.

In spite of the answer on the tip of her tongue,
Not wanting to miss this opportunity to shine, Mantra dug into her soul deeper,
Making sure she was absolutely certain of what was to leave her mouth...

"**You are not simply the gatekeeper of this realm,**
The gardener of this kingdom,
An educator to the Illiterates,
Or, merely a healer of broken souls.
You are so, so, so much more than that!"
Recollecting Param's and Aatma's words, the prudent macaque went on,

"**You are the guardian to everyone!**
You are the protector of everybody!
You are the teacher we all seek!
You are the surgeon needed to put us out of our misery!"
Tears of gratitude left her twinkling eyes as she continued counting her blessings.

"You are the calming darkness!
You are the soothing light!
You are my day and you are my night!
You are the sun and the moon;
The one who never fails to light up my path!

You are the breeze that breaks my fall!
You are the Divine nurturer!
Both mother and father in one!
You are whoever you want to be...
When you want to be...
You are me and I am you!
TOGETHER, WE ARE ONE!"

Beautifully, the bright soul summed up her thoughts glowing like never before!

"Just like Dhairu clarified earlier,
You are all in one and one in all!
One in all and all in one!"

Khatru couldn't help himself but jump with joy grateful for the lessons he'd learnt!

"Someone has been paying attention, I see!"

The God and Goddess were impressed by the wolf's unexpected progress.

Turning their attention to Gayatri,
Whose radiant smile lit up the already dazzling dome, the God asked,
"So, how would you explain what you see in front of you, Gayatri?"

Bowing before the Divine paying her respect, she expressed her feelings,
"Me attempting to explain your Divinity will take many lifetimes, Your
Holiness!
For, my mortal mind fails to fathom your glory!
Yet,
I feel utterly privileged, to be standing in your presence!
Although I never envisioned this scenario in my wildest of dreams,
Humbled by your love, I realize that I was born for this meeting!"

Awestruck, she continued her honest sharing.

"I love my darling, Dhairya!
I adore my beautiful daughter Mantra!
And, I cherish my brother Khatru!
But the way I feel when you look at me, I cannot explain!?!
My mere mortal existence fails to find words to do you justice...
Because, our vocabulary is limited and our language restricted.

Yet, since your wish is my command, I will try to express myself;
But if I fail which I most certainly might,
Your Holiness, please don't hold me in contempt..."
Kneeling before them, she humbly asked for their forgiveness...
Melting the hearts of the ones she unknowingly worshipped.

"Your existence is pure bliss!
Your appearance is mesmerizing!
Your charisma is captivating!
But, above all,
You are in touch, with your soul!"
Seeing the divine feathers scale up and shine on that note,
Instantly reminded of the double rainbows and dainty cobras, she added,

"Literally and figuratively, I must add,
You are the most bewitching creation living as one!

My God and Goddess,
You are bound together for eternity!
Because, you dared to embrace the *Ultimate Union*!"
Proud of the chosen one's profound words,
The still mysterious entities hooked together, decided to reveal themselves!

Displaying the power of a thought...
They played with the new members of their tribe,
By turning the lustrous dome dark as night,
And, created more suspense, by emitting odourless smoke!

On cue, all the souls present in that realm huddled together again with poise,
hearing the drumroll which no soul in any dimension was fortunate to hear before.
Under all the haze was a lot of magic!
And, the magicians were eager to start the show!

Feeling all their hearts beat as one,
The supreme beings detached, presenting their individual selves.
Blowing the spectators minds!

Quickly giving the audience a rundown of all their forms,
They captivated their attention, forcing them to watch without blinking an eye.

At first, the mortal spirits saw the obvious; their minds pointed out to,
A *dove* and a *pigeon* stood next to each other with wings entwined!
Smoothly transitioning into the *Trees of Devotion,*
The *Celestial Bodies* grooved to the music of its leaves!
Then, they transformed into the dainty *cobras* entangled from hip to tail!
Emerging as the *double rainbows* imbibing in the others glory,
They circled the entire dome in haste, and headed back to the fiery throne!
Whose flames, were now extinguished.

Rendering their already astonished spectators speechless; furthermore,
The Almighty souls infused as one;
This time showcasing themselves to be *Gayatri* and *Dhairya*!

Seeing their mortal bodies in front of their eyes, at first, the langurs were baffled;
Then, witnessing themselves attach into two perfect halves, they were absolutely
rattled. *"What are we doing on that pedestal?"* as one mind they wondered.

"Look, uncle wolf... That's Ma and Pa on the throne!"
Forgetting, that their spirits were still rubbing shoulders with her...
Mantra lit up seeing her parents filling in the shoes of the Gods!

"I am you and you are me!
Together, we are, whatever we want to be!"
The Goddess smiled giving a slight twist to Mantra's wise words.

"All you have to do is listen; Listen to your heart!
Because, we beat as one!
Listen to your inner voice!
Because, that is how we connect!"
The Almighty enlightened his tribe,
While the opulent dome echoed with their wisdom.
Then, without warning, he vanished behind the clouds along with his soul!

Unaware, they were being prepared all along to get to this stage…
The teachings of the Divine were now imprinted upon their mortal souls with a chalk!
A chalk, which could never be erased!

CHAPTER 25

While the rest of the souls present wondered, '*who these mortals spirits were?*' Dhairya scanned his surroundings to see if his eyes could spot the one he sought.

His head drooped in disappointment not finding her there;
However, his grounded spirit lifted when she whispered in his ear,
"You were here on a mission;
But, I hope you realise that your mission goes beyond my well-being!"

Dadima's departed soul took Dhairya by surprise.
"You were on a quest to reach me! And, here you are, my boy!
Making me so very proud!
I always knew you were the chosen one!
Born at the exact second, when magic was at its prime!"

Before Dadima could finish her piece,
A blast from his near past interrupted her giving Dhairya the chills...

"Your mission was to find this Dome of Healing you think?
I hope, after all that you've seen, you understand that your presence here,
Emphasises the grave dangers lurking around the corner.
Dangers, which you, and you alone, can rescue us from." The anxiety and desperation in Raksha's deep voice shocked Gayatri. Who, not so long ago, had held her dear friend in her arms at the *Temple of Spirits* and left her side with a very heavy heart, hoping to reunite soon. *But never under circumstances like these.*

Recognizing the esteemed matriarch of the langur clan,
Who never hesitated to put the wicked wolf in his place,
Khatru immediately knelt before Dadima,
Seeking forgiveness for his trespasses of the past.

Already shocked to see him there, she smiled.

Because, in Dhairya's company, even the wicked wolf looked like a saint!

Stroking him affectionately, the one who desperately sought her grandson's forgiveness, gestured him to dive into her smoky arms.

While Dhairya rushed towards his grandmother,

Gayatri drifted towards her best mate; and Mantra,

Her innocent eyes searched for Suraksha.

But, fortunately unfortunately, she was nowhere in sight.

The baby bat had survived the disaster at the holy temple, thanks to her mother who sacrificed her life just like their ancestors, to treasure its secrets.

"What happened after we left, Raksha???"

Gayatri's broken spirit cried, dreading the worst.

"The despicable humans!" The bat tried in vain to contain her fury.

"I had visions, or nightmares, must I say,

Of villainous beings encroaching the sacred grounds of our temple,

To quench their thirst for eternal life.

They want to be invincible. They want to live forever,

Those fools!" Acknowledging her burning emotions, Raksha took a few deep breaths in order to regain her balance.

"I was afraid that day was gonna come. But, so soon, I never dreamt in my wildest of dreams..." Reliving the atrocity, Raksha flew higher and higher. Losing herself in the dome meant to relieve her of her pain.

"A few days before the nightmares began,

A vagrant stumbled upon our Temple of Spirits...

I pitied him since he could barely carry the weight of his scrawny self.

He looked famished and parched.

He seemed like he had hit a rough patch in his existence;

And, the deteriorating jungles were in no position to meet his needs.

Normally I never encouraged unwelcome visitors, you know that right?"

Instantly reminded of their prank on Dhairya, Gayatri nodded.

"But, this time, I decided to make an exception. And, that choice led to my demise." The bat, who always took pride in her foresight, was embarrassed to admit she was fooled,
"I eased his pain by bestowing fruity blessings upon him.
I even led him to the Well of Divinity where he drew himself some water...

After gaining some strength,
He loitered around the temple inspecting the ancient statues.
I should have understood then. I should have;
However, I was too focused on the good that I was doing to notice his evil mind.

He was no homeless or even a drifter,
He was a cruel gypsy on a sadist mission.
His eavesdropping ears had stumbled upon a folklore beyond our boundaries, which bragged about the Well of Divinity to be well hidden within the Temple grounds of an enchanted forest. Our forest!" She cried acknowledging her stupidity.

"Chasing his desire to acquire wealth and soak in power,
He who regularly put himself in harm's way,
Wandered into unchartered territory on a witch hunt.
My heart went out to him seeing his condition...
Which now I understand he rightly deserved.
Because, he carried nothing but darkness behind his charismatic façade."
She was infuriated.

"Ungrateful as these humans are known to have become,
He who made a deal with the devil long ago,
Came back a few days after you headed towards the Valley of Hope.
I was feeding the batlings of a sister who never returned from her expedition;
Her children had become my priority keeping me from guarding my post.

Little distractions were signs,
Things were not aligned the way they should be.
But, giving into mortal obligations, I silenced the voice,

I'd never dismissed before..." She admitted her shortcomings, with a heavy heart.

"Disrespecting the sanctity of our glorious grounds,
The doppelganger returned with dozens of men at his disposal, provided by an obese man, whose stallion was on the verge of collapsing, due to his riders' outrageous weight.
Recklessly hacking through dense bushes with monstrous machetes, they destroyed the enchanting creepers which had been spreading joy in our lives, and enhancing the glory of our Temple at night..." Raksha wept, feeling their pain.

"Guided by the delusions of two demented men, the hired help followed the impersonator to our doorstep carrying massive barrels to devour the holy water. But, our resident spirits stopped the unruly humans from crossing that threshold by spooking the jeepers out of the fearful, forcing them helter skelter.

By the time I flew to my post, they had lost all their footmen.
The overbearing stallion had dropped his load,
Aimlessly taking off into the forest jolted by the ruckus.
There was no way the greedy men were getting what they wanted that day;
So, they backtracked their stumbling steps petrified."
Gayatri was relieved to hear that. Yet, Raksha grieved...

"Since that incident, I stood there, day and night, guarding my post.
When the kids felt me getting distant, Suku insisted that I train her and her cousins for the uncertainties which lay ahead. My child is already making me proud! The way she is handling herself, by taking charge of my mission at this young age!"
Raksha concealed her worry, with an awkward smile.

"A month ago, I heard unusual monsters charge into our forest.
Our enchanted forest which had begun to lose its magic.
This time, the cowards attacked from a distance,
Knowing well that the spirits didn't cross certain boundaries.

Destroying the outer structure of our sacred space by bombarding it with cannons,
They shook the foundation of the Temple forcing it to crumble.

Everything happened so fast;
There was no time to salvage anything but the Well of Divinity.
Some spirits retreated into the mythical statutes bringing them to life;
Repositioning them around the well, they intended to mislead the mortals.
Our angels did the best they could to protect the elixir!

It seemed like everything was under control. Yet, it wasn't.
My brilliant little soul was prepared for this unfortunate moment.
She understood more than I gave her credit for!
Seconds before the divine structure disintegrated itself around the Well of Divinity masking it for good, Suku escorted her friends underground into our secret cave. Through the flurry of settling rubble, as I turned around to take one last look at the monsters, a huge cannonball, struck the spot where we last spent our night, blowing me into pieces."

Visualizing the entire scene, Gayatri was stumped.

"Feeling responsible for the havoc I caused…
Here I am, seeking redemption for my mistakes.
My mistake of not being able to look through the deceit,
Of the cunning mankind.
Mankind whose kindness has gone down the drain;
While man has turned himself into a monster.

With no love or empathy left in their hearts,
They are ever ready to destroy lives;
Ever willing to claim kingdoms not theirs to claim.

Acting worse than savage beasts,
They fail to preserve the real treasures.
All because greed has corrupted their menial minds.

Although I am fortunate to receive a chance at redemption,
While healing my soul from the pain, I inflict upon myself every moment...
I fear, that they are getting closer to destroying dimensions invisible to their eyes.
I see them shamelessly encroaching into our territory day in and day out.
It won't be too long before their evil eyes fall upon this magical place,
Disrupting the balance of this Universe."
Raksha's tattered spirit spill her guts eyeballing her saviour to make things right.

Instantly gloomy in a glorious space,
Gayatri turned towards her soul mate for comfort,
Only to find him console his weeping grandmother at a distance.

Dadima and Dhairya were having a heartfelt moment of their own,
And, it was clearly visible that their roles in life had now reversed.
Because, Dhairya was the one,
Trying to shut the floodgates to the dam his beloved grandma let overflow.

CHAPTER 26

"**D**on't be so hard on yourself Dadima,
    I've been hard on myself too...
Do believe me when I say; Holding myself responsible for another's action,
brought me nothing but immense pain." Dhairya comforted the one who
always wiped his tears when he was a child.

"That's very kind of you my boy!
I know you say these words to cause me relief...
But, I'd be fooling myself if I let you convince me that it wasn't my fault."
The adulated soul, spoke her heart.

"I understand the turmoil you face because of the choices you made.
I've been through similar emotions, which broke me down and drove me
insane.
This is no time to dwell on what has transpired,
Because, sadly, it is out of our control.
What we could do moving forward is not to repeat the same mistakes."
Forgetting the pain he suffered at her hands, he showed nothing but compassion!

"I want you to know I was there,
Not at that very moment when the monstrosity occurred...
But, sent back in time to feel your heartbeat.
Your heart beat in my name!

The ones blinded by their delusions couldn't feel your sorrow...
But, I guess, you already know of the fate they met.

Bhram was my idol growing up!
My big brother is who I aspired to be.
Therefore, imagine the shattering of my heart witnessing his duplicity.
Visualise me beat myself up regretting I kept mum.

Had I defended myself the day I was blamed for his wrongdoings,
I might have been able to influence his misguided actions.
He was a fool lost in love, we know...
I wonder, if he knew of her betrayal when he took his last breath?"
Dadima's soul was impressed to see the clarity her daring Dhairya had
attained.

"I was hoping to cross paths with you somehow...
So, I could humbly request you to let go of all the baggage.
Baggage which is weighing down your beautiful soul.
You are the bravest and toughest langur I've ever known to live!
Will you please Dadima, find it in you to forgive yourself?!?"
Bound by the colours of the rainbow still,
His soulful eyes shone bright, penetrating her mourning soul.

Her soul had lingered in the Dome of Healing for as long as it did, because,
His forgiveness is what she sought, feeling responsible for his banishment.
And, here he was, before it was too late,
Holding her close,
Asking her to forgive herself!

Touched by an angel she helped raise, Dadima cried again.
However, this time she was blissful!
Because, just like Raksha, she had understood,
Dhairya was the answer to all their prayers!

He was the chosen one they had been desperately waiting for to arrive.
Now, he was here with his own army - his most beloved tribe!

Letting them say their piece in peace, Mantra patiently waited,
To be introduced to another important Goddess in her Pa's life.

Noticing a little Macaque staring at them from a distance,
Dadima inquired, **"Who exactly is that cheeky monkey?"**

Filling her in on his selfless deeds, he made his grandmother proud!

Delighted by his accomplishments, her drooping spirit lifted, and she happily glided towards his extraordinary family with open arms.

Unlike the union Gayatri, Mantra and Dhairya had each imagined when they set off on this expedition, this unification was beyond their expectation!
In an outlandish space, under uncustomary circumstances,
An unconventional family came together in harmony,
Displaying nothing but unconditional love!

"I've been dreaming of this moment...
Ever since I let a precious gift slip away from my hands." Dadima uttered the truth affectionately sliding her hand over Gayatri's luscious hair.

"And, you. Don't I know you from somewhere?" Teasing the wolf who looked nothing like his original self, the prudent langur gleamed.

"Who must I say this bundle of joy is now?!?"
Striking a conversation with her granddaughter, Dadima's soul was euphoric!

Feeling instantly loved by the tranquil tone of her voice,
Mantra, who always had an answer to everything,
Hid behind her Ma, shy to face her legendary great grandma!

"My, my. Why so shy!?!"
Khatru mocked the little one, who was ever ready for any encounter.

"I'm not shy!"

Mantra asserted herself playfully chasing Khatru, who led her straight to Dadima.
"Or, maybe I am!" camouflaged with Dhairya, she blushed.

"This is the one who you've been bombarding me with questions about!
This is who polished my acrobatic skills!
She is the one you were so eager to meet.
My Dadima!" Dhairya coaxed Mantra, out of her shell.

"Now that you are graced with her presence,
Don't waste a single moment to bond!
We've learnt how unpredictable life can be;
Therefore, my little girl, make the most out of your time!" Seeing her take a few steps towards her great grandma, Dhairya was pleased to make the important introduction of his life!

She wasn't their blood...
Yet, Mantra was so much more than they could ever ask for.
She was a gift from the Gods!
Gods, who knew her potential even before she was born.
To be blessed with a child like her was indeed a privilege!
Therefore, keeping her safe from all harm was their task!
A task, the langurs had excelled in!

Taking responsibility for her actions,
Dadima had found it hard to forgive herself.
But, the compassion Dhairya displayed walking on the path of righteousness,
Had instantly melted her heart!
Shedding all the inhibitions of her past life, Dadima now felt only love!
Love, that made her see everything in a new light.

Just like Raksha, she too had gotten glimpses into the dreadful future,
She knew that darkness was heading their way if no solution was found.

Now that she had finally reconnected with the one she had abandoned on earth,
Dadima knew there was nothing to worry
'Coz she had come to realize,
In the end, everything completes a full circle;
WHAT GOES AROUND, COMES AROUND!

CHAPTER 27

Connecting most of the dots before a brief interaction with Gayatri…
Dhairya gained a better insight into Raksha's agony after a gut wrenching synopsis.

Attempting to piece together a never ending puzzle,
He desperately desired an elusive meeting with the divinely bound duo,
Because, he had caught an alarming glimpse, into the future too.

Nature, who he regarded as his Mother,
Was being insensibly destroyed under the pretence of progress.
Flourishing life, was being banished out of their habitat ruthlessly,
Forcing the fierce to suffer an unfortunately aberrational fate.
Resources were depleting drastically;
Indispensable treasures were being looted;
All, in order to satisfy the insatiable appetite of self-indulgent homo sapiens,
Who chose to remain deluded, in the pursuit of illusionary power.

Dreading the demise of his planet,
Just like the one which shook them to the core,
Dhairya hungered to attain direction before it was too late.

Facing a dilemma as to how to address the enigmatic Gods,
He sought guidance from the souls who had been there a bit longer.

Raksha and Dadima simply smiled, since his question wasn't relevant.
Their mentors were extremely mysterious...
Therefore, there was no specific answer.

Sensing his heart and soul yearning for an union,
A chirpy snow angel appeared out of thin air,
Enunciating her enthusiasm while singing a magical song!

"The Sibylline Fabricators of Abundance!
Extend their gracious, invitationnnnnn!
Urging all of you to hurry,
Towards, their Marvellous Creationnnnnn!
Oh, Passionate Pioneer!
Huddle up, your Pundits!!!

Because, you are soon to venture into the vastness!
To find your Cosmic, Connectionnnnnnnnnnn!"

Snapping her fingers while tapping her toes, the seraphim ushered two revered souls and four remarkable mortal spirits beneath the extramundane brilliance of the Healing Dome. Encouraging them to follow her lead!

Spreading her delicate arms out wide,
Exhorting the fascinated explorers to do the same,
She spiralled around her own axis, generating a whirlwind of magic!

By unanimously causing uncontrollable friction,
Together, they gave birth to a prodigious phenomenon never monitored before!
A ferocious fountain of lava erupted from under them fossilizing the crust,
Shooting its riders straight out of one dimension…
Making them disappear into the cryptic cosmos!

Siphoned into outer space with pleasure,
The animals were in ataraxia rocketing through millions of galaxies…
Never imagined in their wildest of dreams!

"There you are!"
A heavenly voice echoed through infinitude…
Making them come to a halt.

"We were wondering if we would hear from you again!"
The supernatural wonders conveyed their concern,
From two different corners of a corner-less expanse.

"Your perseverance is an indication of your resolute devotion!
For this unconditional love you shower upon us…
We are eternally beholden!"

The visitors were humbled by the grace their divine hosts displayed.

"Unlike many gifted fools,
Who have faltered from their calling in the past…
You did not waver to embark upon what the restricted minds,
Might consider to be 'a preposterous mission'."
The Goddess, concealing herself within the dainty dove,
Shed light in the darkness with her magnificent aura!

"Our only concern was, if you were prepared?!?
Prepared to inculcate our perennial vision!"

Basking in her glory, the ecstatic God emerged as the unparalleled pigeon,
Emitting rays, just like the sun would.

"Instead of retiring back to the dwindling land you come from…
You impressed us, by volunteering to investigate further!"
Drawing a curtain of wonder, the God and Goddess infused together eclipsing
their special spectators and forcing every magical motion to come to a standstill.

Presenting a platform for an open and honest dialogue, the immortal souls
enthralled their visitants in the quietude of their enchanting creation, encouraging
Dhairya to take centre stage!

"Oh no, Supreme Souls,
Or, Sibylline Sources, must I say?!?

We are indebted to be in your powerful presence!
Why would we ever want to return to a land where nobody cares?"
He went on to elaborate his feelings, in all openness,

"A land, where it is no longer the survival of the fittest,
A land where morals have succumbed to the tyranny of the richest.
A land, where sacred idols have become mere statutes,
A land where money has taken precedence burying all their virtues.
A land, where thoughtfulness has gone down the drain,
A land where compassion is absolutely lost…
A land, where its inhabitants are blinded with false pride,
A land where sympathy is faked.
A land, where the deluded show no mercy…
Stooping to the lowest level, they trample the meek exuding no empathy.
Why would we want to go back to that land which is swiftly losing its charm?
Why would I want to put my loved ones in the way of any harm???"
Disturbed by the long list of troubles, his eyes moistened.

"There is not much left for us to do there, but to save the ones in plight.
You are the Originator!
You are the Creator!

You are the Fabricator!
You are the Holy Priest and Priestess in one!
You are the esteemed Emperor and Empress with a magic touch!
You are the Almighty who, I believe, will ultimately make things right!"
On his knee, Dhariya bent as if waiting to be knighted by Divinity itself.
"In your glory, forever I wish for us to bask;
For, your eternal love I devote myself willing to take up any task!"

Expecting nothing less than what they heard, the celestial forces hovered over his spirit while his family anticipated their response.

"Your devotion to the nature you regard as your Mother,
Touched our hearts since you were first conceived!
It is not this life that you know of which we talk about,
It is the thousands of lifetimes before this,
You have shown us the same love!

An insight into your past, which you are soon to receive,
Might bewilder many mortal minds;
But, you my child, aren't any ordinary soul.
Believe it or not, you are, our first born!"

Neither of them listening could comprehend their words,
Still, they eyed Dhairya with admiration.

"Your contribution towards your mission, has always been quintessential!
Your love for the Universe is no coincidence!
Your zest for living life to its fullest is no fluke!
Your passion towards your calling is innate!
You have, forever, been the forerunner.
You just don't know it yet!"
The Ethereal Souls enlightened them some more!

"You have passed numerous hurdles to get to where we are standing...
You are here, because not once have you failed!
We are elated by your determination and devotion!

You woo our hearts in every form that you take!
Yes, you have bit your tongue when you should have spoken,
However, given the situation, you did what you thought was best.
You never intentionally ignored one's suffering;
Whenever you smelt trouble, you risked your life to save the rest!"
The proud parents, made their deific son blush, by their revelations.

"This wolf, who stands here looking so stumped,
Is an example of the huge heart you bear.

It was no accident for you to cross paths whenever you did;
For, this is one of your divine siblings!
Sent to support you in your consequential journey!
A journey which goes beyond, this lifetime."

Flushed, feeling all eyes on him, Khatru didn't know how to process his emotions.
Was he to hug his long lost brother, a langur,
Or, fall into the arms of the Source who were his progenitors?
His mortal spirit, was baffled.

"Dadima and Raksha, join us in this conclave;
Because, they were sent by us to watch over you through all your births.
Their dedication has been exemplary in the past;
But, even the best of the best have strayed in this current lifetime,
Since the world, as you described so well,
Is going to hell."

Surprised to discover their actual purposes of all their lifetimes, Dadima and Raksha didn't know how to react, considering both were beating themselves up for the mistakes they had made.

Illuminating their family on what they had forgotten over infinite lifetimes,
The Sibylline Sources continued their monologue,
"*'Where exactly is heaven?!?*
How scary is this hell???'
Mankind often wonders!

Mankind...
Who was gifted with the privilege of expression and consciousness.
The same Mankind,
Now blatantly disregard their blessings and misuse their intelligence.

Forgetting that,
Heaven lies within every soul who feels nothing but love!
The highest degree of one's consciousness aligned with their thoughtful actions, pure thoughts and unbiased emotions, is where heaven lies!
When, your overall vibrations are in sync with the Universe's Blueprint,
You don't have to look too far.
Because, where you stand, there heaven is!"

Forcing them to go over all their actions of the only lifetime they remember,
The Creators, continued,
"Now let's talk about hell, shall we?
When one's selfish wants and desires in their physical state,
Overpower their ability to be awakened at all times,
And, they easily stray away from staying true to their souls...
Is when suffering presents itself,
Transforming a gifted life into a living hell.

To those who find themselves in this hell,
Death doesn't come easily!
Because, their life of distress,
Is a price to be paid for all their disdainful choices."
The prudent guardians of the Universe imparted clarity upon the departed souls, while the mortal spirits simply stared into a dark future of their fellow earthlings.

"Stay self-centred was our message when we created them all!
SELF-CENTRED, as in maintaining perfect balance within!
Not, selfishly accumulating material possessions.
SELF-ABSORBING, was their secret tool to thrive!
Absorbing the love and awareness divulged by their inner Goddess!
Not narcissistically put their own flesh on the pedestal!?!"
Disappointment reflected in their demeanor as they continued...

"Instead of understanding, the deeper meaning, of these beautiful words…
The self-proclaimed 'intelligent beings,'
Lost themselves in the superficial world they created.
All because they allowed outside forces,
To seep into their already rocky existence,
Forcing them to lose their equilibrium to a point of no return.

In this vicious cycle, they crossed all boundaries of sanity,
By twisting our 'words' and manipulating their 'brethren'.
Words which were meant to be treasured,
Brethren, who were supposed to be treated,
With the same love and respect they themselves desired.

Unable to find clarity, peace and love,
While, many are busy chasing illusions,
In the name of their perceptions…
Other fools on a similar ego trip,
Wonder where they have gone wrong?"
Portraying issues for what they were, their openness embarrassed their children.

"If you were all flawless, it would have been magic indeed!
However, we most definitely made a mistake.
A mistake, by underestimating the foolishness of this species…
This species who constantly choose to entangle themselves,
In their own web of deceit and trickery.

We need to rectify our errors.
Otherwise, they are going to self-destruct.
Self-destruct, because they've reached a stage,
Where they thoughtlessly place their greed on the altar."
The Prophetic Forces were saddened by the mess the humans had made.

"Although Dadima and Raksha lost focus,
They also acknowledged their shortcomings, in all honesty.
Which is why, despite their blunders in this tumultuous lifespan,
They are present here with us today!"

Dadima and Raksha were now under the radiant spotlight,
Shedding tears of repentance, for their contribution to the mess…
Grateful, for an opportunity given to redeem themselves.

Attempting to lift their breaking spirits,
The Protectors of the Universe addressed their first born!

'These two lovely ladies by your side who we have yet to acknowledge,
Since inception, you have been bound together as a family!
Therefore, you have connected in situations surreal!!!
Dadima, was meant to be your protector.
Raksha, your cupid!

Gayatri! Gayatri is the one that forever keeps you strong!
And, Mantra, she keeps you grounded!
Their roles, have been intertwined for millions of lifetimes,
But, Dhairya, you our boy!
You are the CONSTANT!
Their single point of attraction!!!"

Speechless at the secrets being spilt, none of them interrupted the Empyrean
entities by asking inapposite questions.

"By now, you very well understand the significance and power of the code,
You deciphered on your way here.
For, you are,
ALL IN ONE and ONE IN ALL!
ONE IN ALL, and, ALL IN ONE!
Together, you are meant to forever stand tall!
And, when you selflessly do what you must,
We will make sure you never fall!
Never fall!
Never fall!"

As soon as the Divine said their piece,
Their last assuring words echoed throughout the cosmos…
Transmitting powerful energies into the Vastness,
Forcing a significant change, in the already serene space!

A space where emerald waters cascaded into the stillness of the night skies.
Skies, although dark, were clearer than one's reflection in an unambiguous mirror.
A mirror that reflected not only into the galaxy but the entire cosmos.
A cosmos, which was beyond the imagination of a mortal mind.
A mortal mind that inflicted unnecessary anguish...
Anguish resulting in unfathomable misery.
Misery, which was to follow them throughout their numerous lifetimes,
If their wrongs, weren't righted.

CHAPTER 28

Changing colours like the magical orb they had concocted before,
The poised pigeon and the dazzling dove in the Celestial Body,
Transformed into an Oracle only Dhairya had known to be!

Witnessing the imperial Eagle-Owl staring them down,
The rest of his tribe were in glee!

"Vaani!"
Dhairya's spirit was elated to see his saviour again!

This time though, the distinction of her splendorous stature was definable,
Because there were no distractions in the quietude of their vast expanse!

Dividing her deep colours,
Painting patterns on her wings of swaying scales,
She reminded her descendants of the colossal cobras doused in passion!
Then, partitioning herself,
Vaani dropped her colourful cloak,
Making room for her beloved Vidur, to step in!

Her beloved!
His father!
Who Dhairya had failed to notice during their initial encounter of this lifetime,
Simply because, he was blinded by absolute grief.

With his senses all sharpened after the many tools he'd collected along the way,
Dhairya could now distinguish, Him from Her!

Just as Vaani had commanded his full attention by the river bed,
Vidur's powerful presence, accentuated his astonishing appearance!

Paying close attention to yet another transformation of the sublime source...

This time, he saw clearly, her purity!
Purity that reflected not only in her loving, nurturing, endearing eyes,
But also in the opulence of the rare white owl that she became!
And he, Vidur!
He was in rhapsody, to be the most dominant harpy eagle!
An eagle brave enough to unleash his might, in order to tame untamed beasts.

Dhairya was blessed around every corner and at every nook;
Because, his divine parents were out there keeping him safe,
In spite his ignorance.

Fortunate to experience the marvels of their creation,
While, sharing the same space as them!
He took the opportunity to thank the Oracle,
Who had abruptly vanished before his eyes,
Giving him a glimpse into their nightmare.

"Thank you, for taking me under your wing, and guiding my way!
I was certain that it was you who bestowed meaty blessings upon Khatru!
When I failed to quench his thirst...
Conflicted with myself that day."

Wrapping their wondrous wings around him for the third time in this life,
The almighty force comforted their boy expressing their relief.

"It's been a struggle in the past to get you together, standing still as you stand
right now. All because, your physical existence always drove you in opposite
ways.

In every human form you received,
You repelled over and over and over again...
So, in this life, we tried something different,
Bringing you back as the primogenitors!"
The Ethereal entities took pride in their choice.

"You needed a little nudge in the right direction,
Because, your sensitive soul was suffering soaked in all that pain.
And, Khatru, in spite of a long list of his faux pas, he needed to heal.
Heal, in order to find his way.
Which he did, because here you stand before us all united!
Like, you should have done lifetimes ago."
The Oracle, painted a picture, of their struggles.

"Now that we have you here all together,
Let's clarify certain points, shall we?
Firstly, get this.
No matter where life takes you, and what obstacles we throw your way,

You must always remain connected!
Secondly,
'Time is of the essence,' you keep saying.
But, time, as you know it, doesn't exist in our realms!"

Spotting confusion, on all their faces, the Marvellous Wonders elaborated…

"Humans divided this cycle of life for their own convenience.
To be productive is what they initially had in mind.
Gradually, in 'time,'
They learnt to pose as angels in the light of day.
And, at night they enabled their nasty demons to come forth and play.

Strangling their inner voice while suffocating their conscience…
These ignoramuses rapidly lost control.
Lost control, we say,
That's because we observe them every day,
Constantly battling themselves to 'simply be'.
Be one with the Force!
Be one with the Source!" They looked at their disciples carefully, wondering if they understood the true meaning of their words.

"We would love for you all to stay here with us!
Yet, that isn't our priority.
The planet you walk on is soon to perish…
If the gnarly earthlings don't change their godforsaken ways."

Consumed by anxiety, little Mantra politely interrupted,
"Forgive my intrusion, my eternal grandparents!
Pardon me, for I am not sure how to address you yet…
We caught a few glimpses into worlds direly in need of help.
The most heart-breaking was the one where… Where…"

The pure soul found it hard to describe a nightmare.
Still, she dug deep drawing a dreadful picture of what she saw.

"Where not a single tree was visible…
Breathing freshness back into the air.
There was no pure oxygen left for them to breathe;
Only deadly toxins engulfed their atmosphere.
Mountains of garbage stank up their skies defying gravity,
Making all their birds and animals disappear.
There was no fresh water for them to drink;
Only disgusting fluids flowed everywhere…
Inconceivable sewage seeped through their dwellings,
Still, the mutating inhabitants and savage beasts staggered along,
Giving an impression that they didn't seem to care!

Is that how our earth is going to be???
Are we going to meet the same unfortunate fate as them???"
Terrified of the future, Mantra was in tears.

Consoling the one who was supposed to salvage the future of all dimensions,
Vaani, along with her counterpart, Vidur, spoke in unison,
"No. Not if you do what u are meant to do!
Not if you become who you are meant to be!
There is always hope to restore balance;
Provided, you don't allow the planet, which helps you sustain, to wither."

Taking the prodigy under their enchanted wing, they carried on…

"Every calamity they blame upon the wrath of God.
Every misery they pin on the one sitting above.
All we hear these days are complaints…
All we see everywhere is sulking and suffering.
It is not us who are responsible for their misery and hardships;
They have brought it all upon themselves.
In spite of evolving into 'brilliant beings,'
The growth of humanity, conveniently, doesn't seem to matter to them."

Disheartened by the mess of their creation, they continued to shed light,

"They pretend to lack awareness...
They disregard the consequences of their individual actions...
Accustomed to play the blame game, they pass along the buck.
No wonder, as one happy community, they fail to co-exist.

Taking advantage of every pure soul has become their horrible habit.
All they keep doing these days is reproduce like rabbits,
Aiming to carry on their ancestral legacy!
A legacy, which isn't one to be proud of anymore."

Their tribe nodded in agreement.

"It is easy for the ignorant to look the other way,
Pacifying themselves; that it isn't their responsibility.
But, the educated?!?!?

For them, to presume others will clean up their mess is disheartening.
If they keep up these antics,
They are most certainly going to self-destruct!

We often wonder if they've forgotten,they are perishable goods;
That they all, come with an expiry date.
Our wonders don't!

Facing hardships at the hands of their own choices,
They will all evaporate into the poison they help produce in the future.
When the soil and oxygen, which helps them nourish and flourish, is destroyed,
The halfwits' demise as a race is inevitable."

Watching Mantra's tears of terror trickle down her cheek,
They cast their shadow upon her comforting her pure spirit.

"Although you've seen a future that terrorises you...
Please, understand,
We are the loving parents one might seek in times of distress.

If our children turn their lives around,
There is still a chance they will avert major catastrophes.
If they play their part right,
Like princes and princesses, them we will treat!
But, if disrespected in anyway…
We might just do what the humans always like to say we do,
'Unleash our wrath'
Devouring every savage beast!"
The caring and loving Father and Mother of the Universe,
Smiled at themselves, at the end of their dramatic delivery!

"But, if they are already doomed,
How do u expect us to save them???
Shall we pray for their souls?!?" Khatru, was conflicted.

"They've tortured you by torturing your creation;
Then, why do you not wipe them off the face of this planet,
Putting an end to all their madness, once and for all?"
Raksha's tone was vengeful.

"Why must we help those who are set in their unholy ways???
Why do we even try in vain to save them…
When they are adamant to hurt you, in ways unbearable to us?"
Dadima, who was burnt by Bhram, not so long ago,
Failed to contain her fury.

"It is not for us to save those, who aren't willing to save themselves…
That would be a waste of our precious energy!" Gayatri was calm.

"I think, what their Holinesses mean is…
We have to do our best to protect their creation,
While aiming to rekindle the lost love among those who still have hope!"
The radiant soul looked to her mystical in-laws for asseveration.

"We hear you. All of you!
However, your worries are unnecessary!

And, as expected,
Gayatri has expressed herself beautifully!"
They took pride in the one they chose to be their son's rock.

"It is not the planet Earth we are concerned about!
She is well endowed to equalize herself,
Whenever there is an extreme imbalance.

If you are fearful that she might not survive the disasters foreign to her,
Please do understand,
She is our masterpiece!
And, as the Fabricators of this cosmos,
We appreciate your cosmoses!
We really do!" Vidur and Vaani, grinned.

"What you need to register at this crucial meeting is that,
There is a lot more magic where our creations come from!
When the need arises, we can conceive them again!
Start fresh aiming to seek perfection!

Our concern is humanity.
Although the human race might fail to regard Nature as their Mother,
We never forget that they are our children!
Children who have miserably lost their way to false pride.

Therefore, as any parent would be,
We are worried for their wellbeing.
Not of our origination!

No, no, no, no, no!
It is their suffering we intend to minimize...
Not ours.
No matter what comes our way,
We will forever be in Eternal Bliss!"
The concerned nurturers, addressed their tribe!
Then, spiralled around Mantra giving her wings!

Fulfilling her secret desire, to be one, with the wind!

"On our behalf,
It is you who has to save the day!
You can never let demonic darkness overpower your light;
Because, you are our warriors!
You are our tribe!

Together, you have to keep coming back for as long as it takes,
To encourage your brethren to do what is right!
You have to come back as one,
In order to save innocent souls!
Souls who find themselves stuck in this mayhem.
Them, you have to rescue from unimaginable plight!

Since every lifetime will spring unexpected challenges,
You must prepare yourselves to face them all!
Your mission is to restore balance...
While staying balanced yourselves!

Our vision,
Is to nurse Earth back to health along with the lost souls!
For that to become a possibility,
You have to plant seeds!
Literally and figuratively!
All, so, this precious planet does not go to waste!

It might seem like an undoable task, given what you've seen.
However, always remember...
Nothing is impossible in life!
All you need is the courage to take that first step with grace!

Those mortals who are afraid of challenges,
Or, even those who half-heartedly begin any quest,
Might quickly lose hope and retreat into their caves,
Since, accepting defeat would have become their second nature."

In their indirectness, the Sibylline Forces,
Directly addressed Dadima, Rakha and Khatru.
Because, even though it seemed like they weren't being watched,
Divinity had caught them frowning.

"Imagine a world,
Where seeds are planted, when any mortal perishes...
Their souls will transcend peacefully,
Knowing that their memory will be honoured and respected!

However,
To earn that respect and honour from the ones still breathing in flesh,
Their actions will have to match their vibrations when they live.
Since honour,
Cannot be commanded...
And, respect cannot be demanded,
What happens in the end is all in their hands!
If they choose to ignore the gifts of life,
They will have no one but themselves to blame."

Spelling out the obvious, the unparalleled entities came to the point.

"Which is where you, our tribe, play an important role,
Rescuing the lost souls from an abyss...
You have to guide them towards the light!
Because, every soul on every planet moving or still,
Is a part of us, and we are a part of them!"

Painting a picture of the divine connection,
Vidur and Vaani, reminded them of the constant!

Moving along, they emphasized on certain shortcomings,
In order to focus on finding a perfect solution!

"Blindly allowing themselves to be brainwashed and bullied,
The naive spirits empower the demons residing in disturbed minds...
To shamelessly manipulate our existence.

Aimlessly following those with immoral intentions further and farther away from reality, the weak and the meek choose to fall prey to the wicked predators...

Those are the facts of the world you live in;
THE HUMAN WORLD.
You've encountered these predators too, haven't you?!?"

The dynamic duo, tested their tribe's knowledge of the dark world they lived in.
In dismay, their children bobbed their heads;
Yet, had hope in their eyes waiting to hear more...

"Our Children are living in denial,
Assuming they are better than the rest.
All because false pride is clouding their judgement,
And, arrogance is leading them to fail every test.

Encouraging their delusions, to take precedence over sanity,
They are authorizing their egos to lead them astray...

No one else is to blame!

Refusing to acknowledge their shortcomings,
They continue to fool themselves, causing further damage.
Permitting their superficial lives to shove them into darkness...
Our lost sheep tend to forget,
All they have to do is 'simply be aware'!
Aware of our presence in them, at all times!"

Owlishly, the Prophets spilt more secrets...
Encouraging all souls to share their light,
Instead of not selfishly confining its radiance.

"As long as one's intentions are pure, and they remain grounded,
We will give them wings!
Sincerely, proceeding in the right direction...

Eventually, as they tap onto their optimum potential,
We will, teach them to fly!

Provided,
They are willing to devote themselves to the higher power!
The higher power, dwelling within themselves!
Without a single trace of doubt!

For, there is no fast track in this process.
Just as there is no shortcut to success.

Exploring their divine connection has to become their only priority.
For that, they, voluntarily, have to put in the required effort!
Only then, will they be able to recognise and acknowledge The Divine,
Who resides in each and every one of our children!

By worshipping idols created by man...
They have reduced their faith into a piece of fascinating art,
Forgetting that every image is a depiction of a learned man's imagination.
Imagination, which came to fruition because of the Divine inspiration.
Which, in return, came to life in the form of a story!

A story that was told in order to impart wisdom.
Wisdom, so mankind could register the moral messages!
And, by following the idol of their choice,
They could all walk in their God or Goddesses footsteps!
Originating as role models themselves.

Role models who would act in alignment to their words,
Aiming to nourish and flourish each other as one righteous family!

Alas, like Chinese whispers,
The learnings were lost in translation.
And, idols and role models merely became objects and subjects to their mortal
fascination."

Wanting to wash away all images...
Images, they themselves once created to captivate their children's attention,
The Wondrous Entities, once again, worked their wonders,
Transforming themselves into Sublime Supremacy,
Showcasing, nothing, but endless infinitude...

'The infinitude,
Where a gazillion planets were serenaded by their own Gods and Goddesses!

Some had more than a dozen moons, orbiting around their marvels!
While the others had multiple suns, illuminating everyone's existence,
By engulfing them in their majestic rays of brilliance...
While the vividly vibrant shades of lustre continuously invigorated all senses!'

Giving their children, a glimpse into the vastness of their expanse,
The Luminary Legends illuminated their first born,
Putting him right under their luminous spotlight...

"Dhairya! Oh, Dhairya! Our Miracle Child!
You unknowingly pledge your allegiance to the Universe!
Making us, oh, so proud!

In order to Explore One's Divine Connection...
Your brethren must commit in ways similar,
Keeping in mind nothing can ever be forced.

One cannot simply hop onto our wagon and expect a miracle...
This journey isn't a walk in the park, nor a picnic or a fancy celebration...
As you have discovered for yourself,
Their devotion too, must naturally flow!

Although we have a soft spot for everyone,
We cannot be fooled!
We sniff a liar and a cheat even before it knows the evil it's capable of.
So, we want to make it very clear,
Selfish reasons and ulterior motives will never be entertained.

Hence, it is entirely up to them to choose...
Choose if they intend to embark upon an adventure,
Without worrying about what's to come in the future!
Or, simply succumb to their disdained delusions, like always!"

Making him aware of his growth,
The spectrum of double rainbows appeared yet again,
Circling around his already beaming aura.

"Dhairya, our daring darling!
We know you yearn to be knighted by us.
What you don't realize…
Is that, you already are our knight in shining armour!
Knighted the very moment,
You fought darkness with great fortitude!"

He who was still basking in their glory, blushed like a boy hearing the truth.

"You set the bar really high, champion!
Because, now, the ones seeking our attention,
Will have to be willing to fit in your pious shoes!"

Humbled by the love showered upon him by the Sovereign Souls,
Dhairya allowed his tears of joy to flow freely!

"Yes you have, Champion! Yes you have!"
The proud parents acknowledged his love!

"Whenever you allow yours tears of gratitude to flow in abundance,
Showering us with your unconditional love…
In all honesty and with great joy! The same way as you do now…
Believe us son, your devotion has also made us cry!

'You are the source!
I am the channel!'
You said with utmost conviction…"
Brimming with love, they reminded him of his words!

Touched to hear, they shed tears with him too.
In harmony with them, he pledged himself to their service yet again!
"Together we are one!!!
You are the inventor!
And, I am your tool!
Use me as you see fit,
My divine creator!

I am at your disposal not only for now;
At your disposal, I will forever be!
I dedicate all my lifetimes to you,
Because, we are in this together,
SINCE FOREVER, INTO INFINITY, BEYOND ETERNITY!!!
BEYOND ETERNITY!!!
BEYOND ETERNITY!!
BEYOND ETERNITY!

Just as these last words had echoed throughout the animal kingdom,
Before they left on this life-altering, yet enlightening voyage...
Similarly, moments ago, the Sibylline Sources' declaration,
Had penetrated through the space, waking every sleeping soul!!!
Dhairya's heartfelt proclamation, also echoed into the cosmos loud and clear!
Alarming every soul, on every minute planet, in every little galaxy, that...
The 'Chosen One' was here!

CHAPTER 29...
THE CONCLUSION: PART ONE!

"Wow! That's incredible, Dadu!
Does that mean you are like God or something?!?
I always wondered why you looked so mysterious;
Now, I know!"

Losing himself in Dadu's flashback,
As if he was next to the valiant Dhairya at all times…
The ever enthusiastic Kela, forced Dadu out of his spell,
Forgetting all about the scolding he received only a few hours ago.

Unable to contain his excitement, the ever curious soul bombarded his adulated
granduncle with questions, even before Dadu could recover from the travels into
his past.
"So, where are Dadima and Dadi Gayatri now?
What happened to Aunty Mantra?!?
And, that wolf who was supposed to be your brother,
What became of him???
Did he go back to his old ways gobbling the meek for dinner?

I have a feeling he did…
I think I have seen a wolf with red spots terrorising animals,
Deep in the heart of this jungle…"

Kela could have gone on and on, but Akeli pleaded for him to stop.

"Oh, poor little Akeli, am I scaring you again?!?
Am I? Am I?"
He who was always easily distracted,
Mocked his cousin embodying the fictional wolf he had mentioned.

"When will you ever grow up, Kela???
Can you please give Dadu a minute to breathe?
You've been enjoying Dadu's adventures for hours now;
Could you be thoughtful and offer him some water, maybe?!?"
She who rarely uttered a few words unless she was spoken to,
Looked different in the eyes of the one,
Who seemed to have forgotten, for a brief moment, where he was.

Chucking the plastic glasses and glass bottles in the same blue plastic bag,
Which had given birth to her dearest Dadu's anxiety…
Akeli had placed them out of his sight, making an effort to minimize his angst.
Later, she gathered some coconut shells planning for the future!

Filling the same coconut shells with every last drop of rain water,
Resting on every refreshed leaf in that patch of the jungle…
Akeli stayed close all along not intending to miss a word.

Offering her beloved grandfather the elixir of her love,
She watched him finish every last drop of the precious water in that shell.
Then, she quickly offered him another, wanting to quench his thirst to the fullest.

Enjoying the blessings bestowed upon him by the twinkle of his eye,
He looked up, to thank his beloved parents for their generosity too.
Which was when he was caught off guard to see a congregation of birds, monkeys
and all other species of animals in their kingdom watch his every move.

His thunderous voice of distress had echoed throughout the valley inviting every
living soul and departed spirit to his council, in search of some answers…

Overwhelmed, feeling all eyes on him,
His tears flowed rapidly causing a chain reaction.
Soon, all one could hear were the sniffles of the one sitting next to them.
Because, they had sensed his joy whilst, simultaneously, feeling his sorrow.

Scanning the vicinity some more,
Dadu's, sharp eyes caught a few glimpses of the blasts from his past,
Waving at him from a distance making him aware of their presence!

Both, departed souls and living spirits who had once been touched by the angel,
Had gathered around with love to listen to the most awaited story of all time.

Unsure of how to react to this odd situation he found himself in,
He had to remind himself,
'Nothing was ever a coincidence; everything was a sign!'

Although he attempted to tame the beast that his worried mind had become,
All kinds of thoughts consumed his anxious being,
'They have been here watching me all this while?
Then, why have we failed to reconnect earlier?
Are my lovely ladies and stubborn brother watching me too?'

Hoping to discern the pillars of his lost world, he regretted the loss of precious time.

'No. Lifetimes...
All those precious lifetimes!'
He corrected himself still weeping searching some more...

By now, his vision was too blurry to be able to see anything clearly;
So, he closed his eyes like he did before.
Anticipating the voice of the Divine within him,
To whisper into his ear some magic words of wisdom.

Upset, seeing him drag himself into a bottomless pit,
When she did speak in the past...
He failed, to pay attention.
All because his mind had been preoccupied.

Even though he had pretended to be tough, he was all broken inside,
Always praying, somehow he'd manage to fix himself...

The ones he was hoping to see weren't around to soothe his agony.
Therefore, unknowingly, he gave up instead of exploring again,
Doing exactly opposite of what his Prophetic parents had asked of him.

Just like an angel sent to save the day,
Out of nowhere, a huge bat with a swollen belly appeared before him,
Commanding his full awareness.

"Raksha! *Is that you, Raksha?"*
He promptly rose to his feet wishing it was her.
However, he was left a bit disappointed,
Because it wasn't Raksha seeking his consciousness,
It was her brave and fearless daughter, Suraksha!
Who they fondly called, Suku,
Waiting to be acknowledged.

Surviving the hardships and challenges life had tossed her way,
After the untimely passing of her endearing mother…
Suku, had grown to be the most glorious bat ever known to live.
Making her ancestors, oh so proud!

Although, to any other eye, all bats looked the same,
The astute langur had recognised the tiny white mark on her belly.
A mark resembling the Temple of Spirits passed along to all its protectors!
Protectors, who were still active on duty.

In spite of his failed efforts for centuries…
To reconnect, with a soul who now walked in her mother's footsteps,
His spirit sparkled when she stooped down from higher groundsn the light of day,
seeking his blessings!

"I always wondered,
If you were my uncle Dhairu. I did!
But, for reasons insane,
I never gathered the courage to clarify my doubts.
I thought, if you weren't who I thought you were…
I'd be deemed crazy just like the rest of the spirits.
Spirits, who are still walking the face of this planet,
Looking for a miracle."
With no one to guide her thoughts, she faced her own dilemma refraining from
doing what she was supposed to do. Just like Dhairya, lost in Dadu's desolate
body.

Touched by her presence, her uncle Dhairu didn't know where to begin;
Which is when a deafening cry interrupted their long awaited union.

A venturous leopard strode in full speed from the peak of a nearby mountain,
Scaring the jeepers of all the animals who were accustomed to live in fear.

All pumped by Dhairya's tales of gallantry,
Kela charged towards the leopard in full force,
Senselessly screaming on top of his lungs, ***"Stop right there, you savage beast!* Or**
else, my Dadu will make you regret the day you were born."

Almost butting heads as they abruptly came to a halt,
The wind picked up announcing a 'bout,'
A bout featuring David and Goliath!

Roaring, like he had never roared before…
The always misunderstood leopard, sent the feisty langur running for cover
behind his granduncle begging to be saved.

Causing the earth to quake, with each tenacious step that he took,
The leopard flaunted his razor sharp nails in Dadu's face.

Unlike Kela, whose quivering existence now simply froze,
Akeli, stepped forward acting as a shield to protect her Dadu from harm,
Staring the dreaded feline defiantly deep into his mesmerizing golden eyes,
Strangely, she found herself to be at peace;
Observing her reflection,
Looking into his soul!

Although, she didn't recollect their connection…
He somehow felt, she was no stranger to him like he was no stranger to her.

Stepping aside all flushed, Akeli took charge of her mind;
Making room for the estranged souls to reconnect.
Reconnect, under circumstances so surreal!

"Capu, my boy! You've grown so tall!
Yet, you've managed to stay hidden for all these years?!?"
Dadu couldn't help but wonder.
'Why was it that they never crossed paths before that day?
Or, had they passed each other?'

His once sharp mind had lost its mojo…
Ever since his mortal state had been consumed by his self-inflicted suffering.
Nevertheless, he did what he had learnt to do best,
Beat himself up, dwelling on one thought…
'How had he not been able to identify,
This beautiful, compassionate creature he helped raise?'

Snapping out of his mind maze, where he was so used to being trapped…
In all honesty, he admitted to his mistake,
"I'm sorry, my boy! I'm sorry for not finding you sooner.
Trust me, I looked and looked;
I looked for you everywhere; for you, and the rest of our tribe.

However, everyone vanished on me all at once,
Leaving no trace.

Where did you disappear, my boy?!? Where???
Where is the rest of the family? Is everybody in good spirits?
And, Ravi??? Where is Ravi?
Did he do his best to keep you all safe?!?"

Dadu recollected Dhairya's plight, and shed a few more tears.
It had been so long that he failed to recollect, *'who had abandoned whom?'*
Yet, feeling responsible, he apologized.
Shocking everybody present.

The love that reflected in their eyes towards the other, was astonishing!
Their bond, although lost due to the games life played,
Was now clearly visible!
The revered langur and a lionhearted leopard, gleamed in each other's glory,
Happy to be sharing the same space again!

"Capu? As in the cub you rescued from the fire all those years ago???
This is that same Capu?!?" Kela seemed relieved and excited too!

A thrill seeker that he was, he had stayed up all night,
Dreaming of riding mystical dolphins in deep blue waters,
After Dadu had mentioned their existence the previous day.

Then, having heard of little Mantra riding on a leopard,
The dolphins had vanished from his thoughts…
And, he'd envisioned himself mounting this wild beast displaying his bravado.

All choked up to be in the presence of the only father he once knew,
The leopard tried in vain, to inquire about the rest of his family,
Because, words wouldn't seem to make past his scarred mouth.

Holding onto her frivolous cousin who was to ruin this heartfelt reunion,
Akeli surprised Kela with her sudden burst of strength.
He fought hard to break free of her grip.
But his antics were no match to her determination.

Sensing something had horribly gone wrong all those years ago,
The once shy and timid outcast, Akeli, was adamant to let her Dadu make peace
with all the demons of his past which, obviously, still haunted him.

Unsure of whom to turn to first, Dadu gestured them all to huddle close.
Obedient as they had always been, his wish was their command!

Taking their spots before the one they adored, irrespective of his failures,
They made him very proud!
Affectionately running his fingers on Suku's swollen belly,
He softly spoke of her Mother, Raksha.

**"She loved you a lot, you know?
She still loves you wherever she is. I'm sure she does!"**
Dadu recollected his last meeting with Raksha with a heavy heart.

**"We were meant to meet again when she came into mortal existence,
But, somehow, that never happened..."** he seemed dejected.

Turning his attention to Capu,
Who was concerned for his mother's and sister's well-being,
Dadu, went on to tell his story,
**"After our surreal encounter with the forces of this Universe,
Who, we were stunned to discover were our Eternal Parents,
We were thrilled to take charge of the mission we were born for!**

Understanding the gravity of the situation,

Together, we took an oath before we left the sacred space!
Pledging our lives in service of the Divine.
We vowed, to always stay connected!
Connected, in order, to fulfil the prophecies of the Sibylline Sources!

Everyone was elated when we left the quietude of the brilliant cosmos!
All the magic we experienced was beyond our mortal imagination!
Our lives now had a purpose!
We were given great directions!
All we were to do was to remain grounded while staying on track."

Dadu's soulful eyes exuded radiance addressing Divinity to be his parents,
But, as he re lived his past, he started to lose that light...

"Once, we were sent back, to the Dome of Healing,
We, mortal spirits, were meant to find our way back to the Redemption
Bridge,
Where our flesh and bones eagerly waited to reunite with our souls!
Dadima and Raksha were to continue their healing process,
Under the expert guidance of the Ultimate Healers!

Everything was planned for us according to the Almighty's wishes;
All we had to do was to diligently follow in their footsteps.
However,
Everything went wrong as soon as one of us lost focus.
Everything;
Nothing was ever the same again.
Nothing..."

Struck with immense grief, Dadu directly spoke to Akeli who stood there in
disbelief.
"I am the one to be blamed for all my nightmares;
No one else, my love.
For, it is all my fault;
It is all my fault!
Had I not indulged in Gayatri's curiosity to explore the Dome of Healing,

None of this would have happened.
None of this."

Holding himself accountable for all their suffering, Dadu addressed his tribe,
"I wouldn't have lost everyone I love in a split second,
Had I anchored them together...
There is no one to blame, but me. Because, it is, my fault.
I very well knew that there would be distractions to divert us from our mission.
All we had to do was stick together, and be aware of every step we took.
Alas! I couldn't even do that much."

He who was known to hold his composure in the gravest of situations,
Was shattered blaming himself for the battles he lost in the past.

Reliving the nightmares that he couldn't bring himself to share,
He etched into his wounds causing himself more harm.
Making it clear to the one waiting to bear his burden,
He was deeply disturbed by whatever transpired in that Dome meant to heal.

Unable to lock eyes with the pure soul who loved him unconditionally, Dadu
turned to answer Kela's question. Kela had, by then, managed to free himself from
Akeli's firm grip as soon as she felt weak.

"Kela, you asked me if I am like God or something?
I am something, alright,
But, understand,
I am nowhere close to God.

Had I been as wise as my immortal parents,
I would have most definitely had the ability to see through the demons;
Demons, lurking around the corner waiting to tear us apart.

As you can see, I am simply a mere mortal,
Stuck in this body, cursed with the anxiety of separation."
His humble words bewildered them all arising more curiosity.

"So, Dadu tell us what happened in that Dome of Healing???
Tell us where Gayatri went?
Sorry, Grandma Gayatri, where did she go?!?
Did she get lost in the Dome?
And, Mantra…"
Knocking himself on his thick head failing to address his elders properly,
Kela apologized,
"Sorry! Aunty Mantra, I mean.
Did she follow in Grandma's footsteps???
They were attached together at all times you said,
Weren't they literally joined to the hip?!?
Is that how you lost them all at once?"

Picking up on certain words which made no sense to him,
Kela had visualized Gayatri and Mantra literally joined to their hips all along,
Missing certain plots whilst baffling his pea sized brain.

"Yes, Dadu,
Please tell us what happened in that Dome of Healing?!?"
Akeli, who wished to help in any way she could,
Tried coaxing the love of her life into narrating his gruesome history.
A history due to which Dadu was in eternal despair.

"I hear the concern in your voice, my beautiful angels!
I know you are looking out for me,
Yearning to soothe my suffering,"
Confusing Kela some more, Dadu hinted at Akeli.
"But, that story remains to be told…
Another day, perhaps!
For it is longer, much, much longer.
Than the one I accidentally blurted out loud.

Night is to fall upon us soon,
So let us not waste another second reminiscing over my past.
Let's head home and connect with our loved ones, before…,"

"Before what, Dadu???
Before the humans come and slay us all?"
Kela interrupted his grand uncle yet again.
"Is that what you were going to say?!?
Did they find the secret passage into that realm???
Like the Temple of Spirits, did they shoot a cannonball into the Dome?
Tell me, Dadu! Tell me!"

Adamant to keep the chronicles going, Kela refused to budge.

"All our loved ones are here!
Haven't you already noticed?
Therefore, we are not heading anywhere.
We are not afraid of those weird two legged primates anymore.
Now, we have Capu on our team!
He will help us gobble them all!
Won't you, Capu?!? Sorry, sorry! Uncle Capu!"
Taking pride in calling a mighty leopard his uncle, Kela drew Dadu's attention to
all the eager ears waiting to know what happened next.

Choosing his words wisely and not intending to ignite unnecessary fire,
Dadu figured that the best way to get out of that situation for then,
Was to leave Kela's peculiar mind with another intense thought.

"Alright! Alright!
Since every precious soul and valiant spirit is lending me their ear...,
Let me spell it out loud and clear!

I am hard on myself because I know I've committed mistakes;
I have failed to redeem myself over all these years.
And, that is what gives me nightmares!

Reliving, my life's journey by venturing into the past,
I have come to realize that I am my own worst enemy!
Because, I have failed to utilize the tools at my disposal.
Tools, which were a gift from the Divine.

The Divine who I half-heartedly acknowledged,
Ever since my life turned upside down."

Admitting his shortcoming out loud, he shocked the audience.
Nonetheless, he felt the load lift off his chest;
So, taking the opportunity to heal himself some more, he continued,

"It was up to me to stay focused.
It was up to me to stay on track.
Yet, restricted in this physical state…
Overpowered by my limited mind…
As soon as a major obstacle presented itself,
I wavered.
Wavered even though we were warned;
Warned about the tests we'd have to endure along the way.

I allowed myself to get rattled;
And, by doing so, I wasted my life fighting meaningless battles.

I had everything I needed to make things right again.
Yet, I failed and miserably at that…
Why?
Because, I permitted my grief to taint my judgement,
And, authorized hatred to overpower the love I have."
Dadu shook his head, acknowledging his own stupidity.

"Therefore, my children…
I humbly request you to not let my sorrow,
Influence your mortal minds.

Whatever just happened hours ago making me tick like a bomb,
I now understand, was a blessing in disguise!

Because, had I not exploded the way I did,
I would have most certainly imploded!
Causing harm not only to myself but also my loved ones…

Every emotion, every feeling and every action of mine,
Should have come from a place of love!
Instead, I lost my balance to the extreme imbalance,
Created by no one else but me.

When I loved, I wholeheartedly loved.
When I despised, I passionately despised...
Empowering my past to affect my present,
Was absolutely foolish of me;
I see that clearly now!
All thanks to this angel who keeps me going,
While I wait, for my other angels to show up!"

Seeing her Dadu's lost smile back,
Akeli, hopped onto his lap in glee encouraging him to go on.

"My Gayatri and Mantra, are very special to me! Yes, they are!" Dadu couldn't help himself but wrap his arms around Akeli bestowing his affection on her like he'd do to Mantra.
"They still are;
Their presence, their existence, their love, their devotion;
Is way more exemplary than you make mine to be.
Never a moment goes by without them in my thoughts!
I've been waiting for them patiently...

Well that's not true, is it?"
Her cheeky laughter lightened up the grim atmosphere, as he corrected himself,

"I've been, forever, waiting restlessly...
To reconnect with them in some way, shape or form.
Still, I haven't crossed paths with them yet,
Or, maybe I did!
I did but I was too blinded by my misery to see clearly.

Who knows if my Gayatri and Mantra, Khatru, Dadima and Raksha,
Have been in front of my eyes, all this time.

I've been holding onto their image I have in my head,
When I should have known better...
They could be in any soul who has brought a smile on my face!
In any spirit that's been kind..."

Dadu's eyes were fixated on Akeli,
Until Kela sought his attention,
Enacting a duel pretending, for a stick to be his sword.

"Detesting these obnoxious homo sapiens, and,
Keeping a record of all the bloodshed and mayhem they've caused,
I've allowed them to seep into my existence and wear me down.

Therefore, I urge you not to repeat my mistake.
Don't foolishly hold a grudge, and label them all to be the same...

Just like we have all kinds in our kingdom,
The kind, the compassionate, the feisty, the brave,
The bullies, the cunning, the greedy and the cowards,
Similarly, they do too.

Not everyone is as spoilt as the next.
Not everyone is as cold as the rest.
There are souls who aim to support us!
We simply haven't crossed paths with them yet.

All because, we have been,
Pardon me again for my silliness!
I'm thoughtlessly dragging you down with me...
That isn't fair to you!

I have been...
All because I have been,
Fixated upon their darkness since I failed to find my light.

These humans have evolved over the years.
They've learnt to read and write;

Ride and fly.
They've even landed on our mother moon, a long time ago."

Holding firmly his prop, Kela looked up at the sky…
Wondering, '*how was that even possible?*'

"Capitalising more, achieving more, conquering more,
Their overall greed has rubbed onto the simpletons.
Causing more suffering and perturbation to their kind.

We have our worries; Yes, we do.
But, don't you see,
What they are putting themselves through?

Still, being brainwashed,
Still, being fooled!
Blindly following the herd as always,
Allowing themselves to be conditioned by an immoral world,
They are carrying the baggage of all their wrong choices;
Just like me,
Like, I never should have!

This life is a gift!
A divine blessing!
Yet, we outrageously, manage to turn it into a curse."
Wanting all the souls present to pay grave attention to what was coming next,
Dadu gestured all the younglings closer.

Always aiming for the best spot, best meal and the best of everything,
Kela shoved himself in front of his siblings Narangi and Mosambee,
With whom he usually dreaded rubbing shoulders when alone,
Giving Dadu the perfect opportunity to reach out and grab his sword.

Gaining Kela's undivided attention with his toy out of his hand,
The wise one held onto the stick engaging his grandnephew in a personal chat,
"The *Gift*, you were so eager to receive yesterday,

Was showered upon us by the Gods,
In the form of rain!

The most precious *Gift*, I said, you received 11 months ago,
Is the *Gift* of Life granted to you with so much love!

I know it might not seem so to those children,
Who've been abandoned by their mortal parents...
Nevertheless, think about the magician hiding behind the clouds,
Who has given us infinite gifts ever since we were born!"

Dadu's focus shifted to the parentless child, Akeli, as he handed Kela back his toy.

"Constantly counting all of our sufferings,
Instead of happily making a list of our joy,
It is us; each one of us,
Who fail to accept our benefactions with grace.

We might feel our life is a burden on others,
Because, some spirits intentionally impose their ignorance upon us.
But, who is anyone to belittle this miracle?
A Miracle conferred upon us by Divinity!
In the form of our precious life."

Having felt Akeli's angst, given the bullying she faced at the hands of her cousins and uncle, Dadu's one look was enough for all of them to register his message.

"This garbage that aggravated me and got all your attention,
That, is not all the rubbish we intended to tackle...
Our limited minds were rusting, turning into junk,
Binding us all in pernicious shackles.

This chaos could have been organized, if I simply did what I was meant to do.
Had I stayed on track as I was supposed to,
I wouldn't find myself in a quandary.
Had I cleaned my surroundings responsibly,
All this mess I complain of wouldn't transform into this mishmash.

Adamant to bring change into the lost world,
We failed to stay connected with each other.
Moreover, we neglected the Divine Goddess,
Who resides in our body and commutes via our soul.

This withering planet would have been a paradise by now,
Had my tribe and I not strayed from our undertaking.

In anguish, I abandoned my operation...
By giving up hope, I failed not only you, but Mankind too.
Hence, I still smoulder in agony,
Because, I am the one to be held accountable,
For burying my Divine parents' ethereal vision."

Scrutinizing the swiftly darkening sky, his eyes twitched,
Making an impression that he was looking for something.
Little did they know the long pause Dadu took,
Was to reach out to the Forces of this Universe,
Asking for their forgiveness!

"Thoughtlessly, I succumbed to the demons ruling my every move.
Had I put an end to their madness then,
I wouldn't be preaching this gospel now, would I?
I wouldn't be the one deemed insane.

All this while, who have I been waiting for???
It is my responsibility to clean up the mess I've made.

Our surroundings are in disarray.
Unruly waste is all around us.
Impenetrable debris has accumulated inside our brain.
Untraversable toxins are creeping into our system.

Let's forget our Mother Earth for a second, shall we,
And mourn our own demise.
Because, we have literally turned our sacred temple into a garbage dump...

Aren't we all proud of what we have achieved?"
Caught up in the horror, their lives had become, Dadu gasped for breath.
Instantaneously reminding himself to practise what he preached.

His sincerity showed when he gently closed his soulful eyes!
In all authenticity aiming to bring Dhairya back to life...
Virtuously, he shed every single one of his baggage!

Surrendering all his turmoil in the hands of the Sibylline Sources,
He gracefully softened his existence! Opening his hearing!

For the first time in a long time,
He didn't yearn to hear his lovely ladies whisper in his ears.
Instead, he consciously took a deep breath in hopes for his disciples to follow.
Because, after all those years of petulance,
He was finally heading towards the Empyrean, to bond with his kindred spirits.

Binding the spectators in his brilliant smile, he lost himself in bliss...
Exuding an exceptional aura into the Universe!
Becoming one with nature;
The deific Dhairya emerged, smoothening Dadu's wrinkled skin.
Making all their jaws drop in unison!

"Planting seeds, is what I was told to do,
However, I lost my way combating my own demons.
Therefore, tell me, Kela,
Who would you like to slay?"
Dumbfounded, seeing his elderly Dadu's instant transformation,
The mischievous monkey dropped his sword gawking at his grand uncle.

"The humans,
Who are corrupting everything they lay eyes on?
The devil,
Who keeps me away from my goal?
Or, I,
Who ratifies the evil lodging inside my head to treat me like a puppet?

Answer me, Kela!
Who would you pick?
Somebody? Anybody?
Is there anyone who would like to retort to my query?"

With Dhairya getting to work as soon as he emerged,
Everyone witnessing magic, got something to think about.
And, Dadu, he took the liberty to lose himself in their thoughts again.

THE CONCLUSION: PART TWO!

At first, Dadu's heartfelt story had captivated his interest!
But, heading into the wondrous kingdoms and supernatural realms,
He had deemed it all to be his grand uncle's delusions.

The notion of a valorous Dhairya's extant,
Was no more than fabricated fiction to him.

Fiction which he had thoroughly enjoyed!
As he did any other fascinating tale that kept him on his toes.

Habituated to interrupt any intellectual gathering,
While his preoccupied mind rummaged through dirt,
He covertly considered himself to be the brightest pea in the pod.
However, his inability to perceive one's psyche for what it really was,
Kept him far away from ever understanding the other's reality.

Therefore, decoding secret messages,
And deciphering the deeper meanings of one's wisdom,
Was never truly his priority.
Because, in the end, he was deluded to think that he knew it all!

Losing track of what was being said, his frivolous mind had taken him places.
But, when his wandering eyes witnessed divine magic unfold before him,
He was rendered speechless.

Ever enthusiastic to embark upon intriguing adventures…
He secretly thanked the ultimate magician hiding behind the mysterious clouds,
Forever grateful, to be initiated to Dhairya's enchanted tribe!
A tribe that was destined to achieve more than greatness!

With that belief now embedded in his soul,
Kela, who was very often left bewildered…
Bewildered by the wonders of the world he lived in,
Was now bewitched by its constantly unravelling mysteries!

It was indeed a miracle!
A miracle only those fortunate to witness would appreciate!

After staying hidden, for so very long,
The doughty Dhairya had now resurrected from under Dadu's deterring existence,
Spellbinding them all!

Especially those, whose faith in the higher power remained intact, no matter what obstacle they faced in their tumultuous lives.
Like Akeli!

Her journey of this lifetime had only just begun;
Yet, she had been passed around like a parcel,
Lost without a designated point of origin or delivery.

Her existence was a mystery to her;
One which she desperately wished to unfold.
Nevertheless, taking her Dadu's feelings into account,
She thoughtfully refrained from seeking answers.

His emotional well-being was of the utmost importance to her.
So, she chose not to upset him by asking, '*why she had been rejected?*'
Rejected by the parents who were obviously not normal.
Since, nothing about her appearance was.

At a very young age, she was abandoned by those she had no memory of.
At a very young age, she faced discrimination at the hands of those she loved.
Having often wondered, '*if she was indeed cursed?*'
Dadu's wise words had pierced her heart, just moments ago, making her realise,
She was no bad omen.
She was a blessed soul!
Blessed, to have received this precious gift of life!

A Gift, which her brethren seemed to take for granted.

What she didn't know was,
By blaming himself for the mistakes he thought he made,
Her beloved grandpa had also lost his trail.
And, by constantly inflicting pain upon himself,
He too had taken this divine gift for granted.

Saddened by the loss of his loved ones,
Young Dadu left no stone unturned searching for them.

He was looking in all the wrong places he did realise in time,
Still, he tricked himself into believing that he was doing everything right.

She is simply testing my patience,
He often told himself;
But, the reality of the situation was that he lost his connection.
All because he was fixating on his broken heart, and blaming the world.

He possessed all the tools to mend his fences!
But, they were left aside simply gathering dust.
All because he failed to practice what he passionately preached.

"Obstacles arise where goodness is in store.
So, do temptations test you to the core?
Which is when it is a must,
That you dig deep within!"
These profound words of wisdom, he always delivered with great conviction.
Yet, in his times of distress, he miserably failed to stay on the right track.

He blamed himself; indeed, he did.
However, he was consumed by animosity.
That mistake, cost him not only one but hundreds of lifetimes…
To see what he was meant to see, way back then.

Was he being too harsh on himself?
Was he misleading his tribe from their goal?
Was he causing them more harm, than relief?

All kinds of conflicts continuously crashed his disturbed mind.

Nonetheless, when his stars aligned with his purest emotions, that day,
The most awaited magical moment presented itself,
Enticing him to turn into his original self.

That particular moment was one of great significance!
They were to rewrite history!

Accepting responsibility for his misled actions,
While acknowledging his flaws out loud,
As he peeled away all the layers of sadness, dejection and blame,
He simultaneously wiped his slate clean shedding tears of repentance.

Aiming to rectify his errors;
Errors, that came with major consequences,
He unknowingly invoked his mystical Goddess,
Who was forever longing to be called!

No sooner, did he open his channels,
Allowing her eternal love to flow freely,
She graced him with her Divine presence emerging as a rainbow!

A ray of hope, which he had been yearning to see all this while,
Was reflecting light into his soul!
A light, whose warmth he most certainly felt!
But, his damp eyes impeded his vision,
Forcing the radiant spectrum of colours,
To penetrate his mortal existence
Bringing back to the present,
A blast from Dadu's past!
Transfixing, every member in the audience!

Dhairya, had returned to claim his kingdom!
Soon, his Queen would also arrive to repossess her throne.
Holding close to her heart a very precious key.
A key, which was lost, for over an eternity!

While Dadu was going through a major transformation…
Capu recollected a fascinating dream of his own!
A dream which had oddly slipped his sharp mind.

All excited by a wonderful revelation,
In ecstasy, he leaped towards Akeli embracing her from behind.
"Come, little angel! Come, hop on to my back!!!

It's been too long. Way too long,
Since we've explored the wonders of this nature together!
Hop on little angel!
Grant me the pleasure of taking you on an adventurous ride!"

Unsure of what he meant, since, they had only just met,
Akeli looked at him all stumped.
Which was when a wolf howled, from inside the striking leopard's body!
Shocking everyone listening, while surprising Capu himself,
Who quickly placed his paws on his mouth, in order to stop that madness.

The Divine Magic was still lingering in the air!
Eagerly waiting to unveil another secret,
A secret Capu didn't consciously know he was carrying.

No wonder, in the past few years,
When the magnificent Moon met her full potential,
Bringing absolute delight in his lonesome life,
The leopard found himself on one particular rock overlooking the dying jungle.

Naturally bewitched by her beatific beauty,
His occasional roars, would mysteriously turn into everlasting howls...
Yet, Capu never seemed to remember the events of those precious meetings,
No matter how hard he always tried.

It was no coincidence 'that sacred union' occurred the way it did!
Khatru needed a body to carry his aimlessly loitering spirit;
And, Capu needed a miracle to save his withering existence.
They both needed each other in order to carry on with their lives' mission.
Because ultimately, 'their point of attraction' was the same!

Khatru roughly knew what he was getting himself into,
However, Capu, remained clueless to the intrusion of his entity.
Strangely, the wolf instantly felt at home residing in a leopard's body,
For reasons unknown to him...
Up until that moment!

Hearing Capu address Akeli the way he would do, Mantra,
All of the Khatru's questions were, at once, answered!
They were destined to become one! Indeed they were!
They had much more in common than either of them could begin to imagine!

Once upon a time,
The leopard and the wolf had each taken little Mantra for a ride!
And, on one special occasion, they'd entertained Akeli too!
But, that memory, only one of them had.

Akeli, was no Mantra; they were both unique entities!
However, just like Khatru hiding in Capu…
Mantra, was most likely living in Akeli!

Even though the Valley of Hope had transformed into a Valley of Despair,
A few chosen souls were brought back to life at the auspicious hour!
In hopes of making it into the hands of their saviour.

At that miraculous instant,
As if they were being summoned by their Queen herself,
Capu's feet drew him to Khatru's favourite spot earlier than usual.
No sooner did the charmer start wooing his Goddess,
He heard his howls echo, unlike ever before…

Paying close attention to where the voice was reverberating from,
Khatru stumbled upon an outlandish creature mimicking his cries.

Her features were so distinct that it made it impossible to distinguish,
Who she might belong to?

Subconsciously drawn,
To an elderly langur hiding immense pain behind those soulful eyes,
Khatru often pondered,
If, that was, his long lost Dhairu?!?

Mostly finding him alone…
Endlessly gazing at the open sky,

As if waiting for someone to drop something from high up above,
Khatru figured,
A baby in Dadu's hands would certainly bring back his lost spark!
Thereafter, filling a big void in his seemingly empty life.

Without Capu's full awareness,
Khatru rescued the abandoned newborn,
From the relentless conditions of that 'unusually' cold night.
Keeping her warm in the leopard's furry arms,
He waited until the break of dawn, praying, Capu would not snap out of his spell.

Supported by the ones directing his every move,
Safely securing the tiny little soul on Capu's back with mystical vines,
Khatru scaled the distance from one end of the Valley to the other end of the jungle where Dadu dwelled, within no time. Whilst the alien infant, thoroughly enjoyed her first glorious ride!

Carefully sliding Capu's stubby paw exhibiting deadly nails,
Over a peculiar line partitioning her precious face,
Unintentionally he ended up scaring her nose.
Apologizing to the fast asleep baby for his big blunder, Khatru's existence melted, when the extraordinary being locked eyes, with his spirit!

The thought of raising her himself crossed his mind that second!
Yet, unsure of his host's reaction to fresh meat,
He brushed of that idea deciding to stick to the plan.

Wrapping her nicely in dried lotus leaves,
Promising to stay forever connected…
He carefully placed the eccentric soul in Dadu's path.
The path, leading to a bone dry pond, he knew, Dadu explored every morning.

The tales told, of Akeli being found by the river…
Weren't all tales!
Still, the chain of events,
Leading to her finding solace in Dadu's arms….
A complex mind could never being to comprehend.

It wasn't Kela's figment of imagination as he secretly thought it to be, when she mentioned, a wolf with red spots causing mayhem in the heart of the jungle...

On one particular full moon,

Tucking Capu in bed, Khatru had come out to play with his fellow spirits!

That is when, Kela's sleepy eyes had caught a glimpse of the sublime sorcery!

Nothing about either of their union was 'normal' in terms of mortal standards.

Therefore, those who lacked courage, to venture beyond the boundaries of their superficial lives...

Would, most definitely, have to be spoon fed!

THE CONCLUSION: PART THREE!

*A*s if, 'announcing,'
They were closer to solving a divine mystery of their times...
The sun shone brighter than ever whitening up the darkened clouds!

And, out of nowhere,

Ensnaring its spectators by its spectacular sparks…

A huge bolt of lightning,
Drew a horizontal line,
In the cottony white sky,
Instantly followed by a deafening roar of endless thunder!
Commanding everyone's absolute attention.

The enchanted rainbow which had gone unnoticed,
By the ones who needed to see it the most…
Had now returned with its counterpart!
Forming a double spectrum of dazzling light.
Enhancing the glory of the once gloomy sky!

In awe of its radiant beauty,
Every awakened soul was instantly gratified!

Suraksha, unlike any other bat known to live,
Soared towards the arch of colours to soak in its wonder!

Since, the objective was to fill in some of the mysterious blanks…
Unveiling the little secret hidden inside Capu some more,
His blackish brown breathtaking spots;
Slowly transformed into a ravishing, ruby red!

Displaying their Divine powers,
By seeping into Dadu's untainted spirit!
The sorcerers at work had baffled every soul,
Making them witness;
Dadu's every wrinkle…
Gradually disappear!

Binding her magic along with her soul mate's…
The sorcerer was adamant to restore Dadu's diminished sight too.
All, so he could see, *'what he needed to see'*, in a whole new light!

Akeli was no ordinary soul, Dadu had known that all along.
Yet, influenced by his shortcomings…

He overlooked the obvious, which stared him in the face, daily.

Dhairya, had seen, what Dadu yearned to see...
He had also read, between the lines, with great ease!
But, since he was aging in Dadu's mortal body...,
For them to attain flawless clarity,
It was of the utmost importance they infused as one.

Or else, their struggles would continue;
Unable to read the same page.

Hearing their children's every heartbeat, Divinity got to work right way!

Unlike the astonishing moments,
When a rainbow appears and fades away in time...
These arches of brilliance deepened their colours,
Eagerly inching their way towards Akeli!

With all eyes in that space engrossed watching the double rainbows every step,
The enigma, created by the God's, came to a halt.
Instantly encompassing the special soul, in their luminous spotlight!
Secretly fulfilling, her unrevealed desire to bask in their glory!

Unsure of how to react, Akeli blushed noticing all eyes fixated upon her.
Which is when, the *progenitors* she wasn't introduced to yet,
Dropped illusionary blinds around her, so she could express herself freely!

Clapping, while jumping with joy,
She was in euphoria just like little Mantra in Dadu's story!

Having paid close attention to every word,
She lifted her hands above her head like a chalice, and rejoiced!

"Thank you, Universe!
I love you so much!!!
Thank you for making my wish come true!!!

Thank you, for making my cup overflow with your eternal love!!!"

Besides the glorious spectrums of light that caressed her existence,
There was no one else in her sight; not even Dadu.
That didn't mean she wasn't being seen by those drawn to her charisma.

Blinding each and every entity in her refulgent aura…
Her distinct vibrations drew Dadu's ecstatic soul towards her love!
Their love!
To be precise.

Because, she wasn't alone…
She never was!

She always felt, that she was different from the rest…
At that moment, it was clear as to *why*?

Those who she considered to be her imaginary friends…
Weren't simply fragments of her creativity or mere voices in her head!
They were a major part of her existence,
Just as she was a huge part of them!

Akeli was no ordinary soul or spirit…
Unlike her brethren who struggled to take a big leap,
She was destined to spread her wings and fly!

She wasn't just different from the rest,
She was unique! She was one of a kind!
She was, indeed, very, very special!

Because, in her mortal existence, she held the key to the kingdom;
The key which would fit perfectly in the Almighty's master plan!

Just like,
Vaani and Vidur!
Param and Aatma!

The dove and the pigeon!
The dainty cobras and the dazzling trees!
The spectres hidden within the double rainbows!
Each dedicating their every breath, every heartbeat and every song they ever created in
the name of love, to their everlasting connections!

In solidarity, stood before the love of their life his Goddesses!
Reflecting nothing but divine radiance!!!
Yearning to unite again!
Eager to be embraced!
Longing, to be loved!!!

Although he failed to acknowledge their different manifestations, time and time
again,
They never, for once, gave up on him!

Sacrificing the life they'd been given,
They kept coming back to seek his attention!
Alas, blinded by grief, Dadu always chose to ignore them.

They were the ones whose absence had driven Dhairya insane...
Insane to the point, where he disillusioned himself to be unworthy!
Unworthy, of fulfilling, his only given mission.
In return, relinquishing his ethereal parents' Divine vision.
All because he foolishly thought that he lost them forever.

'What was their once brilliant langur searching for?'
Their immortal entities failed to understand...

Therefore, with a little help from Divinity itself,
They stood before him as one body, three souls!
Serenading him with the same love...
Like they had each serenaded him with before!

Making it dawn upon their saviour...
Why he felt the way he did,

When he looked into Akeli's different coloured eyes...
When she stroked his back with affection, to calm his mind...
When he stared admirably at her distinguished features...
When she ran her delicate fingers, on his ancient scars...

Opening his channels was the best thing he did in a long, long time!
Because, now, he could clearly distinguish one from the other!

Standing in the midst of his enchanted luminaries!
Gawking at them in disbelief like Kela gawked at Dhairya...
The words of his wondrous Vaani, echoed in his ears!
"Snap out of it, Mr. Langur.
Didn't your mama ever tell you it is rude to stare?!?"

Laughing and crying all at once!
Hugging and kissing Akeli like he had never done before!
His exhilaration knew no bounds!

"Oh, my lovely ladies, here you are!
All in one! One in all!
One in all! All in one!"

In Spite of listening to his chronicles closely,
Some sceptics reluctant to surrender to the unknown,
Reckoned that the adulated langur had suddenly lost his mind.

In denial of the unparalleled universe,
Clouding their mind with further speculation,
Their mortal imagination couldn't fathom the miracle unfolding before their eyes!

Not realising, he too was gifted,
Kela blinked his long lashes profusely.
Then, rubbed his eyelids until they got sore.
All because he was in disbelief of what he saw with his eyes wide open!

Wondering if he was dreaming a surreal dream,

Kela, pinched himself to make sure he was awake.

Then, taking his madness to another level,
Testing if his mind was simply playing a cruel game,
He poked himself with his sword to check if he felt pain.

He couldn't get himself to stop; because, although he didn't say it out loud,
He dreaded the thought of being stuck in a world,
Where Akeli was the Queen, and he became her slave.

Just like he had failed to see the bigger picture the previous day,
Since he was only fixated on the notion of receiving a gift.
His fixation with Akeli's prosperity and his own failure,
Deprived him of seeking blessings from the Goddesses, who resided within her!

**"Oh, my dear loving, caring, forgiving parents,
I know you are laughing at me from above!"**
Raising his hands over his head,
Exactly like Mantra had done lifetimes ago,
And, Akeli had done now,
Dadu lost himself in their eternal love!

**"You know how much I hated being related to you,
When I assumed you tore us apart...
Yet, you bestow me with all these blessings, I consider myself unworthy of!**

**Pardon my stupidity oh you wonderful fabricators of this Universe!
Thank you so much,
For showering me with abundance,
In spite of my failures!**

**I love you!!! You know I do!
I love each and every one of you!!!"**

*Looking out for all their children every step of the way...
The Sibylline Sources worked more magic, hoping to save the day!*

Lifting the curtains of mirage by making the prominent rainbows disappear...
Along with the once lone Akeli, they made Gayatri and Mantra appear!
Showcasing each of his Goddesses individually!

Witnessing three spirits hover over one bizzare body still standing in flesh,
Some were baffled, some were scared and some were left bewildered;
The rest were simply bewitched, by their beguiling existence!

And, those wise souls fortunate to have been touched by these angels,
Instantaneously dropped to their feet in awe of the Supreme!

Suraksha, cried happy tears rubbing her child bearing tummy!
Celebrating the Marvellous Miracle, Capu and Khatru roared and howled in cohesion, inviting the entire kingdom to join their sensational symphony!

Although it took a while for everyone to calm their nerves after all that excitement,
One by one, the entire congregation, got down on their knee...
Hailing to the Goddesses residing in one Queen!

Elated to see the animal kingdom surrender to the higher power...
Dhairya secretly wished,
Mankind would be fortunate to be touched by his angels too.
Which is when, reading his mind,
In Harmony the trio addressed their admirers!

"Wouldn't you consider it to be a foolish act if one was to,
Cross seven seas,
Climb treacherous valleys,
Struggle to get to the peak of a mountain,
Turn their world upside down,
Destroying their sanctity,
Disrupting their peace...
All, in search of the treasures they already possess?"

Having already accepted his idiocy, Dhairya rocked his head back and forth, empathizing with that fool.

"The wonders, we wish to see!
The miracle, we are looking for!
The magic, we yearn to experience!
We hold the power to unfold all of their mysteries!

All we have to do is dive into our souls,
And, most importantly, *stay there*!
For, in that sacred space...
Is where Divinity reigns!

When we treat her right,
She will open all impossible doors!
When we follow in her footsteps...
Together, we can make magic happen!
Together, we can work wonders!

All is possible!!!
As long as we are receptive of their Divine Love!

We, say we,
Because, we know...
No matter how capable some might think they are,
This isn't a one man show!"

"Clearly isn't!" Kela mumbled, consumed by jealousy.

Tapping into his destructive emotions,
Divinity itself took over the platform using Akeli as their microphone.

"Every single soul gathered here this day...
Is destined to achieve greatness!

Yet, we can't all be doing the same thing now, can we?!?

If we all did the same thing,
We would no longer do justice to who we are meant to be.

We would all get lost in the crowd;
We will, most certainly, lose our individuality!

Won't we, Kela?"

The naive one frowned instantly taking offence for being singled out by Akeli,
Unable to look beyond the surface.

"We did obtain a great gift when we were born, Kela!
But, that is not all what we received.

We are all given remarkable abilities!
Abilities to make our journey a memorable one!
It is up to us to approach them with dignity!

Do not aim to climb peaks not meant for you to conquer!
Do not drag down the other who is destined to reach that height!
For, it would be a waste of your precious lifetime.
A lifetime you are meant to make worthwhile!

Be inspired by those who are making their existence fruitful.
Learn to wholeheartedly appreciate!
Tap onto your own truest potential...
By being your purest self!

Always remember, everything must flow naturally!
Nothing can ever be forced!
Because your gift is yours alone to explore,
Just like theirs, is theirs, to accentuate!"

Not ready to accept the Divine teachings openly,
Embarrassed to have his insides exposed in public, Kela wanted to cry.
Picking up on his building anxiety, the perceptive entities continued speaking in
terms he would understand.

"There are so many more gifts waiting to be unwrapped by us!"

Captivating his full attention now, the sagacious bodies gleamed!

"Yes, Kela!
There are plenty of gifts waiting to be unwrapped by you too!

This world is our oyster!
And, the sky!
The sky isn't our limit.
We are destined to venture way beyond that!

You know this already,
Don't you?"
Relieved to see his lost smile plaster his face again,
The Sibylline Sources continued their sermon,
But, not before making their striking presence known!

Elongating Akeli like a lean trunk of devotion, they got everybody looking up.

"The only reason your Dadu and his tribe,
Made it as far as they did way back then,
Is because they flushed out all the demons,
And, filtered their polluting system!
But, as you've heard from the horse's mouth,
And, seen with your Owlish eyes,
Once they fell prey, to their self-induced misery,
They continued to crumble and senselessly suffer.
We know, you won't repeat their mistakes!
Will you?!?"

Recollecting a few known blunders,
As soon as he nodded in sign of agreement,
The Almighty, ceased the opportunity to throw in the punch!

"We know you are a smart boy,
Destined for greatness just like your sister!
If you see her as the Queen,

You have to be her knight!
A knight, in shining armour!"

Tapping upon his desire to get down on his knee,
Like Dhairya yearned to do once upon a time...
They had him where they wanted him to be!

"Yes, every Queen needs a knight,
To keep all her troubles away!

Since we want you to succeed in all your endeavours,
We'd like to share with you our little secret;

Stay centred at all times!
Always maintain your balance!

You already have innate *courage* and *charisma*!
All you have to do is stay focused, dedicated and persevere!
While you do all this, remember to be grounded!
Because,
Appreciation, gratification and compassion will lead you places!!!"

Kela's clamped demeanour changed hearing himself being praised by the Goddess,
Which is when the bomb was dropped.
A bomb he accepted with grace!

"This journey! This adventure! This exclusive ride!
This will lead you to your paradise with pleasure!
All you have to do is never falter;
Never falter in your unconditional devotion!

Because,
Devils disguised in negative emotions,
Are lurking around every corner,
Waiting to catch you in your weak moment.
And, we clearly do not intend for our bright boy,

To be outsmarted, outwitted and outplayed now, do we?!?"

Throwing the ball back in his court, they gave him something to think about,
Indirectly conveying their message, to everybody listening!

With their mission accomplished for now,
The Almighty creators spread their vibrations throughout the Universe...
Calling upon a beguiling bolt of lightning,
To strike the glorious sky with all its might!

Before the thunderous roars could begin their drumming,
Bidding adieu to their enchanted children,
Divinity took off with that glorious flash!

On their way out, they did leave their disciples with another gift!

A gift that would not only make their cups overflow with eternal love,
But also, make their rivers flow in abundance!
All, so no child of theirs would ever forget, the taste of free flowing water again!

Taking the cloud burst above their heads as a cue to disperse,
All creatures looked at Akeli, to check if this memorable meeting was adjourned!

"Go on, my tribe!
Go seek solace in the comfort of your divine space!!!
I am right here whenever you need me!

Nevertheless, for whatever reasons it might be,
If you struggle to find me,
Don't you worry!

Simply, loosen yourself...,
Close your eyes...
Open your hearing...
And, taking a deep breath, call my name!
I will be there!!!"

Blowing kisses their way, she endearingly asked them to hurry!

Astonished to see this new side of Akeli, Dadu admired his Princess!
And, Dhairya, he simply smiled,
Knowing very well that Dadu's little Princess, would never be the same again!
Since all he could hear besides the pitter patter of the rain, was her new tribe
singing praises of their Magnificent Queen Akeli!

The same Magnificent Queen,
Was to be addressed as Matrikali!!!
In the very near future;
They just didn't know that yet.

Surprisingly, Narangi and Mosambee, who forever bullied Akeli,
Suddenly followed in her oversized footsteps seeking her attention!

"Wait, Akeli, wait!!!"
Narangi shouted on top of his voice fighting the sound of the pouring rain!

"That's not only Akeli anymore, Dadi Gayatri and Aunty Mantra are with her too, you fool!" Mosambee tried to outsmart his brother.

"I'm not a fool, you are the fool!"
"No. You are the fool!"
The forever bickering twins forgot they were being watched.

"What is it you want from our Queen???"
Breaking their banter, Kela stepped up, not afraid of his siblings anymore.

"Yes, that's right!
Queen Akeli!!!
From now on, that's how you shall address her!
Comprende?"

Taking the words of the Divine to heart…
He happily proclaimed himself to be his sister's knight in shining armour!

"And, you two better get this straight,
Before you get to her...
You will always have to go through me!"
Placing his toy sword on their scrunched shoulders,
He enrolled them to serve their Queen without seeking their permission!

"Yes, Sire!
Comprende!
Comprende!
Hail to the Queen!!! Hail to the Queen!!! Hail to the Queen!!!"

Without causing any trouble, his once fearsome brothers, bowed before him,
Taking their oath in unison!

Then, carrying on the revelry, happy to be knighted,
They sang on top of their voices, welcoming Akeli!

"Queen of the Kingdom!
Queen of the Kingdom!
Queen of the Kingdom, come!!!
Come, Queen Akeli!
Queen of the Kingdom, come!!!
Queen of the King..,."

"That's a very catchy song!
Has a good ring to it too!
Did you just make that up?!?"
The soon to be mother, Suku, cleverly interrupted their painful performance.

"Yes, I did! Just now!!!" bragged Narangi.

"No, that's not true. We both did. We made it together. Just now!
One line him, one line me!" Mosambee wanted his share of the credit too.

"That's great!
But, your Queen is already on her way home!!!

Where you should be heading too!"
Pointing them in the direction of Akeli who was way ahead of them, Suku laughed!

**"Come on, children!
Getting to the caves is our priority right now.
You can continue your jubilation later!"**
Capu and Khatru completed each other's sentences!
Then, chuckled at the coincidence!

**"But, Uncle Capu, Uncle Khatru,
We want to know what happened to Dadima;
Don't you want to know, Dadu?"**
The hooligans suddenly transformed into innocent monkeys.

"Yes. I do…"
Having often wondered where Dadima lost her way,
Dhairya stood still like a statue,
Waiting for his Goddesses to reply.

Lovingly stroking his back all unified, Akeli directed her attention to those who tormented her, up until the day before.
"Haven't you two heard enough stories for one day?!?"

Excited to meet her new family Mantra's spirit popped out, introducing herself,
**"Hi Narangi! Hi Mosambee!
I am technically your Aunty Mantra but consider me a sister too!"**

Shying away from her spirit, the troublemakers trembled,
As the cold drops of gushing rain, sent chills, through their spine!

"Let's continue this chit chat in the safety of our cave shall we…"
Gayatri's motherly instincts reflected in Akeli's tone.

Noticing all her boys standing there with long faces not ready for the Chronicles to end, Gayatri took a different approach letting her free spirit jiggle over their soaked shoulders!

"Aren't your tiny little brains overloaded,
With everything that you've heard?
Why don't we all head home,
Reliving, the fascinating stories told today!
Instead of freezing in this rain…"

"Although there was some heartache and pain,
There were also so many wonderful lessons to learn!"
Tickling her Pa, who acted like a child,
Mantra joined her Ma to dance in the rain!

"We did share an unconventional journey together,
A journey of a lifetime!

Now that one story is over,
The other is only just beginning!

So, believe me when I say,
We are not going anywhere, brother!"

Spooking Narangi who lost focus for a second,
Mantra glided into Akeli's body settling in her new home!

Amazed that her tiny frame hosted two Wondrous Entities at once, Akeli tapped
her toes!
"Yay! Gayatri Ma, Mantra, Suku, Capu and Khatru;
They are all here to stay!
You know what that means?!?
There are more stories of their adventures coming our way!!!"
Cheekily, she played with her long fingers enticing them all to cheer!

Kela, Chikoo, Kaju, Narangi, Mosambee and the rest of the crew,
Huddled together on that note, all excited, to hear more!

"But not right now, silly!
Let them all take a breath!

Let them all catch up with each other!
They are going to be here with us at all times!
Where else would they go?!?"

Welcoming her new family with delight, she hopped on Capu's back,
Luring Khatru, to howl with glee!

Even though they were convinced that no one was going anywhere else, but home,
They stubbornly stood still.

Which is when, Gayatri Ma's spirit took charge.
Soothing their anxious souls and forcing them to laugh at first,
"Chop chop children! Chop chop!
Big children! Small children!
Young children! Old children!
All of you! All my children!
Pay close attention!

Hop onto my wagon of love!
Allow me take you for a ride!"
Displaying her wit, she hooked them by her charm!

"A ride of lifetime…
One which you will never forget!
However, before we start that journey…
It is important you sharpen your skills!
Accentuate your abilities!
Utilize your divine tools!
Because, for what is to come next…
You must all be prepared!!!

Comprende?!?"

Although the idea of winding up the chronicles wasn't an easy one for them to
digest…
Still,

Respecting their Goddesses' wish,
They followed in the footsteps of their Queen!
Knowing, very soon, will come the day,
When another Divine story will be told,
Unfolding yet another mystery…
Tapping straight into the unknown!

THE END!

To
Oliver !!!!.
May Your Dreams head U
To More Magic !!!

Love

EBELINE 4/12/19